THE POLITICS OF ECONOMIC REGIONALISM

The International Political Economy of New Regionalisms Series

The International Political Economy of New Regionalisms Series presents innovative analyses of a range of novel regional relations and institutions. Going beyond established, formal, interstate economic organizations, this essential series provides informed interdisciplinary and international research and debate about myriad heterogeneous intermediate level interactions.

Reflective of its cosmopolitan and creative orientation, this series is developed by an international editorial team of established and emerging scholars in both the South and North. It reinforces ongoing networks of analysts in both academia and think-tanks as well as international agencies concerned with micro-, meso- and macro-level regionalisms.

Editorial Board

Timothy M. Shaw, University of London, London
Isidro Morales, Universidad de las Américas - Puebla, Mexico
Maria Nzomo, University of Nairobi, Kenya
Nicola Phillips, University of Warwick, UK
Johan Saravanamuttu, Munk Centre for International Studies, Canada
Fredrik Söderbaum, Göteborgs Universitet, Sweden

Other Titles in the Series

European Union and New Regionalism
Edited by Mario Telò
ISBN 0 7546 1748 3

South Africa's Multilateral Diplomacy and Global Change
Edited by Philip Nel, Ian Taylor and Janis van der Westhuizen
ISBN 0 7546 1653 3

Crises of Governance in Asia and Africa
Edited by Sandra J. MacLean, Fahimul Quadir and Timothy M. Shaw
ISBN 0 7546 1410 7

The Politics of Economic Regionalism
Sierra Leone in ECOWAS

DAVID J. FRANCIS
Department of Peace Studies, University of Bradford

LONDON AND NEW YORK

First published 2001 by Ashgate Publishing

Reissued 2018 by Routledge
2 Park Square, Milton Park, Abingdon, Oxon OX14 4RN
711 Third Avenue, New York, NY 10017, USA

Routledge is an imprint of the Taylor & Francis Group, an informa business

Copyright © David J. Francis 2001

All rights reserved. No part of this book may be reprinted or reproduced or utilised in any form or by any electronic, mechanical, or other means, now known or hereafter invented, including photocopying and recording, or in any information storage or retrieval system, without permission in writing from the publishers.

Notice:
Product or corporate names may be trademarks or registered trademarks, and are used only for identification and explanation without intent to infringe.

Publisher's Note
The publisher has gone to great lengths to ensure the quality of this reprint but points out that some imperfections in the original copies may be apparent.

Disclaimer
The publisher has made every effort to trace copyright holders and welcomes correspondence from those they have been unable to contact.

A Library of Congress record exists under LC control number: 2001088776

ISBN 13: 978-1-138-70226-4 (hbk)
ISBN 13: 978-1-138-62916-5 (pbk)
ISBN 13: 978-1-315-20978-4 (ebk)

Contents

List of Maps	*viii*
List of Tables	*ix*
Acknowledgements	*x*
List of Abbreviations	*xi*

Introduction	1
1 Economic Regionalism in West Africa	7
Introduction	7
Political Economy of West Africa	8
Evolution of the Economic Community of West African States (ECOWAS)	13
Formation of ECOWAS: 1972-1975	21
Aims and Objectives, Institutional Framework and Main Features of the Treaty	23
Conceptual Framework: Modernisation, Dependency and Developmental Regionalism	29
Conclusion	34
Notes and References	36
2 Security Regionalism in West Africa	39
Introduction	39
The Creation of ECOMOG: The Liberian Crisis and the International Neglect of Africa	40
ECOWAS Political and Security Co-operation: Redefining Economic and Security Interdependence	43
ECOMOG: Peacekeeping, Peace Enforcement and Conflict Management in West Africa	49
Conceptualising ECOMOG	52
Security Regionalism in West Africa and African International Relations	57
Conclusion	59
Notes and References	59

3 ECOWAS and the New Regionalism	63
Introduction	63
From 'Old' Regionalism to 'New' Regionalism	63
ECOWAS New Regionalism and the Myth of Globalisation	66
ECOWAS and Responses to the New Regionalism	70
Conclusion	73
Notes and References	74
4 Sierra Leone in ECOWAS	76
Introduction	76
Political Economy of Sierra Leone	77
Characterisation of State and the Politics of Decline in Sierra Leone	82
Sierra Leone's Foreign Policy Approach to ECOWAS Regionalism	87
Sierra Leone's Institutional Structure for ECOWAS Responsibilities	92
The Politics of Ratification of ECOWAS Protocols and Decisions	96
Financial and Infrastructural Obligation to ECOWAS	97
Level of Popular Participation in ECOWAS Regionalism	100
Conclusion	104
Notes and References	104
5 Civil War in Sierra Leone: Interpretations	107
Introduction	107
Civil War in Sierra Leone	107
ECOMOG Military Base in Sierra Leone: An Obstacle to Charles Taylor's Presidential Ambition	111
Civil War and its Interpretations	114
Conclusion	120
Notes and References	121
6 Political Economy of Diamonds and Trans-border Regionalisation	123
Introduction	123
Diamonds and the Politics of Underdevelopment	123
Conflict Diamonds, Privatisation of Security and Globalisation	129
Diamonds and Human Security in Post-war Sierra Leone	141

	Conclusion	143
	Notes and References	144
7	Political Implications of Sierra Leone's ECOWAS Regionalism	147
	Introduction	147
	Politico-Diplomatic Relevance of ECOWAS Regionalism	149
	ECOWAS and the Defence of Democracy in Sierra Leone	156
	ECOWAS-UN Co-operative Security in Sierra Leone	165
	ECOWAS and the Erosion of National Sovereignty	178
	Conclusion	184
	Notes and References	185
8	Economic Implications of Sierra Leone's ECOWAS Regionalism	189
	Introduction	189
	Sierra Leone and the Traditional Benefits of Economic Regionalism	190
	Sierra Leone and ECOWAS Trade Liberalisation Programme	196
	Sierra Leone and Intra-Regional Trade	201
	Free Movement and its Pressures on the Economy	204
	Mano River Regionalisation: The Monkey Trade and Smuggling	206
	The ASYCUDA Project and Sierra Leone's Customs Regime	209
	West African Clearing House and its Impact on Sierra Leone	213
	ECOWAS Trade Fair and Private Sector Participation	215
	Sierra Leone and ECOWAS Regional Agricultural Development Strategy	217
	Sierra Leone and ECOWAS Infrastructural Development Strategy	223
	Conclusion	226
	Notes and References	227
Conclusion		231
Bibliography		*238*
Index		*249*

List of Maps

Map of West Africa   xv
Map of Sierra Leone   xvi

List of Tables

1. Basic Indicators for West African States — xvii
2. Conflict Diamonds – Estimate Against Total World Production, 1999 — 131
3. Taxes on International Trade Transactions – ECOWAS Countries — 199
4. Intra-ECOWAS Trade — 202
5. Direction of Sierra Leone's Intra-ECOWAS Trade — 202

Acknowledgements

In the process of writing this book, I have incurred a debt of gratitude to many people who have, in diverse ways, helped to make this project a success. I owe a special debt of gratitude to Peter Calvert and Caroline Thomas, both at Southampton University, for their academic guidance and constant support throughout my doctoral journey. To my West African friends at the ECOWAS headquarters in Abuja and the ECOWAS Fund Secretariat in Lomé, I am grateful for the interviews and numerous discussions we had. I am immensely grateful to Carol Hutson, Mandy Oliver and Vivian Nassar for their technical expertise and eye for details, without which, the production of this book would have been frustratingly torturous.

Friends and loved ones, they say, are a happy part of life. This project would have been impossible without them. I am immensely grateful to Dagmar for her love and constant encouragement, and to Mohamed Kamanda and Mike Ward for their academic and moral support. I also acknowledge the fun and wonderful distractions provided by David Jr. I owe a special gratitude to my brothers and sisters; Peter, Paul, Paulina, Mary, Cecilia and Assumpta for their prayers, affection and patience in trying to understand my excitingly boring life. Above all, I thank my God for making this project possible.

List of Abbreviations

AAF	African Alternative Framework to Structural Adjustment Programmes
AAFC	Allied Armed Forces of the Community
ACP-EEC	African Caribbean Pacific - European Economic Community
ACRI	African Crisis Response Initiative
ADB	African Development Bank
ADMS	Alluvial Diamond Mining Scheme
AEC	African Economic Community
AFRC	Armed Forces Revolutionary Council
AIDS	Acquired Immune Deficiency Syndrome
ANSWE	African Network for Support to Women Entrepreneurs
AOF	Afrique Occidentale Francaise (Federation of French West Africa)
APC	All Peoples Congress
APL	Armed Forces of Liberia
ASEAN	Association of South East Asian Nations
ASYCUDA	Automated System for Customs Data
BADEA	Arab Bank for Economic Development in Africa
BCEAO	Central Bank of West African States
CACM	Central America Common Market
CARIFTA	Caribbean Free Trade Association
CAST	Consolidated African Selection Trust
CBC	Chad Basin Commission
CCC	(ECOWAS) Community Computer Centre
CCC	Customs Co-operation Council (International)
CCMS	Co-operative Contract Mining Scheme
CDF	Civil Defence Force
CEAO	West African Economic Community
CFA	Communaute Financiere Africaine (African Financial Community)
CMS	Contract Mining Scheme
COMESA	Common Market for East and Southern African States
CPLP	Community of Lusophone Countries
CSO	Central Selling Organisation

DRC	Democratic Republic of Congo
EAC	East African Community
EC	European Community
ECA	Economic Commission for Africa
ECCAS	Economic Community of Central African States
ECLA	Economic Commission for Latin America
ECOMOG	ECOWAS Cease-fire Monitoring Group
ECOWAS	Economic Community of West African States
ECSC	European Coal and Steel Community
EEC	European Economic Community
EEZ	Economic Exclusive Zone
EO	Executive Outcomes
EPRU	Economic Policy and Research Unit
EU	European Union
FAO	Food and Agricultural Organisation
FDI	Foreign Direct Investment
GCA	Global Coalition for Africa
GDP	Gross Domestic Product
GGDO	Government Gold and Diamond Office
GNP	Gross National Product
HDI	Human Development Index
HIV	Human Immunodeficiency Virus
HRD	Hoge Raad Voor Diamant
IFIs	International Financial Institutions
IGOs	Inter-Governmental Organisations
IMF	International Monetary Fund
IPE	International Political Economy
ISI	Import Substitution Industrialisation
ISU	Internal Security Unit
KFOR	Kosovo Force
LAIA	Latin America Integration Association
LDCs	Least Developed Countries
LPC	Liberian Peace Council
MCS	Monitoring, Control and Surveillance Mechanism
MNCs	Multinational Corporations
MOD	Ministry of Defence
MPRI	Military Professional Resource Incorporated
MPSSL	Marine Protection Services - Sierra Leone
MRU	Manu River Union

NAFTA	North American Free Trade Area
NAM	Non-Aligned Movement
NDMC	National Diamond Mining Company
NGOs	Non-Governmental Organisations
NIEO	New International Economic Order
NPFL	National Patriotic Front of Liberia
NPRC	National Provisional Ruling Council
NRA	New Regionalism Approach
OAU	Organisation of African Unity
ODA	Official Development Assistance
OERS	Organisation of Senegal River States
OPEC	Organisation of Petroleum Exporting Countries
PAC	Partnership Africa Canada
PADRIGU	Department of Peace and Development Research
PAIGC	Partido Africano da Indpendência da Guiné e Cabo Verde (African Independence Party of Guiné and the Cape Verde Islands)
PMCs	Private Military Companies
PMMC	Precious Metal Mining Company
PTA	Preferential Trade Area
RNC	Niger River Commission
RSLMF	Republic of Sierra Leone Military Forces
RUF	Revolutionary United Front
SACU	Southern African Customs Union
SADC	Southern African Development Community
SADCC	Southern African Development Co-ordination Conference
SAPs	Structural Adjustment Programmes
SCD	Single Customs Document
SDR	Special Drawing Right
SLA	Sierra Leone Army
SLEDIC	Sierra Leone Export Development and Investment Corporation
SLPP	Sierra Leone Peoples Party
SLST	Sierra Leone Selection Trust
SMC	Standing Mediation Committee
SOFA	Status of Forces Agreement
SSATP	Sub-Saharan African Transport Programme
SSD	Special Security Division
TNCs	Transnational Corporations

UA	Unit of Account
UDEAO	Union Douaniere de L'Afrique de L'Ouest
ULIMO	United Liberian Movement for Democracy
UMEOA	West African Economic and Monetary Union
UN	United Nations
UNAMSIL	United Nations Observer Mission in Sierra Leone
UNCLOS	United Nations Convention on the Law of the Sea
UNCTAD	United Nations Conference on Trade and Development
UNDP	United Nations Development Programme
UNEF	United Nations Emergency Force
UNITA	National Union for the Total Independence of Angola
UNOMIL	United Nations Observer Mission in Liberia
UNOSOM	United Nations Observer Mission in Somalia
UNPAAERD	United Nations Programme of Action for the Accelerated Development of Africa
UNPROFOR	United Nations Protection Force
UNTACDA	United Nations Transport and Communication Decade for Africa
UNU	United Nations University
UTRAO	West African Union of Road Transporters
WACH	West African Clearing House
WAMA	West African Manufacturers Association
WAMA	West African Monetary Agency
WIDER	World Institute for Development Economics Research
WTO	World Trade Organisation

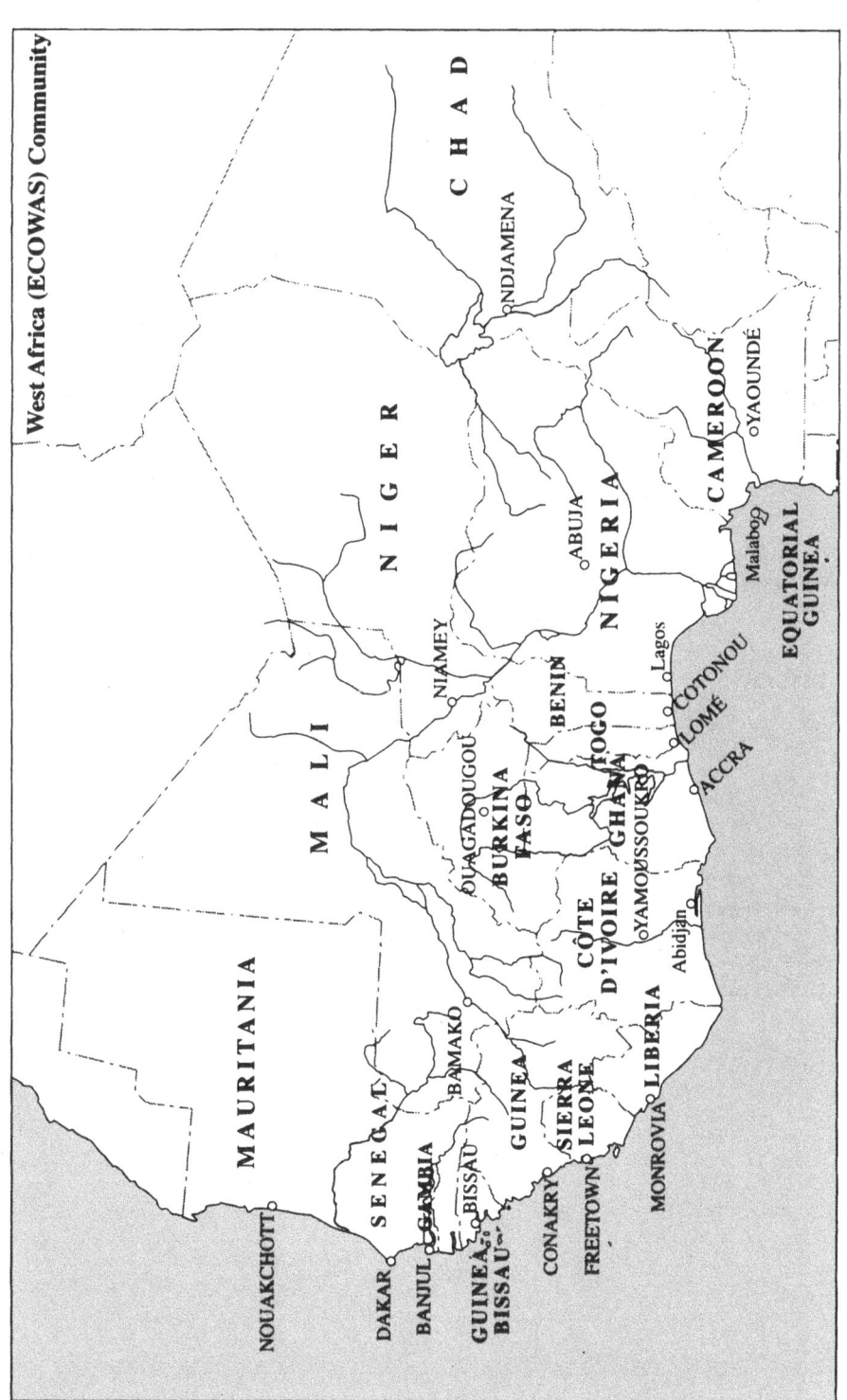

Table 1: Basic Indicators for West African States

Country	Population mid 1998 (millions)	Land area (Thousands of Square Km)	GNP per capita av. annual percentage growth	Life expectancy at birth (years) 1997	Illiteracy (percentage of population 15 years and above) – 1997	Total net ODA per capita 1997	Total external debt - 1997 (millions of US dollars)
Benin	6.0	111.0	0.9	53	66	39	1624
Burkina Faso	10.7	274.0	0.8	44	79	35	1297
Cape Verde	0.4	4.0	0.1	68	29	273	220
Côte d'Ivoire	14.5	318.0	-0.2	47	57	31	15609
Gambia, The	1.2	10.0	-0.9	53	67	35	430
Ghana	18.5	228.0	1.5	60	34	28	5982
Guinea	7.1	246.0	2.4	46	-	55	3520
Guinea-Bissau	1.2	28.0	0.2	44	66	110	921
Liberia	3.0	96.0	-	47	52	33	2012
Mali	10.6	1220.0	0.5	50	65	44	2945
Mauritania	2.5	1025.0	0.8	53	62	102	2453
Niger	10.1	1269.0	-2.0	47	68	35	1579
Nigeria	121.3	911.0	1.3	54	40	2	28455
Senegal	9.0	193.0	-0.1	52	65	49	3671
Sierra Leone	4.9	72.0	-5.7	38	-	27	1149
Togo	4.5	54.0	-1.5	49	47	29	1339

Source: World Bank, *African Development Indicators 2000*, Washington D.C., The World Bank 2000, pp. 6, 176, 329.

For the loving memory of Papa and Sisy

And for Dagmar

Introduction

The primary objective of this book is to provide an analytical understanding of the nature, dynamics and complexity of the politics of economic regionalism through the prism of Sierra Leone in the Economic Community of West African States (ECOWAS). West Africa itself has been pessimistically portrayed by analysts such as Robert Kaplan as the new 'strategic danger'[1] in contemporary world politics because of the many civil wars and intra-communal violence, political instability, fragile economies, poverty and underdevelopment, weak and collapsing states, and environmental problems facing the sub-region. West Africa has therefore been held as a mirror image of Africa and according to the London-based magazine *The Economist*, Africa is simply a 'hopeless continent'.[2] This kind of negative portrayal of West Africa and Africa in general misses the significant developments taking place on the continent. What the West African sub-region reflects is a contradictory element of reversal and advancement. Recent political, economic and security developments in the West African sub-region, and in particular the formation and role of the West African peacekeeping and intervention force in conflict management and peace support operations within the economic community, have brought the regionalism project to the centre stage in the debate on security regionalism in post-Cold War politics.

But what are the imperatives that have forced the ECOWAS regionalism, originally established with common market objectives, to expand into political, security and foreign policy areas? What has become of the economic integration and co-operation objective in ECOWAS? Are the developments in West Africa a continental and global phenomenon? These are some of the critical issues addressed in this book through an analysis of the participation of a single country in an economic regionalism project. *The Politics of Economic Regionalism* is therefore about the interface between economics, development, politics, democratisation, and security issues within a region. In developing regions these issues are inseparable, and if anything, they are mutually reinforcing. Economic regionalism has been the umbrella under which broader regional political, environmental, socio-cultural, security, military and development issues have been addressed. In effect, the purely economic focus of any regionalism project will not sustain or ensure the survival of the regionalist scheme. Louise Fawcett and Andrew Hurrell in fact argue that 'Even if the outward form of regionalism is economic in nature . . . the factors that underpin and sustain such projects are often far from solely economic and economic regionalism may carry with it important geopolitical or security consequences'.[3] This is what the politics of regionalism is about in West Africa, as well as other regionalist projects such as the European Union, Caribbean Common Market, Latin America Free Trade Association, Association of South East Asian Nations and the Southern African Development Community.

Economic regionalism as a political phenomenon is critically analysed within the context of West Africa from a broader international perspective. The view is that the integration of West Africa into the international political system and the global market economy has inevitably made the sub-region a 'beneficiary' or 'loser' in the international processes. What has become evident is the fact that the resurgence of regionalism in contemporary world politics has had considerable impact on the West African regionalism. The expansion of ECOWAS regionalism into the security domain has led to the revival of what has been described as the 'old' regionalism. The resurgence of regionalisms dates back to the late 1980s and is generally associated with the end of the Cold War and the cessation of the bi-polar international system; the economic and technological globalisation and their impact on increasing economic integration; the general adoption of neo-liberal economic policies in many parts of the developing world; the impact of the 'wind' of democratisation; and for many developing regions, the devastating domestic and regional effects of civil wars and state implosion on international peace and security.[4] However, the revival of regionalism is not a new phenomenon. It started with the regionalisation processes in Europe, Africa, Asia and North America. Therefore contemporary regionalism is regarded as a defining characteristic of the post-Cold War international order. In Aaron Friedberg's view, 'the dominant trend in world politics today is towards regionalization rather than globalization'[5] whilst Peter Drucker sees the knowledge-based economy as a phenomenon that 'makes regionalism both inevitable and irresistible'.[6]

But how does the West African regionalism fit within this global phenomenon? It becomes obvious that the contemporary regionalism is different from the 'regional wave in the 1960s' and 1970s of which ECOWAS is a part, because the emerging regionalisms do not focus primarily on economic issues and development co-operation but on diverse regional areas such as security, democratisation, environmental, human security and foreign policy co-operation. The ECOWAS community, far from becoming an 'ageing regionalist dinosaur'[7] has revamped itself in the 1990s and in the process is gradually evolving a regional identity or 'regionness'. This book will therefore highlight the multidimensional character of ECOWAS regionalism through the evaluation of Sierra Leone's West African integration.

It is important to note that the academic preoccupation with regionalism has been largely concerned with theoretical and empirical explanations and predictions about the integration process. As a result, a variety of political, sociological and economic theories have been advanced to explain the phenomenon of regionalism in world politics. Analyses of the impact of regionalism on member states had not occupied much of the attention of integration theorists in the 1960s and 1970s. The general preoccupation with elaborating models of integration during this period made the evaluation of gains and losses for member states a limited priority. However, in many developing regions, the critical issue of benefits and costs from regionalism projects were already leading to the disintegration of the integration schemes. In other words, the problems associated with distributing the benefits and costs of economic regionalism are major political issues and as such, crucial to understanding the integration and disintegration of regionalist projects. An UNCTAD report in 1993 described the crises arising from the benefits and costs of regionalism as the 'Achilles heel' of Third World integration projects.

Regionalist projects in developed and industrialised regions of the world have also been concerned about the costs and benefits of integration. In recognition of this problem, Dudley Seers and Constantine Vaitsos in *Integration and Underdevelopment* (London: Macmillan, 1980) explored the implications of integration for Western Europe. In 1988, the Cecchini Report was commissioned by the European Community on *Studies on the Economics of Integration: The Cost of Non-Europe*. In addition, a special European Commission project under the auspices of the Action and Research Committee in 1990 published a series comprising 12 volumes entitled *European Community Membership Evaluated*. These volumes evaluated the gains and losses of European Community membership for each of the then 12 states.

Unlike ECOWAS, there exists no comprehensive study of the impact of ECOWAS regionalism on Community countries. The majority of the impressive writings on ECOWAS regionalism have mostly focused on regional economic growth, trade liberalisation and intra-regional trade, sectoral development and technical co-operation, dependency and political economy of foreign policy, and regional security and peacekeeping. The novel contribution of this book is that it seeks critically to evaluate Sierra Leone's ECOWAS regionalism. The view is that the evaluation of ECOWAS regionalism for Community partners is a research endeavour that is long overdue. In almost all

ECOWAS countries, the regional organisation has, at different times, generated a great deal of controversial debate, but little or no academic analysis. *The Politics of Economic Regionalism* therefore establishes the basis for further analysis of the implications, costs and benefits of ECOWAS regionalism on member states.

The definition of some relevant terms is important at this stage. 'Regionalism' is a somewhat ambiguous term. It generally describes the degree of economic, political, socio-cultural and organisational interdependence amongst geographically proximate and contiguous states.[8] Regionalism describes the ideas, identities and ideologies related to a regional project, normally perceived as a political project. It is based on the normative assumption that it is a good thing for the region, peoples and the states. 'Regionalisation' on the other hand describes the material aspects and processes of regionalism.[9] It describes the diverse and multidimensional processes of regionalism, and the often 'undirected processes' of social, economic, political interaction within a region. According to Fawcett and Hurrell, regionalisation has been described as 'informal integration' and 'soft integration'.[10] In several respects then, regionalisation reflects the interplay between the formal and informal aspects of regionalism and the rather unconscious direction of the idea of regionalism. 'Regionness' defies any precise definition because of its often rhetorical underpinnings, i.e. the given understanding and meaning associated with a political activity that is described.[11] In Björn Hettne and Fredrik Söderbaum's view 'regionness' is 'the process whereby a geographical region is transformed from a passive object to a subject with capacity to articulate the interests of the emerging region'.[12] But as far as Fawcett and Hurrell are concerned, 'it is how political actors perceive and interpret the idea of a region and notion of regionness that is critical: all regions are socially constructed and hence politically contested'.[13] The defining characteristic of regionnness is the shared perception, whether 'real' or 'imagined', of belonging to a particular region as a result of common socio-cultural, historical, ethno-linguistic or religious traditions. The definition of the term 'Integration' has been a subject of controversy. The term is associated with the 'old' regionalism of the 1950s to 1970s. Integration has been used to describe the official, state-led economic, social and political process of integration amongst geographically proximate states. The term however lacks any 'essentialist' definition because of the divergent views as to whether integration is a 'process' or a 'condition'; what aspects are to be emphasised, i.e., economic, political or socio-psychological; or whether in fact integration points to an end-state, i.e. a teleological nature of integration, for example, a political community or union. Integration is simply defined as regional co-operation resulting from increasing interdependence amongst geographically proximate and contiguous states for the 'achievement of common goals' be it economic, political, developmental, environmental, technical or security.[14] Integration also reflects the non-material dimension of the process itself and hence has ideological underpinnings. For the purposes of this book, and mainly for convenience, the terms 'regionalism' and 'integration' shall be used interchangeably.

The Politics of Economic Regionalism analysed in eight chapters will delve into the following issues. Chapter One looks at the evolution of economic regionalism in West Africa and the conceptual framework for analysis. Chapter Two discusses the expansion of the economic regionalism into the security domain and the nature, dynamics and complexity of the emerging security regionalism in West Africa. Chapter Three links the developments within the West Africa sub-region with those of the transformation of the global economy and international political system by looking at ECOWAS and the 'new' regionalism. Chapter Four sets the basis for the political economy analysis of Sierra Leone's ECOWAS regionalism. The political, economic and security developments within ECOWAS have been regarded by some analysts as a contributing factor to the civil war in Sierra Leone. Chapter Five will therefore provide an interpretation of the civil war in Sierra Leone and how ECOWAS regionalism has or has not contributed to fuelling the war. Chapter Six analytically shows the interface between the civil war in Sierra Leone, the political economy of diamonds, and trans-border regionalisation within the context of ECOWAS regionalism. The objective of Chapter Seven is to evaluate the political implications of Sierra Leone's ECOWAS regionalism. It will discuss the politico-diplomatic relevance of ECOWAS for small states such as Sierra Leone, the ECOWAS democratic intervention and its implications for post-Cold War African international relations, the ECOWAS / ECOMOG - United Nations co-operative security for peacekeeping and conflict management in Sierra Leone and the how ECOWAS regionalism erodes national sovereignty. Chapter Eight assesses the economic implications of Sierra Leone's ECOWAS regionalism and how the country can further exploit the opportunities and advantages of West African integration and co-operation. The chapters that follow in this book therefore explore these diverse but interrelated issues of the politics of economic regionalism within the context of West Africa and the possible international dimensions.

Notes and References

[1] Robert D. Kaplan, 'The Coming Anarchy' *Atlantic Monthly*, February 1994.
[2] 'Hopeless Africa', *The Economist*, 13-19 May 2000.
[3] Louise Fawcett and Andrew Hurrell (eds) *Regionalism in World Politics: Regional Organization and International Order* Oxford: Oxford University Press, 1995, p. 5.
[4] Louise Fawcett and Andrew Hurrell (eds.) *op. cit.* 1995, p. 1, identifies some of the reasons responsible for the resurgence of regionalism in contemporary world politics.
[5] Aaron L. Friedberg, 'Ripe for Rivalry: Prospects for Peace in a Multipolar Asia' *International Security* Vol. 18, No. 3, Winter 1993-4, p. 5.
[6] Peter F. Drucker, *Post-Capitalist Society* London: Butterworth-Heinemann, 1993, p.137.
[7] Fawcett and Hurrell, op. cit. 1995, p. 3.
[8] See Fawcett and Hurrell, p. 5; and also, Joseph S. Nye (ed.) *International Regionalism: Readings* Boston: Little, Brown & Co., 1968.
[9] See M. Marchand, M. Böas and T. Shaw (eds), 'The Political Economy of New Regionalism' *Third World Quarterly* Vol. 20, No. 5, 1999, Special Issue.
[10] Fawcett and Hurrell, p. 39.
[11] Ibid.
[12] B. Hettne and F. Söderbaum, 'The New Regionalism in Approach' *Politeia* Vol. 17, No. 3, 1998, p. 9.
[13] Fawcett and Hurrell, pp. 38-39.
[14] For a variety of definitions of integration see, A. J. R. Groom and Alexis Heraclides, 'Integration and Disintegration' in Groom and Mitchell (eds.) *International Relations Theory* London: Pinter, 1978; Ernst Haas, 'Turbulent Fields and the Theory of Regional Integration' *International Organization* Vol. 3, No. 2, 1975; 'The Study of Regional Integration: Reflections on the Joy and Anguish of Pretheorising' in Leon Lindberg and Stuart Scheingold (eds.) *Regional Integration: Theory and Research* Harvard University Press, 1975; Michael Hodges, 'Integration Theory' in Trevor Taylor (ed.) *Approaches and Theory in International Relations* London: Longman, 1978.

1 Economic Regionalism in West Africa

Introduction

The phenomenon of economic regionalism has been a prominent feature of contemporary international politics. It became a major development concern in the post-Second World War period. The European integration experiment which started with the creation of the European Coal and Steel Community (ECSC) and later the European Economic Community (EEC) in 1957 became an attractive example for political and economic leaders in the Third World. The 1960s and 1970s saw a proliferation of regional economic integration and co-operation groupings in Africa, Asia and Latin America. The United Nations, through its regional economic commissions, such as the Economic Commission for Latin America (ECLA) and the Economic Commission for Africa (ECA) played a leading role in promoting the idea of regional integration and co-operation as a viable mechanism for generating economic development and progress in the Third World.

The majority of the newly independent African states perceived economic regionalism and co-operation as an alternative development strategy that would generate welfare creation, industrialisation and trade expansion at continental and intra-regional levels. Economic regionalism and co-operation became a 'fashionable' ideology for African states which they perceived as a means of reducing their marginalisation in the international division of labour and power. The interest of African leaders in economic regionalisms was based on the recognition that the 'economic integration of the continent is a pre-requisite for the realisation of the objectives of the OAU'. A variety of regional integration and functional co-operation projects were established in Africa. According to a World Bank report, sub-Saharan African has undertaken the most extensive experimentation in regional integration and co-operation than any region in the developing world.[1] The most ambitious economic integration and co-operation projects in Africa include:

i. Common Market for East and Southern African States (COMESA), formerly the Preferential Trade Area (PTA) for East and Southern Africa.
ii. Arab Maghreb Union.
iii. Economic Community of Central African States (ECCAS).
iv. Southern African Development Community (SADC), formerly Southern African Development Co-ordination Conference (SADCC).
v. Economic Community of West African States (ECOWAS).

These economic regionalisms were intended to serve as the foundation for the creation of a continent-wide Common Market, as envisaged in the Lagos Plan of Action of 1980. The Lagos Plan sought to promote the long-term economic development and industrialisation of Africa through the creation first of large sub-regional markets, followed by a continent-wide market through merging the sub-regional markets.[2] In pursuit of this continental objective, the African Economic Community (AEC) was established in 1991.

The West African sub-region is littered with a variety of technical and economic groupings. It is therefore not surprising that the region has been referred to as the 'graveyard' of regional integration projects. This chapter therefore addresses the political economy of West Africa and the evolution of the Economic Community of West African States (ECOWAS).

Political Economy of West Africa

The 'geographical expression' that is West Africa occupies a land area of some 6.5 million sq. kms., with an estimated population of 225 million people (2000). West Africa accounts for approximately 32 per cent of Africa's population. It comprises sixteen independent states, which stretch from Mauritania in the north-west to Niger in the north-east, Nigeria in the south-east, and the gulf of Guinea in the south and south-west. The political map of West Africa consists of three land-locked states of Mali, Burkina Faso and Niger; the island state of Cape Verde, and twelve coastal states of Sierra Leone, Liberia, Guinea, Ghana, The Gambia, Togo, Benin, Nigeria, Senegal, Côte d'Ivoire, Guinea Bissau and Mauritania. The definition of West Africa however seems to defy geographical precision in that Cameroon and Chad are sometimes regarded as part of West Africa. This rather imprecise political geography is at the heart of the diversity and complexity of the West African sub-region. West Africa as a 'region' consists of geographically proximate and contiguous states, emerging as a distinct entity or more precisely, a territorial sub-system.

West Africa exhibits a diverse range of historical, ethnic, cultural, political, economic, religious, ecological, and linguistic differences. The region has a trilingual cultural heritage, i.e., Anglophone, Francophone and Lusophone, a product of European imperialism in Africa. The Berlin Congress of 1885 effectively divided West Africa into different spheres of influence, subsequently known as British West Africa, French West Africa, Portuguese West Africa and German West Africa. European colonialism and partition bequeathed to West Africa the most heterogeneous group of states in Africa. The arbitrary demarcation of political frontiers in West Africa cut across ethnic, linguistic and cultural borders. Thus, the Via speaking people are divided between Sierra Leone and Liberia, the Ewe, between Togo and Ghana, and the Yuroba, between Benin and Nigeria. The map of West Africa therefore presents a picture of uneven states, both in size and resource endowment. For example the size, population and resource endowment of such countries as Nigeria, Ghana, Senegal and Côte d'Ivoire are sharply contrasted with such states as The Gambia, Benin, Cape Verde and Togo. It therefore seems that the most distinguishing feature of West Africa is that the differences between the states are greater than the similarities.

In spite of these differences, the states in West Africa share certain similar characteristics. The general characteristic is that these states can be categorised as least developed and underdeveloped in that they share the common features of low life expectancy, high infant mortality, high levels of illiteracy, low growth rates and per capita incomes, and increasing poverty. However, not all states in West Africa conform to this essentially economic criteria. What is obvious is that West African states are at different levels of development.

The territorial boundaries and organisational structures of West African states are a product of European colonialism. The only African exception is Liberia, which was never formally colonised. The politico-administrative units of these states are a legacy of colonial rule. For example, Sierra Leone's political and administrative structures are patterned on that of the British, whilst Senegal's are the replica of the French. Modern state power in these countries is to a very large extent a reflection of the colonial state power based on bureaucratic control and exploitation of trading and production relations by the ruling and governing class in post-colonial West Africa. Therefore, in the majority of post-colonial states, political ethnicity continues to play a significant role in the nature of domestic politics and the struggle for the control of state power. Another similarity is that the majority of West African states had their political independence in a relatively peaceful manner through political agitation and the mobilisation of nationalist fervour against colonial rule. The only exception is that of Guinea Bissau which had to undertake an armed struggle led by the PAIGC (Partido Africano da Indepêndncia da Guiné e Cabo Verde) against Portuguese imperialism.

Another common feature is that contact with European imperialism incorporated West African economies into the capitalist world system, primarily as producers of raw materials. As export economies, they do not have control over the externally determined market prices, which explains their peripheral status in the world economy and the corresponding limitation to independent socio-economic development. The uneven economic development within West African territories is reflected in the urban and coastal focus of the majority of these economies. This urban-coastal focus also accounts for the patterns of intra-regional migration and some of the regional conflicts of economic interests within and amongst these states.[3]

West African economies are based on:

i. Cash crop economies: agricultural products are the principal foreign exchange earners for most of these states. The products include coffee, palm oil, piassava, pineapples, groundnuts (Senegal and The Gambia are leading producers), and cocoa (Ghana and Côte d'Ivoire are leading world producers).

ii. Extractive-based economies: the West African sub-region is richly endowed with strategic resources such as oil (Nigeria is the sixth-largest producer), bauxite, iron ore, tin, zinc, copper, uranium (Niger), gold, manganese, diamonds and rutile (Sierra Leone, the leading producer).

Industrialisation efforts in West Africa have been a means of diversifying the economic base of the sub-region. These efforts have been hindered by the lack of technological development and manufacturing expertise. West African economies had to rely on Multinational Corporations (MNCs) and bilateral economic co-operation with Western governments for the extraction of these strategic resources. The region's trading pattern is dependent on the outside world, with less than 10 per cent of official trade being intra-regional. This external-dependent nature of West African economies means that they are often in competition with each other for external trading partners, markets, foreign capital and technology. Strategic minerals such as oil, particularly in the post-1973 oil crisis, gave countries like Nigeria important political, economic and diplomatic leverage in international affairs. Ironically, West Africa is a region of poverty and underdevelopment in spite of its huge natural resources. Most of the countries have an annual GNP which economists regard as below the poverty line. The GDP of West African states by 1990 amounted to US $72.53 billion, and has been growing at an annual rate of only 1.6 per cent over the previous ten years.

At independence in the 1960s and 1970s, West African economies generally had a healthy economic growth rate. In the 1980s and 1990s, a combination of external and domestic factors produced unfavourable economic conditions and underdevelopment. It forced most West African governments to implement IMF/World Bank Structural Adjustment Programmes (SAPs) with specific economic objectives and stringent conditionalities. The experiment with SAPs has not generated economic growth and development that is felt in tangible terms for the peoples of West Africa. West Africa therefore has some of the world's poorest nations. The intervention of the IMF and World Bank gave these institutions the opportunity to serve as *de facto* economic and finance ministers of weak West African economies. The IMF/World Bank programmes only exacerbated the debt burden of these states, which by 1997 totalled US $73.206 billion.[4] The 1999 *UN Human Development Report* shows that all the countries in West Africa (with the exception of Ghana and Cape Verde, which are middle-income) are in the low human development category.

In political terms, the immediate post-independence experiment with democratic pluralism, largely based on the political systems of former colonial powers, were to be replaced by centralisation of power through one-party rule and military dictatorships. West Africa has produced a variety of regimes ranging from one-party dictatorship and military juntas to multi-party democracies (Senegal), Socialist and Marxist-Leninist regimes (Guinea, Mali, Ghana [Kwame Nkrumah], Benin) and revolutionary and popularist regimes (Jerry Rawling's Ghana and Thomas Sankara's Burkina Faso). West Africa alone accounts for a large share of military coups in Africa. About 41 successful military coups have taken place in the member states of West Africa between 1963 (Togo) and 1999 (Côte d'Ivoire). Single party politics and military dictatorships heralded the centralisation of power and personalised leadership wherein political power was monopolised by the 'strong man' who controlled state power and its resources. The president became identified as the state for example, Kwame Nkrumah's Ghana, Siaka Steven's Sierra Leone and Houphout-Boigny's Côte d'Ivoire. This trend changed in the late 1980s and 1990s with the 'Third Wave' of democratisation which heralded political liberalisation and multi-party politics in the majority of West African states. The tidal wave of political liberalisation in post-Cold War West Africa, supported by Western governments and international financial institutions such as the IMF and World Bank, swept away one-partyism and some of the autocratic regimes. In some West African states such as Liberia, Mali, Sierra Leone and Guinea Bissau, the effects of the end of the Cold War and the nature of domestic politics in these states led to bloody civil wars and the collapse of the state. State implosion in West Africa and its effects on regional peace and security have led some writers such as Robert Kaplan to paint a rather apocalyptic vision of post-Cold War West Africa in that:

> West Africa is becoming the symbol of world wide democratic, environmental and societal stress, in which criminal anarchy emerges as the real 'strategic' danger. Disease, overpopulation, unprovoked crime, scarcity of resources, refugee migrations, the increasing erosion of nation-states and international borders, and the empowerment of private armies, security firms, and international drug cartels are now most tellingly demonstrated through a West Africa prism.[5]

Although Kaplan's 'Coming Anarchy' raised some serious security issues facing West Africa, it is however an exaggerated account. What is obvious is that post-Cold War West Africa exhibits contradictory elements of reversal (civil wars, poverty, economic underdevelopment etc.) and renewal. Far from 'reverting to the Africa of the Victorian atlas' portrayed by Kaplan, West Africa has re-invented itself by taking responsibility for solving some of its regional problems, though with qualified success.

The political economy analysis of West Africa illustrates the fact that West Africa is marginalised in both the international divisions of labour and of power. As primary producers, West African countries continue to perform their traditional function as 'hewers of stone and drawers of water' in the international economic system. As developing or least developed nations, they operate within a set of international rules and regulations fashioned by the dominant capitalist economies.[6] The economic and political vulnerabilities of West African states explain their propensity for external dependence. These states therefore have to devise strategies of coping in an unfavourable international economic and political system. For instance, the categorisation of West African states as Least Developed Countries (LDCs) provides opportunity for preferential economic and trading agreements with developed regions. Anna Dickson argues that the principle of 'self-election' i.e., electing to remain in the LDCs category, becomes a political ploy to extract preferential trading treatment from the international economic system.[7]

Evolution of the Economic Community of West African States (ECOWAS)

The political economy of West Africa depicts a glaring disparity within and between states in this sub-region. In spite of these differences, West African states committed themselves to establish an economic community that would eventually cut across former colonial boundaries, and bring together the sixteen English, French, Portuguese, and Arab-speaking countries into a scheme aimed at producing a Free Trade Area, Customs Union and a Common Market that would integrate their economies. A variety of factors were responsible for the formation of this West African economic regionalism project.

Economic Factors

Economic imperatives were a driving force for the creation of a West African-wide community. West African states perceived the formation of a regional economic community as a strategy for national and regional development. Economic integration was seen as a means of overcoming the disadvantage of small size, and by establishing economies of scale, would provide opportunities for enhanced economic growth and development. A large consumer market for over 200 million peoples was an attractive proposition for integrating the economies of West Africa. A region-wide economic integration was seen as the best means of maximising the economic advantages to be derived from the economies of scale, comparative advantage and complementarity of goods. A further economic motivation stemmed from the desire to industrialise and advance technological progress that would generate trade expansion, stimulate economic growth and the productive capacity of the region. These economic motivations are shared by all regional integration projects in Asia, Latin America and Europe.

  The idea of a regional economic bloc that would serve as a collective bargaining platform with other economic blocs of the world also provided a powerful motivation. The period of the 1970s was a defining moment for Third World regions in articulating their views on the economic marginalisation in the global economic system. Calls for a New International Economic Order (NIEO) from developing countries was perceived as a viable mechanism of redressing the imbalances inherent in the international economic system. The idea of a regional economic bloc in West Africa was considered by the political leaders as a means to put the region in a better position to negotiate and conclude favourable agreements covering trade, foreign aid and capital investments. The African-Caribbean-Pacific-European Economic Community (ACP-EEC) relations provided a powerful example for the West African community to establish a collective regional economic bargaining blocs. This was also in line with the views expressed by traditional economists who favoured the formation of regional economic blocs to promote industrial growth and trade expansion base on the principle of comparative advantage. It was assumed that within the West African sub-region, economic regionalism as opposed to mere regional co-operation would lead to increased growth in intra-regional trade and potentially stronger status in relation to the outside world.

Economic regionalism in West Africa was regarded as an engine to solve the economic malaise, poverty and underdevelopment in the region. It was assumed that the size and massive population of the region would serve as a development turbine to mobilise internal resources for industrialisation and foreign direct investment. Economic regionalism was therefore perceived as a means of expanding the productive capacity of the region, create welfare and reduce production costs through joint investment in the exploitation and export of the region's resources. Ibrahim Gambari asserts that the main reasons for economic integration in West Africa have little to do with conventional Customs Union theory, such as trade creation and trade diversion. According to Gambari, it has more to do with the impact of the proposed regional market and other economic arrangements on fundamental socio-economic and political problems of the region.[8]

Political Motivations

Political motivations were crucial for the creation of a West African economic community. Economic regionalism was perceived as a political bloc that would enhance the political leverage of West African states. It was the period of Cold War power politics and the emergence of regional blocs sometimes based on the East-West ideological divide. It was generally acknowledged that the formation of a West African economic community would provide a political platform for the sub-region to play an influential role in continental politics and world affairs. It was assumed that a West African community would provide the institutional political framework to conduct the international relations of the sub-region. It was also assumed that a regional community would provide a forum to pursue independent foreign policy strategies under the umbrella of a regional bloc, and at the same time provide further sources of foreign aid. It was further assumed that a region-wide economic community would serve as a political bulwark to counter the intrusive role of extra-regional actors such as France in West Africa. The global economic crisis of the 1970s, notably the oil crisis, had debilitating effects on West African economies. Political and economic leaders in West Africa therefore needed a collective political bargaining bloc to make their voices heard in international politics. It is this perception of being politically and economically marginalised in the global system that conjointly helped in the words of Ernst Haas to 'spur integration as a way of getting from under'. In effect, it was the exigencies of political imperatives and economic underdevelopment that inspired West African leaders with what Haas referred to as 'a shared conception of how and why they need one another'.[9]

Pan-West African solidarity also served as a motivating factor. The idea of a Pan-West African integration, in political and economic terms, could be traced back to the heydays of Pan-Africanism in the 1950s and 1960s. 'Micro-nationalists' (conservatives) who were opposed to 'radical nationalists' such as Kwame Nkrumah, proposed the formation of economic and technical co-operation schemes as the basis for the gradual movement towards African political unity. In fact, some historians trace the genesis of the idea of political and economic co-operation in one form or another, to the early 19th century. During this period, West African nationalists such as Africanus Beale Horton and Casely Harford, translating their ideological and cultural nationalism, advocated 'self-government of West Africa' and a 'National Congress of British West Africa' respectively. It was argued that such colonial co-operation efforts based on the ideology of Pan-Africansim, represent a concrete manifestation of the desire for continental political unity. In post-colonial West Africa, economic regionalism and co-operation were regarded as laying the foundation on which a future united Africa would be built. This saw the emergence of a variety of political alliances and co-operations in West Africa such as the Ghana-Guinea, Ghana-Congo, and Ghana-Guinea-Mali Unions. These were envisaged as the nucleus of a continental union.

The ideology of Pan-Africanism therefore served as attractive political motivations for West African leaders. Concerns for national and regional security, political leverage derived from a collective bargaining bloc, and the domestic political considerations of all the member states played a significant part in the evolution of the West African economic regionalism. However, G. Salgado Penaherrera argues that political motivations in the creation of regional projects in the developing countries are 'of only incidental importance in comparison with . . . economic motivations'.[10] Though it would be difficult to refute the relevance of economic motivations in developing countries' regionalism, Penaherrera's generalisation is however questionable. Political motivations are a crucial factor for the establishment of economic integration and co-operation groupings. Economic integration and co-operation are by definition aspects of development that is essentially political. Put another way, economic integration amongst developing regions such as West Africa is politics by another means. The politics of economic integration illustrate the level of gradual integration or disintegration of the integration projects in developing regions. Even without achieving the economic objectives, the political advantages usually keep these moribund regional economic integration schemes alive.

Third World Ideology and South-South Co-operation

The motivations for the formation of a West African economic community were perceived within the wider context of the Third World ideology of South-South co-operation. South-South co-operation had its roots in the dissatisfaction with the North-South relations and the perception of being marginalised in the international division of labour and of power. The Third World perceived the structure of international economic relations, designed and maintained by the North, as responsible for their marginalisation and permanent peripheral status in the global economy. The Third World therefore demanded a New International Economic Order that would serve as an alternative to the liberal international economic order that was advantageous to the North. The Arab-Israeli war in 1973 and the subsequent OPEC price rises provided a political and economic leverage for the primary oil producers in the South. The OPEC action provided a political forum for united action where the countries of the South 'could exercise commodity power over the North'.[11] The NIEO debate became crystallised in the Third World ideology of empowering the South in the international system. The demonstration effects of OPEC's political power provided a rallying point for regional economic blocs in the South. Already at the United Nations General Assembly and other international fora, the post-colonial African states were flexing their political muscle by voting as a bloc in the name of Third World solidarity.

The failure of NIEO to bring about any significant transformation in the structure of the international economic relations between the North and the South, motivated Third World countries, including the West African sub-region, to focus on bilateral and regional co-operation arrangements for economic development and progress. South-South co-operation was therefore seen as a viable collective strategy based on self-reliance and a means to surmount the imbalance of the North-South divide, whilst at the same time making the international system more responsive to the needs of the South. South-South co-operation created the spirit of Third World solidarity to work collectively to reduce their dependence on the North and at the same time collectively exploit global opportunities to their advantage. West Africa states, like the majority of Third World countries therefore clung to the Third World ideology, most times half-heartedly, as an alternative form of political and economic expression.

Tradition of Functional Co-operation in West Africa

West African states have a long tradition of functional co-operation, which dates back to the pre-colonial period. Historical evidence points to the fact that there existed in pre-colonial West Africa the 'integrative habit'. Some form of functional co-operation had been prevalent between West African 'kingdoms' or states in pre-colonial and colonial periods. Co-operative efforts between these kingdoms and city-states in economic and commercial ventures utilising the waterhead of Senegalese river, Mano river, and the Lake Chad basin had been a feature of West Africa for centuries. *West Africa* magazine argues that the formation of a West African economic community was not a novel idea because the leaders were merely re-creating something that existed in the past. It argues that the region constituting West Africa has had an ancient economic tradition, largely through the Trans-Saharan trade. Thus the idea of an economic community can be regarded as a congeries of areas served by traditional markets and crossed by traditional trade routes for which modern boundaries are irrelevant.[12] However, it is also argued that though the roots of ECOWAS can be traced to ancient trading links in West Africa, the formation of the economic community was the first constructive attempt to integrate the economies of the West African sub-region.

The tradition of functional co-operation was further strengthened during the colonial era when administrative, economic and political expediencies forced the colonial governments to establish inter-territorial and intra-regional politico-administrative and economic structures. The politico-economic and administrative imperatives provided the framework for organising the diverse economic activities of European colonialism in West Africa. For instance, the French in 1946 created an overall government of federation of French West Africa (AOF) and a Francophone West African Customs Union, with a centralised common currency, the CFA Franc Zone whose convertibility was guaranteed by France in 1962. The British for their part, organised common services in Anglophone West Africa and created the West African Currency Board, and the West African

Produce Board to handle the marketing and management of agricultural products. A number of these arrangements extended into the post-colonial era such as the monetary union between Francophone West African countries and France. French West Africa, drawing from their common history of functional co-operation was in the vanguard in establishing several economic unions. These included: the Niger River Commission (RNC); the Chad Basin Commission (CBC); the Union Monetaire de L'Ouest Africain (UMOA); the Union Douanire de L'Afrique de L'Ouest (UDEAO); the Organisation of Senegal River States (OERS); the Senegambia Confederation and the Communaut de Afrique de L'Ouest (CEAO). On the basis of this colonial economic co-operation, Uka Ezenwe argues that:

> given the level of economic integration achieved in West Africa before independence by each colonising power within its area of authority, one might have expected unimpeded progress, even if at a slower pace, towards closer economic co-operation after the achievement of self-rule.[13]

Arguably, the so-called economic integration of West Africa only created dependent economies to serve the interests of the colonial powers. It was not the harmonisation of economic and monetary policies of West African states primarily based on the collective development of the sub-region. It was a pragmatic colonial device to exploit better the resources of the sub-region and as such could hardly be labeled as economic integration. Arthur Hazelwood aptly captures the illusionary colonial economic integration when he states that:

> It was a unity imposed from outside for the administrative convenience of the colonial power - it was unity of Europe in Africa, reflecting the hegemony of the metropolitan country over its various colonies. It was not to be expected that, with the removal of Europe from the scene, the unity would necessarily continue.[14]

The habit of co-operation established during pre-colonial and colonial periods laid the foundation for economic regionalism in West Africa.

Nigeria's Regional Leadership Ambitions

Nigeria, the brain behind the creation of a West African-wide economic community was motivated by a variety of domestic, regional and international considerations the majority of which were economic, political and strategic in nature. Nigeria is Africa's most populous nation with rich strategic resources and regards West Africa as its sphere of political and economic influence. Two events shaped Nigeria's leadership role in the formation of a West African economic community.

i. The Biafra civil war of 1967-70 established the link between national security and regional security. The Biafra secessionists received military and diplomatic support from both West African states and foreign governments such as Ivory Coast (Côte d'Ivoire); Dahomey (Benin); Rhodesia (Zimbabwe); Zambia; Tanzania; France; Israel; and Portugal. The civil war was a turning point in the history of Nigeria in that it shifted its foreign and security policy orientation from 'isolationism' to 'interventionism' in regional affairs.[15] Post-civil war Nigeria initiated the three 'concentric circles' focus of its foreign policy based on regional stability and functional co-operation, a leadership role in African and international affairs.

ii. The oil crisis of 1973 brought Nigeria into the international limelight because of its strategic oil resources. Nigeria became an indispensable oil producer for the West and used the forum provided by OPEC to flex its political muscle in African and international affairs. Oil diplomacy became a major instrument of Nigerian foreign policy.

Nigeria's civil war history and strategic oil resources strengthened its leadership ambitions in West Africa. This was to reinforce a self-image of Nigeria as the hegemonic leader in West Africa with a 'manifest destiny' to lead the sub-region. Nigeria's leadership role in the formation of ECOWAS was therefore in pursuit of achieving the traditional ends of politics, i.e. power, prestige and political influence. According to Naomi Chazan *et al* 'The decision to work for a regional common market was an important step in re-defining West African geo-political space, for it implicated Lagos in matters beyond economic co-operation.'[16] West African economic regionalism was to provide Nigeria with a platform for a more activist diplomacy in African affairs. Further more, Nigeria's West African leadership was geared towards limiting French influence (which rivals Nigeria for leadership of West Africa) in the sub-region. Nigeria has always regarded French influence in West Africa as a threat to its national security and political independence. Therefore, an economic integration project under Nigerian leadership was perceived as a counter-weight to

French influence in West Africa.

Role of Extra-Regional Actors

France is the most influential extra-regional actor in West African integration. French West Africa is a centrepiece of France's African foreign policy. Its considerable economic, military and political involvement in the sub-region dates back to the colonial period. Post-colonial Francophone states maintained a series of interlocking relationships in the form of economic and technical co-operation, all of which were largely dependent on France. In the post independence era, France discouraged any effective socio-economic and political co-operation between the Francophone and Anglophone parts of Africa. For instance, France was instrumental in the formation of the Francophone-based West African Economic Community (CEAO) in 1973. It used its strategic position in the EEC to secure a technical assistance grant for CEAO in the sum total of US $558,000. This served as a positive attraction for the Francophone states to move away from a Nigerian-led West African community. President Georges Pompidou described CEAO as 'a just equilibrium between the Francophone and Anglophone', and claimed that it was proper for the Francophone states to 'harmonise their efforts so as to counter-balance the heavy weight of Nigeria'.[17] Olatunde Ojo argues that France served as the main protagonist of the anti-West African economic community. However, France's anti-West Africa integration stance indirectly served as a stimulus to strengthen the resolve of Anglophone West African states to bring about the formation of a region-wide economic community. France therefore provides the classic example of the role of intrusive power in a regional sub-system in international politics. It also illustrates the dependence of West African states on extra-regional actors. It is instructive to note that the British did nothing to promote or hinder the creation of a West African economic community, whilst America supported economic regionalism in West Africa as it was within the remit of its economic development policy for Africa.

Pro-integrationists in West Africa

A diverse combination of interest groups played a vital role in mobilising domestic support for the formation of a West African economic community. Olatunde Ojo explains that the Nigerian Chamber of Commerce, Industry and Agriculture was instrumental in mobilising support for regional integration amongst its counterparts in other West

African states. This regional co-operation led to the establishment of a West African Chamber of Commerce, Industry, Mines and Agriculture. Julius Okolo therefore argues that 'Anticipating prospect of expanded regional trade and extensive opportunities to compete more favourably against transnational corporations and other foreign firms, indigenous West African industrialists and commercialists grouped together to foster common economic interests'.[18]

There is not enough evidence to illustrate intellectual support for the formation of a regional economic community. Pro-integrationists such as Adebayo Adedeji, then Commissioner for Economic Development, was instrumental in promoting the idea of a West African common market beneficial to Nigeria. Ojo further explains that the military government of General Yakobu Gowon also drew support from his intellectual think-tank, using the logic of functional co-operation to win converts to the integration cause. The view is that the common market argument advanced by the Nigerian Chamber of Commerce was a convenient cover in an attempt to reduce the commercial influence of France in neighbouring Dahomey, Niger and the Nigerian interior bordering these states. However, anti-integrationists argued that Nigeria's large market did not need regional expansion for large-scale industrialisation and that the country was likely to benefit from integration because of the limited intra-regional trade and competitive export commodities.[19] This shows that even within the region, there were forces that opposed the idea of a West African economic integration.

Formation of ECOWAS: 1972-1975

No single actor, domestically or internationally, could be credited for the actual formation of ECOWAS. It was the result of a complex combination of factors and initiatives of regional players. The late president Tubman of Liberia could be credited for leading the diplomatic and political support for the creation of a West African economic community. In his speech on 7 January 1964, he introduced the idea of a free trade area in West Africa and even organised a series of bilateral and multilateral talks with other West African governments to promote this proposal. In August 1964, representatives from Ivory Coast, Guinea and Sierra Leone met in the Liberian capital Monrovia to discuss the possibility of creating a free trade zone. The Liberian initiative encouraged the UN-ECA to organise a West African Summit of free trade zone in Monrovia in 1968. The Francophone states did not attend the ECA sponsored regional free trade summit. This led to the emergence of two rival economic groupings in the sub-region: i. CEAO, whose membership was exclusively Francophone countries; and ii. the Nigeria-Togo Union, which was to serve as the basis for the proposed West African community. Within the Anglophone community, the Mano River Union (MRU) was established in 1973 between Liberia and Sierra Leone (joined by Guinea in 1980). Between 1965-1972, all efforts to achieve the creation of a regional economic community were futile, despite the institutional support given by ECA. The political divide between the Francophone and Anglophone West African states, clash of national interests, and the complex geopolitics considerably hindered the formation of ECOWAS. The Francophone countries preferred the exclusive economic co-operation in CEAO, with close economic and security co-operation with France. President Leopold Sedar Senghor of Senegal was particularly concerned about the potential power and resources Nigeria could wield in a region-wide economic community. In an effort to counter Nigeria's standing in the proposed economic community, Senghor called for the enlargement of ECOWAS beyond the West African limit to include Cameroon, Zaire (Democratic Republic of Congo), and Congo Brazzaville (countries with Francophone sympathy).

General Gowon and President Eyadema of Togo could be credited with spearheading the campaign for the formation of ECOWAS. The creation of CEAO in 1972, which excluded Anglophone countries and gave observer status to Togo, brought a new diplomatic impetus from the two leaders. The Gowon government in the post-civil war era made a determined effort to win over Francophone states that had supported the Biafra secessionists. Meetings between the two Foreign Ministers of Nigeria and Ivory Coast restored cordial diplomatic relations between the two countries. Nigeria was therefore able to remove a potential stumbling block in the negotiations leading to the formation of ECOWAS. To counter the political influence of the Francophone grouping, Gowon proposed an all-West African economic community, and in collaboration with Togo, formed the Nigeria-Togo embryonic West African Economic Community (WAEC) in 1972, with open membership. The Senghor-Houphout-Boingy rapprochement was a major hindrance for the Gowon-Eyandema integration efforts. Nigeria therefore had to win the political support of Francophone states such as Togo, Dahomey (Benin) and Niger by offering interest-free loans, grants and concessionary-priced oil. The oil diplomacy and 'Naira diplomacy' (equivalent of the American 'dollar diplomacy') became effective instruments to counter the negative argument that economic integration would be detrimental to Francophone states. The support for an all-West African economic community generated by Togo,

Dahomey and Niger created the momentum for other Francophone states, particularly Senegal and Ivory Coast, to join ECOWAS. General Gowon also used his position as Chairman of the OAU to mobilise political support for a regional-wide economic community. At the same time, Nigeria's constructive role in the ACP-EEC negotiations of the Lomé convention created regional trust and confidence in its leadership. In some respects, the Nigeria-Togo alliance could be compared to the Franco-German alliance in the evolution of the EEC in 1957.

A series of meetings of West African states from 1964 to 1975 directly led to the establishment of ECOWAS. A draft treaty produced by a regional commission's experts was adopted by West African government ministers meeting in Lomé in 1973 as the basic principle for the economic community. Subsequent intergovernmental meetings in Accra in 1974 and Monrovia in 1975 were preparatory meetings for the adoption and ratification of the treaty establishing ECOWAS. The ECOWAS Treaty was signed in Lagos on 28 May 1975 by the original fifteen member states. Cape Verde, the sixteenth member, joined in 1977 after independence from Portugal. The realist political pursuits of West African states are reflected in their political gains from the formation of ECOWAS. 'Big brother' Nigeria, secured the ECOWAS Secretariat, Togo provided the secretariat for the ECOWAS Fund, whilst Ivory Coast provided the first Executive Secretary for the regional economic community. This therefore set the stage for the future politics of regionalism in West Africa and why it is dominated by the ECOWAS 'big four', i.e., Nigeria, Côte d'Ivoire, Ghana and Senegal. The formation of ECOWAS provided a major organisational framework for regional economic integration and political co-operation in West Africa.

The formation of ECOWAS shows that the regional community shares similar characteristics with other economic regionalisms in that it is an intergovernmental, state-led elitist project. Furthermore, geographical proximity and mutual interdependence, coupled with economic and political imperatives provides the stimulus for the creation of these economic regionalisms.

Aims and Objectives, Institutional Framework and Main Features of the Treaty

The acronym reflects the centrality of economic development in ECOWAS. The primary objective was to establish a common market that focuses on trade liberalisation, harmonisation of economic policies and the removal of barriers to the free movement of factors of production, i.e. people, goods and services. It proposed to achieve this in 'stages', through the establishment of:

i. Free trade area with no tariff (quantitative and qualitative restrictions) on intra-regional trade.
ii. Customs Union with no intra-regional tariff, but a common external tariff towards third countries.
iii. Common market that allows free movement of the factors of production.
iv. Economic integration that would harmonise the economic, monetary, fiscal, and agricultural policies of the community.

The aims of the Community outlined in Article 2 of the 1975 Treaty[20] also proposed to undertake sectoral development programmes in areas such as industry, transport and communication, energy and infrastructural development. To achieve the objective of monetary integration and equitable distribution of the benefits of economic integration and co-operation, the Treaty proposed to establish a fund for co-operation, compensation and development. It is obvious that the economic objectives are protectionist and exclusionary, like the majority of economic integration schemes in other parts of the world.

ECOWAS Institutional Framework

A quintuple institutional system is charged with administering and directing the affairs of the Community. They include:

i. Authority of the Heads of State and Government: The ECOWAS Authority is the highest decision making body which comprises all the sixteen leaders of the member states. The Chair of the Community is based on yearly rotation and the position is often utilised by West African leaders for power-political calculations; i.e. to promote national interests and for international prestige.
ii. Council of Ministers: The Council is made up of two ministers from each member state and is delegated with the responsibility of supervising all subordinate institutions of the Community, monitoring the functioning and development of the regional organisation.
iii. Executive Secretary: The executive secretary is the principal executive officer of the Community, who initiates and proposes

policy measures and programmes to the technical commissions. The executive secretary is directly responsible to the authority. All officers from the member states employed by the Community are regarded as international civil servants, and in principle, owe loyalty to ECOWAS and not to national constituency. They are the equivalent of the EU 'Eurocracts'.

iv. Tribunal of the Community: is delegated with the responsibility to authoritatively interpret the Treaty and other ECOWAS provisions and settle disputes referred to it by member states.
v. Fund for Co-operation, Compensation and Development.

A variety of specialised Commissions have been established and these include: the Trade, Customs, Taxation Statistics, Monetary and Payments Commission; the Industry, Agriculture and National Resources Commission; the Transport, Telecommunications and Energy Commission; and the Social and Cultural Affairs Commission. An additional technical commission is that of the Community Computer Centre (CCC) with the responsibility to computerise the collection, acquisition and management of Community customs and external trade statistical data.

The Revised Treaty of 1993 made important changes to the 1975 Treaty to reflect the changed international political and economic environment. The Revised Treaty added an Economic and Social Council; a Community Parliament and a Community Court of Justice. It also established a specialised technical Commission for Political, Judicial, Regional Security and Immigration.[21] An important provision of the Revised Treaty is that of the principle of supranationality whereby the decisions of the Authority become binding on the institutions of the Community and member states within 90 days after adoption by the chairperson of the Authority. Regional decision making is within the province of the ECOWAS Authority, though this responsibility is shared with the technical experts and Community bureaucrats. The treaty of ECOWAS does not create a supranational entity with power over national economies and member states. The practical implementation of the supranationality provision of the revised treaty is yet questionable. However, there is some degree of pooling of sovereignty among ECOWAS countries as manifested in the intergovernmental political, economic, security and technical co-operation, networks and bargains. Most of the institutions proposed by both treaties are still yet to be established. In fact, some of the provisions of the revised treaty are largely drawn from the EU framework without consideration for its practical implementation within the West African context. The politics of economic regionalism makes the adoption of institutions, such as Community Parliament and Community Court of Justice, an attractive proposition because it lends some semblance of international prestige to ECOWAS.

Main Features of ECOWAS Regionalism

At the heart of ECOWAS integration is the common market objective. To achieve this objective, the treaty provides for liberalisation amongst ECOWAS countries, industrial and sectoral development, a regional Fund for co-operation, compensation and development, and free movement.

Trade Liberalisation

In a bid to promote intra-regional trade and generate trade expansion and industrialisation, the Community embarked on trade liberalisation that would lead to the creation of a free trade area and customs union. Under the trade liberalisation provisions, ECOWAS countries were to accord each other preferential treatment in matters of trade. It was anticipated that by 1980, all quotas, qualitative and administrative restrictions to intra-regional trade were to be removed and a common external tariff imposed on non-community members. However, the achievement of these objectives have proved more difficult than prescribed. By the late 1990s, implementing the objectives of the intra-community trade liberalisation and the external customs tariffs had not been a comprehensive success.

Industrial and Sectoral Development

Industrial development and trade expansion is at the heart of ECOWAS integration. The regional industrial development was based on joint sectoral planning, i.e. allocating to member states or a group of states that have comparative advantage in resource endowment. The rationale was to maximise the productive capacity of the region and avoid unhealthy rivalry between member states for foreign investors. It was assumed that industrial and sectoral development would enhance the balanced and harmonious development of the region. The following areas are prioritised for intra-community industrial development: agriculture, telecommunications, transportation and postal services. In an effort to attract foreign direct investment and mobilise private sector participation in intra-regional industrialisation, a West African Manufacturers Association (WAMA) was established. This increased the prospects of market sharing, regional co-ordination of production, and in some cases, the joint participation of governmental, community and foreign investors in industrial enterprises. A prominent feature of industrialisation in West Africa is its dependence on foreign investment. This reflects the dependent nature of West African economies. Large industrial enterprises in West Africa are generally 'affiliates of foreign corporations that own the bulk of the capital' ranging from 60 to 100 per cent.[22]

Two important aspects relevant to intra-community industrialisation and trade liberalisation are infrastructural development and harmonisation of monetary policies. The multiplicity of currencies (11 in total) in the sub-region has often hindered intra-regional trade. The Francophone zone, through the economic framework of UMEOA had managed some form of monetary integration pegged on the French Franc. It meant any problems in the French economic and financial market will affect the Francophone zone. To enhance monetary and financial collaboration amongst the sub-regional states, the West African Clearing House (WACH) was established in March 1975, initially outside the ECOWAS framework, but subsequently incorporated in conformity with Article 38 of the 1975 Treaty. The objectives were to promote member state currencies for intra-regional trade and other transactions, and to promote monetary co-operation and consultation. In an attempt to forge closer Community monetary co-operation, WACH was replaced in 1996 with the West African Monetary Agency (WAMA). To stimulate growth in intra-regional trade, which is less than 10 per cent (2000), the Community introduced the ECOWAS Travellers Cheque in January 1999 to ease the difficulties in buying, selling of commodities, and payment of bills within West Africa.

To enhance intra-regional trade and strengthen the economic and fiscal capability of the ECOWAS economies, efforts are being made for a closer monetary union in West Africa. In April 2000 an agreement was signed between Guinea and the region's Anglopohone states to create a single currency by 2003. The eventual objective is to merge with the Francophone CFA France zone, a currency backed by France and convertible into Euros and other international currencies. However, the objective of achieving a monetary union in West Africa, in spite of the long tradition established in the Francophone region, is regarded by many political and economic analysts as an unrealistic dream. The scepticism is based on the fact that the convergence criteria for monetary union can hardly be realistically attainable given the level of poor macro-economic performance of some ECOWAS states and the difficult recovery faced by some of these countries emerging from the throes of destructive civil wars.

There has been the growing awareness that trade liberalisation and removal of tariff barriers on intra-community trade would be meaningless without infrastructural integration. The transport and telecommunications sectors have also attained some relative development. To facilitate intra-regional movement of the factors of production and interconnection of member states, two Trans-West African highway networks have been constructed: i. the Trans-West African coastal highway; and ii. the Trans-Sahelian highway. Timothy Shaw however argues that 'these routes tend to reinforce rather than reduce inequalities, with Lagos for instance, being the terminal of three continental routes: Trans-Africa, Trans-Saharan and Trans-coastal'.[23] Telecommunications is the least developed sector. There are very limited direct telephone links between member states. Most calls have to be routed through London or Paris. However, the Community is working to improve this sector as reflected in the Fund's loan portfolio commitment for May 1992, in which telecommunications was allocated the highest budget, i.e. 42.4 per cent of the Fund's sectoral commitment.

ECOWAS Fund for Co-operation, Compensation and Development

The ECOWAS Fund has its headquarters in Lomé and its main responsibility is to fund regional development projects and disburse compensation to member states that suffer losses as a result of trade liberalisation and the location of community enterprises. Compensation for losses due to tariff reductions and the location of community enterprises had to come from member states' contributions to the Fund. The economic criteria for the assessment of member states' contributions is based on a co-efficiency that takes into account the GNP and per capita income of the states. The relatively developed and wealthy member states contribute far more than their less developed partners. The compensation scheme is regarded as an important fiscal mechanism for redressing the problems associated with the distribution of the benefits of integration. The ECOWAS Fund is similar to the UDEAC Solidarity Fund.

Free Movement

Free movement of people is regarded as central to achieving the objective of complete integration of the West African community. It is argued that the ECOWAS Treaty and Protocol on Free Movement are merely building on the foundations established during pre-colonial and colonial periods. The Community treaty envisages the free movement of the factors of production and describes individuals as 'community citizens'. The protocol on free movement signed in 1979 provided for the removal of visa requirements for community citizens intending to stay in any member state for the period of 90 days, and further granted them right of residence and establishment in any community country. However, the treaty did not provide for an unrestricted free movement within the community. The free movement protocol stipulated that the provisions would be implemented without costs to either the labour exporters or importers. It also provided for the state's right to restrictions that will regulate public health and public order. The point should be made that in general population movement in West Africa took place outside the framework of the ECOWAS treaty and protocol. The 'non-visible' border mentality amongst the peoples and their tradition of informal interactions encouraged both traditional and recent population movement in West Africa.

Free movement is the most popular aspect of ECOWAS integration and, not surprisingly, has generated a lot of criticism. It has led to hostility in several states where the labour market is threatened by the influx of intra-regional migration. This hostility became evident between Nigeria and Ghana in 1983 and 1985, which led not only to the closure of the borders between the two countries, but also the expulsion from Nigeria of more than two million West African nationals. Such expulsions are in breach of the ECOWAS free movement protocol. However, it is apparent that member states facing economic and political difficulties very often scapegoat illegal immigrants for their socio-economic problems.

Free movement continues to generate support and commitment from ECOWAS countries, in spite of the general reluctance to open their economies to regional pressure. The freedom to move without visa restrictions within the community is regarded as the most important symbol of the existence of the West African community. However, community citizens have to contend with illegal barriers such as road blocks, and extortion by customs and immigration officers. These limitations have not detracted from the relatively successful achievement of the free movement protocol, when compared with other regional integration projects in Africa.

Conceptual Framework: Modernisation, Dependency and Developmental Regionalism

The proliferation of economic regionalisms in Africa has not been matched by African-orientated research-based conceptual interpretations. The field of economic integration has been dominated by theories used to explain the Western European integration experiment. In general, economic regionalism has been underpinned by the liberal international economic order, broadly perceived as an approach to development through modernisation. Modernisation theory has been used in the 1960s and 1970s to explain development in 'pre-capitalist' societies, for example, former European colonies such as those in West Africa. This conception sees development in the newly independent states as a 'transition between backwardness and modernity'[24] by merely replicating or imitating the same evolutionary path of industrialised countries in the West. W. W. Rostow, rather simplistically, outlined stages which were to be replicated by 'pre-capitalist societies' in order to achieve economic modernity.[25] The majority of states in the developing world have not conformed to Rustow's model of economic development. In most cases, the intrusion from industrialised economies has led to perpetual economic and political marginalisation in the global economic system.

Dissatisfaction with the limitations of modernisation theory of development led to the emergence of an alternative model. The ECLA established in 1948 propounded the neo-Marxist or dependency perspective of development. The main proponents of the dependency perspective, Raul Prebisch, Andre Gunder Frank and others argued that the obstacles to underdevelopment for the Third World were to be found in the nature of the international system. The international system, according to the dependency school, was categorised into: core of dominant capitalist economies; semi-periphery; and periphery.[26] The dependency perspective proposed that the solutions to reducing the vulnerability and underdevelopment of Third World regions were to be found in industrialisation through protectionism and import substitution, state-led economic management and infrastructural development.[27] However, the import-substitution industrialisation (ISI) and inward-oriented development model promoted by the ECLA, as a way of generating industrialisation in developing regions, only placed further obstacles to development in the Third World regions. The dependency perspectives and ECLA's prescriptions were criticised on the basis that ISI only encouraged excessive borrowing and subsequently created balance of payment deficits for developing countries. The protectionist industrial policies created high costs for industrialisation and in turn provided the need for more foreign aid and external loans.[28] Furthermore, it was argued that this capital-intensive industrialisation created in some countries more unemployment, whilst at the same time creating an enclave economy which benefited only a few.

In spite of the limitations of the dependency school, it provided a powerful intellectual attraction for other Third World scholars. African dependency theorists also drew from Frank's model of 'development of underdevelopment'.[29] The African dependency school argued that Africa's underdevelopment could be traced to the manner in which the continent had been incorporated into the global capitalist system, mainly through colonialism. They contend that the dependency of Africa was responsible for its underdevelopment. The only solution out of this uneven development was to formulate alternative strategies. According to Ouatey-Kodjoe, the two prominent strategies are: i. African socialism; and ii. collective self-reliance through regional integration. The formation of ECOWAS is therefore a product of this alternative development strategy, which has its roots in the dependency perspectives. The majority of African regional integration projects share similar characteristics in that they are state-led market integration with protectionist tariffs, implemented variant forms of ISI, and are external capital dependent.

From Neo-functionalism to Developmental Regionalism

The two prominent conceptual interpretations of economic regionalisms in Africa are neo-functionalism and developmental regionalism. Neo-functionalism, as proposed by Ernst Haas, is a modified form of David Mitrany's functionalism which advocates functional co-operation in specific areas across national boundaries.[30] Neo-functionalism as propounded by Haas and others perceives the integration process to be a situation where a group of states decide to co-operate in order to increase their individual and collective interests in the performance of some technical, welfare and relatively non-controversial functions. These initial collaborative endeavours would gradually spillover into a controversial sphere of political activity. The spillover from the economic to the political arena will encourage the emergence of supranational authority and institutional building to manage the crisis of integration.[31] In general, functional and neo-functional theories have been used to explain ECOWAS integration.

It is incontestable that functional co-operation in West Africa had considerably improved peaceful inter-state relations, bridged the gap in terms of political understanding between the Anglophone, Francophone and Lusophone divide, and even limited border conflicts. However, it has not generated any political commitment to what might resemble a 'federalism by instalment' in West Africa. Unlike economic regionalism in developed and industrialised states, the nation states in West Africa, far from retreating, are still the dominant factor in integration. It is therefore difficult to see how regional functional co-operation will lead to a shift in loyalty from the national to a supranational ECOWAS authority. What is obvious is the fact that neo-functionalism is derived from the experiences of the politico-economic systems of the developed industrialised West. It embraces a general view of the functioning of all states. The universalisation of this concept therefore becomes problematic because the 'state' in Africa lacks the capacity and institutional viability to lend itself to the integration process as prescribed by the neo-functionalists. The neo-functional spillover concept when applied to ECOWAS integration is fraught with difficulties. It is difficult to distinguish between what is essentially 'low' (welfare, socio-economic) or 'high' (security, foreign policy) politics. Issues such as industry, agriculture, monetary policies, telecommunications, and trade are pregnant with political implications because they are vital to economic development and as such require the attention of political leaders for solutions. S. K. B. Asante argues that regional integration in West Africa, as in other developing regions, is in many respects a different phenomenon from that which obtains in an economically advanced and industrialised region.[32] Whereas the developed West can afford to treat such economic integration as a 'matter of welfare politics', the situation is often quite different in developing countries. Instead of 'gradual politicisation' as prescribed by Joseph Nye, 'over politicisation'[33] or instant politicisation is what integration in these regions will produce. Politics cannot be divorced from economics in the affairs of developing regions such as West Africa. ECOWAS integration has shown that the traditional political and sociological theories of integration have limited relevance in understanding the regionalisation process.

Economic regionalism in West Africa is therefore perceived as an economic development strategy. It is regarded as developmental regionalism because it is development-oriented and is seen as an approach to the problems of underdevelopment. Regional integration and co-operation has been an important development strategy for the Third World. Development objectives constitute the central objectives as well as the driving force for all joint economic activities in these regions. Developmental regionalism is defined as the concerted efforts of states and non-states actors within a geographical area to enhance the economic efficiency and development of the region as a whole and to improve its position in the world economy.[34] Fredrick Söderbaum sees developmental regionalism as a political response to economic globalisation. A common objective of regional integration and co-operation groupings is the commitment to improve the general welfare of the people in the region. The preamble of the ECOWAS Treaty states that 'conscious of the overriding need to accelerate, foster and encourage the economic and social development of their states in order to improve the living standards of their people . . . .'. ECOWAS regionalism is therefore a development strategy to improve both national and regional economic development, and to increase welfare gains arising from intensified intra-regional trade. From the 1970s onwards, a positive correlation was made between economic regionalism and development in Africa, and there was the prevalent perception that development could be attained through integration. It was argued that pooling of economic sovereignty in West Africa would transform the economies of the sub-region and improve the standard of living of the peoples.

The debate on Africa's development strategy has been between two schools of thought. On the one hand is the view advanced by the OAU and the ECA as reflected in the *Lagos Plan of Action for the Economic Development of Africa (1980-2000) (LPA)* and the *African Alternative Framework to Structural Adjustment Programmes (AAF)* in 1989. Both Africa strategies emphasised a shift away from the export-led development strategy to collective self-reliance. On the other hand were the World Bank and UN development prescriptions for Africa as reflected in the 1981 *Accelerated Development in Sub-Saharan Africa: An Agenda for Action* or the Berg Report, the 1985 *United Nations Programme of Action for the Development of Africa (UNPAAERD)* and the *United Nations Africa Priority Programme for Economic Recovery*, the 1989 World Bank *Sub-Saharan Africa: From Crisis to Sustainable Growth: A long Term Perspective Study*, and the 1996 *UN Special Initiative for Africa*. These development proposals were a combination of short-term and long-term development prescriptions, which emphasised the neoliberal export-led growth strategy for Africa. They called for an economic reform package directed at the domestic level through devaluation, privatisation, deregulation and implementation of SAPs. The World Bank and UN development proposals for Africa inevitably mean that African leaders have to endorse policy reforms consistent with the neoliberal economic philosophy.[35]

The main strategy of developmental regionalism has been market integration. Market integration is underpinned by the a liberal economic development strategy, which emphasises the capitalist sector as the route to economic development and industrialisation in developing regions. The rural economy, according to liberal theorists, should only play a secondary role as an outlet for capital products and a supplier of labour force. The 1985 UN-ECA proposals for strengthening regional integration in West Africa is notable for its emphasis on market integration. But market integration without physical or infrastructural integration has only led to 'negative integration', i.e. merely removing tariff barriers without a corresponding physical integration of member states' economies. In effect, balanced intra-regional trade has not occurred, nor has integration of the critical productive sectors such as agriculture, transport and communications, and industry. The trade-focused model of development has proved inadequate to generate economic benefits that would trickle down to the people, on whose behalf the integration process is established. The ECA proposal minimally stresses production integration, which is crucial to ECOWAS integration. The obvious question is whether the market actually feeds the people. The experience of ECOWAS integration and other Third World regionalisms has shown that the mere integration of markets through the removal of trade barriers, without substantial effort to expand production integration in all sectors, will achieve very little. It is argued that, in some respects, the graves of starving children in West Africa are dug by development strategies that largely neglect the rural economy, food production as opposed to cash crop production, on which the livelihood of the people depend.

The development strategy of ECOWAS integration is based on two rather contradictory models, i.e. economic modernisation or development through the market; and the alternative strategy of collective self-reliance and participatory development. This marriage of convenience which further incorporates West Africa into the global market economy is at the heart of the problems of economic regionalism in the sub-region. John Ravenhill argues that market integration without production integration is an unsuitable development strategy for developing countries because it accentuates regional inequalities and the emergence of regional growth poles.[36] The relatively developed economies tend to attract external capital for industrialisation, thereby making them 'developed poles' whilst other Community partners are reduced to suppliers of raw materials and consumers of manufactured goods produced elsewhere in the region. In comparative terms, the trade polices of the East African Community (EAC) in the 1970s favoured Kenya to the detriment of Tanzania and Uganda, and hence caused the subsequent disintegration of the integration project.

Conclusion

ECOWAS integration is part of the wider process of contemporary regionalism in world politics. ECOWAS has emerged as one of Africa's leading economic regionalism projects. The political and economic considerations and interests of the governments of the sub-region have largely directed ECOWAS regionalism. This state-led regionalism has therefore been a political elitist project. It has been used for strategising alternatives for regime survival and the control of the 'official' state at national level. Though ECOWAS regionalism has been about maximising economic welfare and benefits from intra-community trade and investment, the broad economic objectives have remained unachievable. The failure of ECOWAS economic integration is partly attributed to the fact that the process of regionalisation had been mainly state-centric, top-down and intergovernmental. The disparity in ECOWAS regionalism is often marked by intergovernmental officialdom and the detached attitude of West African citizens most times preoccupied with existential matters outside the ECOWAS framework. The informal and private sectors have been largely neglected. As part of ECOWAS's responses to the challenges of globalisation, it has in the 1990s started to cultivate the participation of the informal and private sector in the regionalisation process. As a direct response to the new regionalism, ECOWAS has revised its 1975 treaty to take on board the imperative of the changed international environment, and at the same time adopted policies of 'open' regionalism, i.e. less protectionism, open-door economic policies and being more inclusive. In the face of the challenges of market globalisation, African economic regionalisms were faced with two stark choices, either to 'reform or die'. For instance, in 1992 SADCC transformed itself to the Southern African Development Community (SADC) and abandoned its sectoral development strategy for open market integration as a means of integrating the region into the global market economy. SADC even extended its inclusiveness to embrace not only East and Central Africa (Tanzania and Democratic Republic of Congo), but also the Indian Ocean Islands of Mauritius and Seychelles.

      The success of ECOWAS integration depends on the viability of the national economies and political systems. The Community, according to the annual report (1999) of the Executive Secretary Lansana Kouyate, has failed to achieve its economic objectives and the implementation of institutional provisions necessary to enhance and strengthen ECOWAS integration. The poor implementation of ECOWAS decisions and protocols to a very large extent explains the politics of economic regionalism. West African leaders are often ready to adopt at summit level whatever policies or programmes that enhance their political credibility and international prestige, even when they know that they collectively lack the political will to implement such programmes. The Nigerian president Olusegun Obansanjo, in a candid comment at the 22nd ECOWAS Summit in December 1999, stated:

If an impartial observer were to say that we have failed to reach the pass mark, it would be understandable .... More tragically, it is observable that we are still very much as divided as we were at independence, namely into Francophone, Anglophone and Lusophone.[37]

ECOWAS countries in the 1990s have been challenged by civil wars in Mali, Liberia, Sierra Leone and Guinea Bissau; political instabilities and ethno-religious tensions and conflicts in Nigeria and military coups in The Gambia, Côte d'Ivoire and Niger. These pressing domestic political and security problems therefore deflect attention away from ECOWAS economic integration. Those member states in turmoil such as Liberia, Sierra Leone and Guinea Bissau that focus their developmental, foreign and security policies towards ECOWAS regionalism, do so because it serves their vested national interests, and potentially ensures regime survival.

Notes and References

[1] World Bank, *Sub-Saharan Africa: From Crisis to Sustainable Growth* Washington DC.: World Bank Publication, 1989, p. 152.
[2] OAU, *Lagos Plan of Action for the Economic Development of Africa, 1980-2000* Addis Ababa, OAU Publication, 1980.
[3] John Dunn (ed.), *West African States: Failure and Promise: A Study in Comparative Politics* Cambridge: Cambridge University Press, 1978, p.17-18.
[4] World Bank, *African Development Indicators 2000*, Washington D.C., The World Bank, 2000.
[5] Robert Kaplan, 'The Coming Anarchy' *Atlantic Monthly*, February 1994, p. 46.
[6] Barry Buzan, 'New Patterns of Global Security in the Twenty First Century' *International Affairs* Vol. 67, No. 3, 1991, pp. 431-451.
[7] Anna K. Dickson, *Development and International Relations: A Critical Introduction* Cambridge: Polity, 1997, p.29.
[8] Ibrahim Gambari, *Political and Economic Dimension of Regional Integration: The Case of ECOWAS* New Jersey: Humanities Press International, 1991.
[9] Ernst Haas, 'Turbulent Fields and the Theory of Regional Integration' *International Organization* Vol. 3, No. 2, 1975, p.186.
[10] G. Salgado Penaherrera, 'Viable Integration and Economic Co-operation Problems in the Developing World' *Journal of Common Market Studies* Vol. XIX, No. 1 & 2, 1980-1981, p.176.
[11] Anna K. Dickson, *Development and International Relations* 1997, p. 27. According to Caroline Thomas, 'it provided hope where previously there had been nothing but despair' *In Search of Security: The Third World in International Relations*, Hemel Hempstead: Harvester Wheatsheaf, 1987, p. 75.
[12] *West Africa* 30 June 1975, p. 730.
[13] Uka Ezenwa, *ECOWAS and the Economic Integration of West Africa* London: C. Hurst & Co., 1983, 5.

[14] Arthur Hazelwood (ed.), *African Integration and Disintegration* Oxford: Oxford University Press, 1967, p. 5.
[15] David J. Francis, 'Nigeria and West Africa' in Darryl Howlett and John Glenn (ed.) *Realism Versus Culture*, Aldershot: Ashgate, 2001 forthcoming.
[16] Naomi Chazan, Peter Lewis, Robert A. Mortimer, Rothchild, D. and Stedman, S. *Politics and Society in Contemporary Africa 3rd Edition* Boulder: Lynne Rienner, 1999, p. 371.
[17] Olatunde Ojo, 'Nigeria and the Formation of ECOWAS' *International Organization* Vol. 34, No. 4, 1980, p. 596.
[18] Julius E. Okolo & Steven Wright (eds.), *West African Regional Co-operation and Development*, San Francisco, Westview Press Ins, 1990, p. 26.
[19] This section on the evolution of ECOWAS draws extensively from Olatunde Ojo, 'Nigeria and the Formation of ECOWAS' *International Organization* 1980, *op. cit.*
[20] *Treaty of the Economic Community of West African States (ECOWAS), 1975* Lagos: ECOWAS Secretariat, 1975.
[21] *Economic Community of West African States (ECOWAS) - Revised Treaty* Abuja: ECOWAS Secretariat, 1993.
[22] Julius Okolo & Steven Wright, *West African Regional Co-operation and Development* 1990, p. 32.
[23] Timothy Shaw, 'Towards a Political Economy of Regionalism in Africa' in R. I. Onuwuka & A. Sesay (eds.), *Future of Regionalism in Africa* Basingstoke: Macmillan, 1985, p.12.
[24] Anna Dickson, *Development and International Relations*, 1997, p. 34.
[25] W. W. Rostow, *The Stages of Economic Growth* Cambridge: Cambridge University Press, 1960.
[26] Raul Presbish, *The Economic Development of Latin America and its Principal Problems* New York; United Nations, 1950. Andre Gunder Frank, *Capitalism and Underdevelopment in Latin America* New York: Monthly Review Press, 1969.
[27] Ian Mclean, *Oxford Concise Dictionary of Politics*, Oxford: Oxford University Press, 1996, pp. 134-5.
[28] Anna Dickson, *Development and International Relations op. cit.* pp. 38-39.
[29] Samir Amin, *Unequal Development* New York: Monthly Review Press, 1976. Walter Rodney, *How Europe Underdeveloped Africa* London: Bogle L'Ouverture, 1972.
[30] David Mitrany, *A Working Peace System* Chicago: Quad, 1966.
[31] Ernest Haas, *The Uniting of Europe* Stanford: Stanford University Press, 1968; 'The Study of Regional Integration: Reflections on the Joy and Anguish of Pretheorising' in Leon Lindberg & Stuart A. Scheingold (eds.), *Regional Integration: Theory and Research* Harvard University Press, 1975; 'Turbulent Fields and the Theory of Regional Integration' *International Organization* Vol. 3, No. 2, 1975.
[32] S. K. B. Asante, *The Political Economy of Regionalism in Africa: A Decade of Economic Community of West African States* New York: Praeger, 1986.
[33] Joseph S. Nye Jr., 'Comparing Common Markets: A Revised Neo-Functionalist Model' *International Organization* Vol. 24, No. 4, pp. 796-835.
[34] Fredrick Söderbaum, 'The new regionalism in Southern Africa' *Politeia* Vol. 17, No. 3, 1998, p. 91.

[35] For further discussion see: J. N'yangoro & T. Shaw (eds.), *Beyond Structural Adjustment in Africa: The Political Economy of Sustainable and Democratic Development* London: Praeger, 1992; Fantu Cheru, *The Silent Revolution in Africa: Debt, Development and Democracy* London: Zed Books, 1989.

[36] John Ravenhill, in *Future of Regionalism*, 1985, p. 207-8.

[37] 'In search of a new vision' *West Africa,* 20 December 1999- 9 January 2000, p. 49.

2 Security Regionalism in West Africa

Introduction

The political and security dimensions of ECOWAS regionalism have, until recently, been fairly muted. This is understandable given its economic integration origins. But the phenomenon of violent intra-state conflicts in West Africa have brought home the realisation that the economic integration objectives are unattainable in an environment of political instability and societal conflicts. The West African sub-region in the 1990s has become the new theatre of violent civil wars in Liberia, Mali, Sierra Leone and Guinea Bissau. These domestic conflicts threaten not only regional and international peace and security, but also challenge the capacity of the United Nation and regional organisations in managing and resolving these conflicts. Thought these civil wars are domestic in nature, they often have regional and international dimension and ramifications. The most serious threat to regional peace and security in West Africa is the 'contagion effect' of civil wars. These domestic conflicts are perceived with apprehension as the 'fire next door', a bush fire that does not respect national boundaries because its consequences are felt far beyond the state's borders.[1] These brutal intra-state conflicts have led to state collapse and their contagion effects threaten the national and regional security of the sub-region mainly due to the influx of refugees and the proliferation of small arms. It is the concern for regime survival, national and regional security that has forced West African leaders to take an active role in managing and resolving' these regional conflagrations. They have therefore appropriated collective solidarity as the mechanism to intervene and put out these threatening regional 'fires'. It is the imperative for regional peace and security as a precondition for achieving the economic integration objectives, that has forced the political leaders in West Africa to create a home-grown regional security and conflict management mechanism in 1990.

The formation of the ECOWAS Cease-fire Monitoring Group, ECOMOG, has generated popular debate, as well as, academic and policy analyses. The experiment with ECOMOG security regionalism means that political and security issues have dominated the ECOWAS economic integration agenda. The transformation of ECOWAS, i.e., taking on the mantle of security regionalism, is part of the wider responses of regional groupings to the challenges of economic globalisation and the changed international conflict environment of the 1990s. This Chapter will look at the evolution of ECOMOG and the implications for ECOWAS regionalism, as well as, the regional and international dimensions of ECOMOG security regionalism in post-Cold War politics.

The Creation of ECOMOG: The Liberian Crisis and the International Neglect of Africa

The expansion of ECOWAS into the security domain was made possible by two crucial imperatives. The outbreak of the Liberian civil war and the response of the international community led to a new thinking in West Africa on how to address regional security and economic crises.

The Liberian Civil War

The immediate cause for the Liberian civil war was the rebel invasion led by Charles Taylor of the National Patriotic Front of Liberia (NPFL) on Christmas Eve in 1989. The insurgency was against the nearly ten years tyrannical rule of President Samuel Doe who, in 1980, as a Master-Sergeant, led a bloody military coup against President Tolbert. Doe's military, cum-civilian regime, covertly supported by America, during his tenure of office, became infamous for gross violations of human rights, political chicanery, economic mismanagement and the informalisation of the 'official' state of Liberia. Due to the level of state weakness and economic impoverishment, Taylor's invasion, in less than a year, succeeded in controlling 90 per cent of the country, i.e., 12 out of the 13 counties, which he later called 'Greater Liberia' and proclaimed himself president. During this period, Liberia effectively degenerated into chaos and anarchy, and the authority of President Doe did not extend beyond the Executive Mansion where he was besieged. He was subsequently captured and killed by the rival Independent National Patriotic Front of Liberia (INPFL) led by 'General' Prince Johnson, whilst on an 'official mission' to the ECOMOG headquarters.[2]

The reasons for the outbreak of the Liberian conflict could be traced to the nature of post-colonial political and economic system that maintained the Americo-Liberian hegemony (freed slaves deported from

America); and the politics of ethnicity and clientelism established by the Doe regime. George Klay Kieh, Jr. traces the root causes of state implosion and societal fragmentation in Liberia to the nature and type of state formation, anti-democratic political framework, socio-economic inequalities and underdevelopment instituted by the Americo-Liberians since the 1800s.[3] The reign of terror of President Doe, 1980 - 1989, further impoverished the populace, privatised the state apparatus and other institutions of governance to serve the private interest of his Krahn tribesmen and their supporters. Leonard Brehun conclusion is that 'in terms of the loss of Liberia's image abroad and in terms of destruction of everything that Liberia had built over the centuries including lives and property, President Doe carried the championship'.[4] Charles Taylor's rebellion therefore reflected some element of popular revulsion against Doe's dictatorship. Taylor had been a member of Doe's government as Director of General Services responsible for government procurement. Taylor feel out with Doe because of accusation of embezzlement and had to flee into exile where he orchestrated his guerrilla war against Doe's regime.

For a variety of personal interests and political considerations, Taylor's' rebellion war supported by Burkina Faso, Côte d'Ivoire (both ECOWAS members) and Col. Muammar Qaddafi of Libya. The level of human carnage and destruction during the civil war led to massive influx of refugees and created a humanitarian catastrophe. According to a US State Department Report in 1990 'All combatants routinely engage in indiscriminate killing and abuse of civilians, looting and ethnically based executions, with one of the worst single episodes occurring in July When AFL soldiers killed approximately 600 persons taking refuge in the courtyard of St. Peter's Church'.[5] West African nationals were also targeted for brutal reprisals by all parties to the conflict for allegedly supporting their opponents. This brutal civil war and humanitarian catastrophe created directly threatened regional peace and security.

International Neglect of post-Cold War Africa

The Liberian civil war had important implications for the response of the international community to violent intra-state conflicts in Africa. When the war broke out, numerous calls for the United States and the UN to intervene went unheeded. The US in particular, had a special relationship with Liberia because of the country's strategic and economic advantages during the Cold War. By the mid-1980s, Liberia was the largest per capita recipient of US aid in sub-Saharan Africa, estimated at US $500 million between 1980 and 1988. The changed international environment of the post-Cold War era meant that the only form of foreign intervention was limited to the protective evacuation of Western nationals by US marines.

The international response to the Liberian civil war was to set the pattern of international neglect of African conflicts in the post-Cold War period. The Liberian conflict coincided with the end of the Cold War and the outbreak of the Gulf war which attracted the attention of the international community. The end of the Cold War adversely affected Africa in that there was general reluctance amongst major powers to continue the traditional practice of unilateral intervention in African conflicts. Also, Africa, during this period was of limited strategic, political and economic relevance to the major powers. Economic globalisation and other policy imperatives amongst Western governments led to limited aid flow and capital flight from Africa. The UN, in spite of its preoccupation with the Gulf war, was vastly over-burdened with new post-Cold War responsibilities. President Clinton of America stated that the 'United Nations simply can not become engaged in everyone of the world's conflict'.[6] The so-called new world order and the post-Cold War peace dividend did not considerably impact on international response to African conflicts such as the Liberian civil war.

The international neglect and differential treatment of African conflicts created the space for West African leaders to develop new ideas and home-grown approaches to regional security and conflict management, devoid of Cold War ideological divide.

The Birth of ECOMOG

The ECOWAS community assumed responsibility for regional security by default. The Nigerian president, General Ibrahim Babangida, in an impromptu briefing on the Liberian crisis in 1990 stated that; 'When certain events occur in the sub-region depending on their intensity and magnitude, which are bound to affect Nigeria's politico-military and socio-economic environment, we should not stand by as helpless and hapless spectators'.[7] Nigeria took the political and diplomatic initiative in convening the ECOWAS Standing Mediation Committee (SMC)[8] because it perceived the Liberia crisis as a threat to national and regional security. An ECOWAS peace plan was designed for Liberia as a framework to resolve the civil war. It provided for an immediate cease-fire; the establishment and deployment of ECOWAS Cease-fire Monitoring Group (ECOMOG) as a multinational intervention force to monitor the observance of cease-fire; the establishment of an interim government of national unity as a prelude for the holding of democratic elections under international supervision. The

ECOWAS peace plan for Liberia was supported by both the OAU and the UN.

The peace plan was outrightly rejected by Taylor's NPFL, and his Francophone supporters, Côte d'Ivoire and Burkina Faso, on the grounds that it was a Pax-Nigeriana attempt to continue to dominate the sub-region. The mandate of ECOMOG was to 'conduct military operations for the purpose of monitoring the cease-fire, restore law and order . . .'.[9] ECOMOG's mandate embraced elements of peacekeeping and enforcement, hence the justification for military intervention. However, when the ECOMOG 'Operation Liberty' landed in Monrovia on 24 August 1990, it was without the consent of one of the main parties to the conflict, the NPFL. There was no peace to keep or cease-fire to observe, nor any previous experience in peacekeeping, as such, the ECOMOG intervention force inevitably got embroiled in the Liberian imbroglio. This was to have serious implications for the peacekeeping force to serve as a neutral inter-positionary force in the conflict. The initial ECOMOG contingent that landed in Monrovia included Nigeria, Ghana, Guinea, The Gambia and Sierra Leone. Noticeably absent were Togo and Mali who, as members of the SMC, had formulated the ECOWAS peace plan. Though the Togolese and Malian presidents were initially willing to send troops, it is alleged that the pressure from the Ivoirian President, Houphouet-Boigny, forced them to change their policy. This reflects the ever present Anglophone-Francophone divide, and the complex geo-politics in West Africa.

However, some analysts argue that intervention in Liberia transcended concerns for regional security and humanitarian considerations.[10] The Liberian civil war was a 'clear and present' danger to the regimes in West Africa, most of whom are of dubious legitimacy. These West African leaders were therefore not ready to entertain the domino effect of the Liberian example. Political realists would argue that the struggle for regime survival was the primary motif for the rather unusual regional military concert to respond to 'regional' security threat.

ECOWAS Political and Security Co-operation: Redefining Economic and Security Interdependence

The politics of economic regionalism had ensured ECOWAS preoccupation with regional political co-operation and confidence building especially in such areas as peaceful resolution of inter-state disputes and forging a common position on international affairs. ECOWAS foreign policy response to inter-state disputes and other threats to regional security have been based on mobilising regional solidarity to mediate peaceful resolution of dispute and to forge a common ECOWAS position on controversial global issues. The pursuit of national interests under the guise of regional co-operation had provided the opportunity for ECOWAS members to articulate a common foreign policy, when they deem it necessary. However, the willingness to pool their sovereignties goes beyond the simple realist interpretation. The pooling of sovereignty is a recognition of their mutual political, economic and security interdependence which had been the driving force for collective action.[11]

The political aspects of economic regionalism have been more prominent than its economic integration policies. ECOWAS regional diplomacy and political co-operation had been geared towards limiting the negative effects of the Anglophone - Francophone divide, whilst at the same time, finding a regional balance of power or consensus acceptable to member states. The situation of ECOWAS is not peculiar as other examples of economic regionalism in Asia, Latin America and Europe show that economic regionalism is also about politics.

The ECOWAS experiment with security regionalism has provided a platform for the regional organisation to formulate and articulate a common foreign policy on security and conflict management issues. At the December 1999 ECOWAS summit in Togo, two important issues relating to regional security were adopted:

i. protocol establishing a permanent mechanism for conflict prevention, management and resolution, peace and security; and,
ii. supported regional moratorium on the importation, exportation and manufacture of light weapons.

ECOWAS regionalism has therefore provided a regional framework for institutionalised co-operation at political, economic, security and diplomatic levels.

Tradition of Regional Security Co-operation

Though ECOWAS regionalism has been primarily preoccupied with economic regionalism, regional peace and security considerations have never been lost on member states. The 1975 Treaty did not make any provision for political and security co-operation. To fill this security vacuum, a Protocol on Non-Aggression of 1978 and a Protocol on Mutual Assistance in Defence of 1981 were signed by Community members. These defence protocols were confidence-building mechanisms for peaceful co-existence. It reflected the recognition that regional peace and security were a necessary prerequisite for economic development and socio-political progress. In particular, the 1981 Defence Pact provided for permissible armed intervention by ECOWAS, but only in defence of member states against external aggression. This was an unprecedented provision for legitimate intervention in the internal affairs of member states. However, this 'co-operative protection'[12] against civil strife was directed against proxy wars and externally orchestrated civil wars. The conformity with the principle on non-intervention in domestic affairs of member states as provided for in the UN and OAU Charters militarily barred ECOWAS from intervening in any such conflicts. Furthermore, the institutional mechanisms established by the 1981 Protocol such as the Defence Council, Defence Commission, and the Allied Armed Forces of the Community (AAFC) were never implemented. The Liberian civil war forced on ECOWAS leaders the need to formulate a regional policy approach on the propriety of military intervention in domestic conflicts. The ECOWAS extra-ordinary summit in Mali in 1990 established the rules of engagement for the threat and use of force by the regional community. The 1993 Revised ECOWAS Treaty, in an attempt to respond to the imperatives of regional security, and specifically provided for regional political and security co-operation.[13]

Approaches to African Security and Conflict Management

The West African intervention in the Liberian civil war highlighted the debate on approaches to African security and conflict management. Two schools of thought have dominated the debate; the UN favoured approach because of the comparative advantage of the world body; and the 'Try Africa First' approach advocated by the OAU. The failure of both the UN and OAU as security provider in African is a familiar story. From Somalia to Rwanda and Sierra Leone, the story is the same. In the 1990s, the UN's capacity as global policeman is increasingly being questioned. The UN, in the post-cold War era, is vastly over-burdened with diverse responsibilities. The 'strategic over-stretch' of the UN[14] have led to task-sharing and security co-operation with regional organisations and regional powers as a 'way of addressing the growing gap between demand and supply, and reducing the burden on the United Nations'.[15] The former UN Secretary-General Boutrous-Ghali, in his *Agenda for Peace* advocated for task-sharing and co-operation with regional entities on issues relating to regional conflicts, peace and security. The *Agenda for Peace* states:

> Under the Charter, the Security Council has and will continue to have primary responsibility to maintaining international peace and security, but regional action, as a matter of democratization, delegation and co-operation with United Nations efforts could not only lighten the burden of the Security Council, but also contribute to a deeper sense of participation, consensus, and democratisation in international affairs. Regional arrangements and agencies have not in recent decades been considered in this light . . . Today a new sense exists that they have contributions to make.[16]

The failure of UN in maintaining peace and security in African has given credence to the regional approach to conflict management. Other alternative approaches to African security and conflict management have been put forward such as the American-sponsored African Crisis Response Initiative (ACRI). The Clinton government proposed to establish a 10,000 member Pan-African rapid reaction force that would cost about US $20 million. The objective ACRI is to enhance capacity building within the African militaries for peacekeeping operations. In October 2000, US military instructors started the training of 400 Senegalese soldiers under the ACRI programe. The training covers such areas as peacekeeping, humanitarian assistance doctrine, combat support and services, and military decision-making process. The American-sponsored Pan African force was rejected because of conflict over ownership and control. It was perceived as an 'American attempt to establish a peace-keeping force for Africa unilaterally, without consulting either the OAU or sub regional organizations'.[17] In addition, the ACRI has been criticised by African military analysts as the attempt by the West to prevent sending their soldiers in African conflict zones. This could be regarded as a reflection of the 'Somalia syndrome' when US soldiers were killed in the Somalia conflict in 1993.

In addition, mercenary interventions have been advanced as an alternative framework for African security and conflict management because of their strategic impact. The intervention of mercenary outfits or private military companies such as Executive Outcomes, Military Professional Resource Incorporated (MPRI) and Sandline International in Sierra Leone, Angola and Democratic Republic of Congo (former Zaire) have proved not to be in the long-term stability and security of African states.[18]

In the post-Cold War period, it has increasingly become apparent that the solution to Africa's security and conflict management problems should be domestic efforts, conceptualised as try Africa first,[19] of which ECOMOG is a novel example. The rationale for the creation of ECOMOG is based on the assumption that a regional security body has comparative advantages which a continental or world body might not necessarily possess. It was base on the premise that the regional organisation has shared interest and a common purpose in the management and resolution of regional conflicts because of their contagion effects. It was also argued that the regional organisation potentially provide legitimacy, recognition and a credible platform for co-operation amongst regional states. Another advantage of such a regional security concert was that it presumably have local knowledge, and familiar with the history, culture and possibly the terrain of the country in crisis. The regional security organ also provide resources in the form of military personnel or combat contingents. Regional organisations such as ECOWAS therefore have valuable assets which could be supportive of conflict management and peacekeeping. Muthiah Alagappa argues that in theory, regionalism should 'facilitate communication, and socialization, information sharing, increase in consensual knowledge, increase in power through pooling of resources, and collective action'.[20]

However, the assumed advantages of regional security and conflict management do not normally reflect the reality. They often lack mandate for the use force, and securing this mandate from the UN Security Council is normally time consuming. They also have limited resources, for example, the majority of ECOMOG's contributing countries are underdeveloped and cash-strapped economies, with mostly small conventional armies. They also find it difficult to forge a common regional position or political consensus as a result of the complex geo-politics. The critical disadvantage is that they often find it difficult to maintain impartiality. It is therefore argued that the complexity and dynamics of domestic conflicts severely limit the impact of regional organisations as conflict managers. Regional organisations are most times supporters of the status quo, and as such often intervene on behalf of incumbent governments for example ECOMOG's initial intervention was to prop up the Doe regime. This protection of the status quo is therefore anti-change. The comments of the late president of Tanzania, Julius Nyerere with reference to the OAU is as well applicable to ECOWAS; 'The OAU exists only for the protection of the African heads of state'.[21]

Re-defining Security in West Africa: Linking Economic and Security Regionalism

Civil wars in West Africa and their threat to regional peace and security have led to the need to redefine the notion of security. With the end of the

Cold War, Africa was literally on 'fire' as manifested by the multiplicity of intra-states conflicts. The regionalisation of these domestic conflicts is made possible because the majority of these 'fragile polities, by definition, are easily permeable. Therefore, internal issues in Third World societies . .
get transformed into inter-state issues quite readily.[22] In the post-Cold War period, political instabilities and state implosion have become the prominent feature of the continent's political landscape. The lid placed on Africa's simmering conflicts during the Cold War era was now removed, as support for clients states were no longer forthcoming. Insurgency groups therefore took up arms to contest state hegemony or the dominance of a small ruling and governing class. The result has been catastrophic in Africa, for example state collapse and societal fragmentation in Somalia, DCR, Liberia, Sierra Leone and Rwanda.

However, ECOWAS, like the OAU, has been preoccupied with the traditional state-centric and military conception of security. Territorial boundary disputes have dominated not only the West African security agenda, but much of the politics of post-independence Africa. The Ghana-Togo border disputes, Mali-Burkina Faso, and Nigeria-Cameroon border skirmishes made the military and external notion of security threat more prominent. In spite of this preoccupation with external military threats, the Congo crisis and the Biafra civil war in Nigeria had demonstrated the threats posed by internal conflicts and the potential for the internationalisation of these domestic wars.

The imperatives to redefine the conception of security in post-Cold War Africa were therefore pressing. In West Africa, the emerging non-military security threats range from crime, drugs, AIDS/HIV, small arms proliferation, poverty, resource scarcity, religious, environmental problems and ethnic oppression. The state could on longer continue to be the single referent object of security, and the traditional response to solve security threats are grossly inadequate to deal with the multiplicity of security threats in the changed conflict environment of the 1990s. The Liberian conflict impacted on the redefinition of security in the West African sub-region. The OAU, for its part, after decades of perceiving security in traditional military and external terms, finally acknowledged at its Dakar, Senegal summit in 1992 that 'there is a link between security, stability, development and co-operation in Africa'.[23] The African Leadership Forum stated that:

> The concept of security goes beyond military consideration. It embraces all aspects of the society including economic, political and social dimensions of individual, family, community, local and national life. The

security of a nation must be constructed in terms of the security of the individual citizen to live in peace with access to basic necessities of life while fully participating in the affairs of his/her society in freedom and enjoying all fundamental human rights.[24]

Insecurity in West Africa have been the product of both internal fissures and fission, as well as external factors. Therefore, the formation of ECOMOG manifest the interplay between 'economic development, regional security, democratization and conflict management in Africa as a whole'.[25] However, the changing focus of the security problematic in the West African sub-region is part of the wider concern with rethinking security, i.e., broadening and deepening the conception of security.[26] Although military security still remains important, for the majority of peoples in West Africa, human, environmental, economic and food security are more serious threats to their security than the traditional inter-state wars.

ECOMOG: Peacekeeping, Peace Enforcement and Conflict Management in West Africa

The West African experiment with security regionalism has led to involvement in peace support operations and conflict management in Liberia (1990 - 1997); Sierra Leone (1997 - 2000) and Guinea Bissau (1999). The expansion of ECOWAS regionalism into the security domain was an ad hoc coalition to respond to regional security threats posed by the Liberian conflict. However, 'adhocery' characterises all coalitions that have come together to conduct complex emergency operations.[27] The creation of the first UN peace keeping operations was formulated on an ad hoc basis in response to the Suez crisis in 1956. The United Nations Emergency Force (UNEF) which started as an ad hoc operation became a model for UN peacekeeping forces.

It could be argued that the contagion effects streaming from the influx of refugees, the spread of national dissidents, arms proliferation and a militarised West Africa were enough reasons to force the member states to band together to prevent the spread of instability. The ECOMOG coalition was therefore a rational approach to serve the national interests of Community members. The range of incentives were enough to coerce ECOWAS leaders to overcome their differences and political rivalries, and under the banner of ECOWAS to collectively address regional security issues, whilst at the same time, securing the fragile stability of some of the illegitimate governments and weak states.

ECOMOG's interventions in West Africa have been generally cast in humanitarian terms, both forcible and non-forcible humanitarian intervention. These complex emergency operations ranges from peacekeeping, peace enforcement, democratic intervention, humanitarian relief assistance and helping to restore collapse states. The ECOMOG experiment reflects the emerging phenomenon of intervention in domestic conflicts by intergovernmental collective security arrangements in the 1990s, for example, the American-led UN intervention in Haiti, UNPROFOR in Bosnia, UNOMSOM I & II in Somalia and KFOR in Kosovo. These multinational interventions in international conflicts are not only costly, but also contravenes the norms of international society.

Peacekeeping and Conflict Management in Liberia

The Liberian crisis provided the first opportunity for ECOWAS' foray in international peacekeeping and conflict management as envisaged in Chapter VIII of the UN Charter. The intervention of ECOMOG into Liberia, without a formal peace agreement or cease-fire compounded the regional forces' peacekeeping capability. ECOMOG therefore found its expedient to constantly change its mandate from peacekeeping to peace enforcement based on the military and humanitarian situation on the ground. This was to compromise ECOMOG's neutrality. The coercive diplomacy approach adopted by ECOMOG saw the intervention force militarily co-operating with other warring factions such as the United Liberian Movement for Democracy (ULIMO), the Liberian Peace Council (LPC) and the Armed Forces of Liberia (AFL) as a strategy to limit the military dominance of the NPFL and also maintain a military balance among the warring factions. Through UN-ECOWAS co-operative security, a United Nations Observer Mission (UNOMIL) was sent to Liberia to legitimise and facilitate the mandate of ECOMOG.

The ECOWAS and ECOMOG twin-track conflict management strategy of political negotiation and military pressure led to series of peace talks from Banjul to Bamako, Geneva, Lomé, Yammassoukru, Cotonou, Akosmobo and Abuja. The coercive diplomacy adopted by ECOMOG led to the signing of series of cease-fire agreements and the eventual commencement of disarmament and demobilisation of warring factions. The ECOWAS peace plan for Liberia was politically and diplomatically supported by the UN, OAU and key western governments and institutions. Through diplomacy backed by force, the ECOWAS peace plan for Liberia succeeded in its primary objective of holding democratic elections in July

1997, under the supervision of ECOWAS and other international observers. The elections were won by Charles Taylor, with the tacit support of the sub-regional hegemon, Nigeria. ECOMOG's peacekeeping, enforcement, and conflict management success in Liberia have implications for Africa and UN in terms of maintaining regional and international peace and security. According to the ECOMOG Field Commander General Victor Malu:

> ... if the experiment here (Liberia) had failed, it would have been a disaster. It is only now that other sub-regions are trying to put regional security forces to assist them in solving their problems. I think ECOMOG is a good example of how this can be done, and I believe we have something to give to the world to copy from.[28]

Though ECOMOG's intervention did not solve the underlying root causes of the conflict or eliminated the potential for relapse into further conflict, it nevertheless brought a deadly civil war to an end, and not only help to stabilise war-torn Liberia, but also stopped the humanitarian disaster, assist with engineering the restoration of the collapse state, and ensured democratic governance based on respect for the rule of law, and not 'gun law'.

Democratic Intervention and Peace Enforcement in Sierra Leone

The contagion effect of the Liberian civil war was felt in Sierra Leone, when Corporal Foday Sankoh's Revolutionary United Front (RUF), supported by Charles Taylor, invaded the eastern borders of the country in March 1991. The Taylor-sponsored RUF insurgency eventually led to the overthrow of the All Peoples Congress Party (APC) regime in 1992 by a military junta, the National Provisional Ruling Council (NPRC). The re-introduction of democratic governance in 1996 was aborted by the intervention of the military in May 1997. The ECOWAS mediation led to the signing of the Conakry Peace Accord for Sierra Leone. Failure to implement the peace agreement provided the opportunity for ECOMOG's military intervention that led to the overthrow of the Armed Forces Revolutionary Council (AFRC) military junta and the restoration of constitutional order in Sierra Leone. ECOMOG intervention in Sierra Leone therefore helped to restore constitutional order, an unprecedented example in the political history of West Africa, negotiated a political settlement to the nine-year old brutal civil war, and provided security for the state. President Kabbah in his address to parliament stated that; ' ... ECOMOG has demonstrated that it has the potential to become a regional peacekeeping and enforcement organisation at par with any force anywhere in the world'.[29] The political and security aspects of Sierra Leone's ECOWAS regionalism are extensively discussed later in this book.

Co-operative Peace Broker in Guinea Bissau

The civil war in Guinea Bissau was the product of both internal and external factors. The insurgency led by General Ansumana Mane against the authoritarian regime of President Bernado Nino Viera was mainly the product of the politics of underdevelopment established by post-independence regimes in Guinea Bissau. The sacking of General Mane as head of the army by President Viera on allegations of arms sales to the Senegalese separatist movement in Casamance led to armed revolt by loyal soldiers. This led to intervention by neighbouring Senegal and Guinea, under the auspices on ECOWAS, on behalf of the beleaguered President Viera. Senegal's intervention in Guinea Bissau was considered a national interest because of the impact of the Casamance separatist rebellion in southern Senegal.

President Viera's appeal to ECOWAS led to the formation of an ECOWAS Committee of seven to facilitate a negotiated settlement of the conflict, and the security mandate of ECOMOG was expanded to cover Guinea Bissau. A cease-fire and a peace agreement between Viera's regime and his former army chief was signed in Praia, Cape Verde. The peace accord was jointly brokered by ECOWAS and the Portuguese-speaking countries, the Community of Lusophone Countries (CPLP).[30] The Senegalese-led ECOMOG observer mission was entrusted with the responsibility to monitor the cease-fire agreement. However, the military superiority of the rebel army led to the overthrow of the Viera government and the setting up of a government of national unity. The military had since returned to the barracks after organising domestic elections. In the internal conflict in Guinea Bissau, ECOWAS diplomacy contributed to the ending the fierce fighting and through co-operation with the CPLP and the UN, contributed to post-war peacebuilding and reconstruction.

Conceptualising ECOMOG

The ECOMOG experiment in West Africa has led to the need to provide a conceptual understanding of this novel development. ECOMOG has been variously described as a security regionalism, a collective security arrangement and an emerging security community.

Security Regionalism

The peacekeeping, enforcement and conflict management operations of ECOMOG in West Africa have led to the description of the intervention force and the role of ECOWAS as a manifestation of security regionalism. Security regionalism is generally defined as security co-operation amongst geographically proximate states, usually acting under the auspices of a regional organisation. Co-operation amongst these regional states may also include increasing economic interdependence and other issues areas. It embraces the notion of enhancing national and regional well-being through collective action.[31] Underpinning the notion of co-operative security at regional level is the principle of non-intervention. However, the tragedy of failed and collapsed states in the 1990s have increasingly eroded this principle. Implicit in the notion of ECOWAS security regionalism is the assumption that economic interdependence, development, social progress, democratization and good governance, environmental protection and respect for human rights are impossible in an environment of wars and conflicts. ECOWAS security regionalism is the post-Cold War resurgence of regionalism in contemporary World politics. Regional organisations such as ECOWAS and its military wing ECOMOG, are increasingly becoming prominent players in world affairs. Muthiah Alalgappa argues that the reasons that generally inform the debate on security regionalism are mainly due to the regionalisation of world politics, the collapse of the Cold War security architecture, the inability of one state or organisation to manage the post-Cold War security problematic, the growth of regional powers and the desire on their part as well as other regional states to seek greater control over their strategic environment, and growth of economic regionmalism.[32] ECOMOG has therefore became part of the policy and academic debate on security regionalism in world politics.

Collective Security or Pragmatic Incrementalism

ECOWAS security regionalism has been described as a collective security arrangement.[33] The notion of collective security in Africa dates back to the early 1960s when the Ghanaian president, Kwame Nkrumah advocated for the formation of an African High Command, a sort of collective defence mechanism to protect the newly independent African states from external aggression and re-colonisation.[34] This concept of collective defence established the basis that African security could best be managed by Africans themselves. However, ECOWAS security regionalism is not the same as collective security for several reasons. Collective security embraces the notion of collective defence against external aggressor.[35] This traditional state-centric military conception of security is no longer applicable in West Africa because of the many civil wars and internal conflicts. Thought military security still remains important, threat to security is from within the states and the states themselves have become sources of insecurity. ECOWAS security regionalism is not a collective defence system designed to deter a common external enemy.

ECOWAS security regionalism therefore do not fit the traditional notion of collective security. It is a regional concert designed to respond to inter-state disputes and most importantly, to internal wars and their spillover effects. There is no formal agreement in ECOWAS that internal wars and state collapse warrants collective intervention from the regional community. ECOWAS collective security, to use the term loosely, approximates the concept of public good. Nigeria, as the sub-regional hegemon, is more inclined to provide this public good through collective action for a variety of reasons. The dominant role of Nigeria in ECOWAS security regionalism is conceptually akin to Karl Deutsch and Bruce Russet's 'core-state' thesis as the driving force for regional integration.[36]

The expansion of ECOWAS regionalism into the security domain reflects the logic of pragmatic Incrementalism, i.e., the recognition that security is an indispensable element for economic regionalism. Pragmatic interest politics or incremental pragmatism is used here to provide understanding of the evolving security regionalism in West Africa. The evolution and gradual integration of economic and security regionalism in West Africa reflects the convergence of political and economic motivations, complementarity of elite values and high level of political support. The West African integrative system reflects a purposeful pattern of common regional attitudes, mutual economic and security interdependence, and some form of collective decision making provided by the ECOWAS institutional framework. The politics of economic regionalism and co-operation in West Africa progresses along pragmatic and incremental lines. This explains the gradual expansion of ECOWAS from an exclusively economic grouping with common market objectives to taking on security responsibility. The pooling of the economic and security sovereignties of ECOWAS countries have been made possible because of pragmatic incrementalism. ECOWAS integration, like other regionalisms have adopted incrementalism to address the problems of premature politicisation and the disintegration of the integration scheme. It has made it possible for ECOWAS countries to gradually pool their economic and security sovereignties without the 'dangerous' erosion of national sovereignty. Thus, every stage *en route* from ECOWAS to ECOMOG, has been one of pragmatic incrementalism. Therefore, ECOWAS regionalism, described as pragmatic incrementalism is a 'movement towards collective action based on consensual values for the achievement of common values'.[37] ECOWAS countries are willing to pool their sovereignties because they do not envisage that the final stage in their integrative endeavour is political unification, an aspect they fiercely resist. Clement Adibe's conclusion is that 'the complexity of the ECOWAS sub-region requires a greater methodological and analytical rigour to enhance our understanding of the intricate connections between the particularities of politics and economics, power and interdependence, nationalism and internationalism, *security and conflict management* (sic).[38]

Security Community Debate

The emerging security community in West Africa has been located within the debate on the role and contribution of security communities in developing 'dependable expectations of peaceful change'. Karl Deutsch defines security community as a group of states or people that have achieved a level of integration to the point that they avoid the use of force in their relations and have developed expectations of peaceful change.[39] The ECOWAS security regionalism could be conceptualised as an evolving, but limited security community that has developed specific disposition in its inter-state relations and the settlement of disputes. The institutionalised system of co-operation and increasing socio-psychological transactions are gradually developing dependable expectations of peaceful change in inter-state relations. This is a contentious claim because West Africa, like the majority of developing regions is hardly the conducive environment for the evolution of the Deutschain idea of security community. In fact, Emmanuel Adler and Michael Barnett's seminal work on *Security Communities* is notable not only for its ground breaking contribution to the 'second generation' security community debate, but also for its omission.[40] The book's 13 chapters, exploring the historical and regional context of security communities has nothing on Africa. It gives the impression of foreclosing or prejudging the debate on the possibility of the emergence of security communities in Africa, or *a priori* Africa is hardly the region to look for security communities. Amitav Acharya argues that theorists 'who have used the concept since, have taken serious note of the possibility of security communities in the developing world'.[41] The plausible reason is that West Africa, like much of tropical Africa, lacks the two essential variables for the emergence of security community, i.e., liberal politics and economics. Furthermore, the sub-region lacks the normative and structural or institutional values that may sustain a secure community.

However, ECOWAS regionalism has led to the development of institutional and inter-governmental co-operation based on economic and security interdependence. This has led to increased socio-cultural transactions underpinned by Pan-African values or identity. The sub-region has therefore benefited from the pacific effects of interdependence and the West African culture of peaceful co-existence. Since 1975, ECOWAS countries have not fought a war against each other, and even with border skirmishes such as the Mali - Burkina Faso; Ghana - Togo; and Nigerian - Cameroon border clashes, they have been resolved by peaceful settlement through ECOWAS and OAU mediation.

With the changed conflict environment of the 1990s in West Africa, i.e., from inter-state to intra-state wars, ECOWAS has responded to regional security threat and the management of conflict through collective action. What is evident is the fact that ECOWAS like 'members of ASEAN may have evolved towards a security community without sharing liberal democratic values or a substantial degree of intra-regional economic interdependence'.[42] The evolving security community in West Africa promotes norms and principles relating to inter-state relations, enhanced community information-sharing, and built not only on confidence building mechanism, but also constraints on unilateral intervention or preferences. The nascent security community in West Africa is represented by a common external (pre-1990) and internal (post-1990) threat perception, expectation of mutual benefits and shared West African or Pan-African identity. However, Community members do not perceive themselves as homogeneous, nor do they implicitly have common agreement on threat perception. In addition, ECOWAS security regionalism is not seen as a security community organised against a common external threat. Also the idea of a sub-regional hegemon, Nigeria, do not sit comfortably with the notion of security community. ECOWAS norms also do not seem to have influenced the behaviour of member states in terms of peaceful inter-state relations. For instance the covert role of Burkina Faso, Côte d'Ivoire and Liberia in the civil wars in Sierra Leone and Liberia clearly undermines the ECOWAS norms of peaceful inter-state relations.

ECOWAS conceptualised as a nascent security community, has developed in a manner quite different from the path outlined by Deutsch, and its consolidation is taking place in a climate of fairly low intra-regional transaction and interdependence. ECOWAS is a product of a different context of security community and the 'mere existence of disputes and conflicts within a group does not necessarily undermine its claim to be a security community. The distinguishing feature of a security community is its ability to manage any conflicts within regions peacefully, rather than the absence of conflict per se'.[43]

Security Regionalism in West Africa and African International Relations

The evolving security regionalism in West Africa have relevant implications for African and international politics. When this ad hoc multinational intervention force was created, it was criticised by political analysts and media commentators of how not to conduct peacekeeping operations outside the traditional UN framework.[44] ECOWAS security regionalism has shown relative success in peace support operations and conflict management. As a regional intergovernmental collective security organisation, it has assumed a dynamics of its own and has therefore affected the nature of African international relations. The phenomenon of regional intergovernmental collective security organisations such as ECOWAS will continue to play a more salient role in the management and settlement of conflicts in contemporary world politics. The ECOMOG conflict management experiment has major implications for the understanding of post-Cold War African politics. It has moved the regional community beyond its primary state-centric focus to a pluralistic conception of domestic and international politics. In the management of the West African crises, ECOWAS had to deal not only with collapsed states, but also civil society organisations, warlords and extra-regional actors.

ECOWAS conflict management experiment in West Africa has important implication for the concept of humanitarian intervention. ECOWAS interventions have been cast in terms of forcible and non-forcible humanitarian intervention. ECOWAS leaders have learnt from their complex emergency operations in West Africa that humanitarian intervention is inherently political, and if not managed properly, can intensify or prolong the internal conflict. The ECOMOG humanitarian intervention is a collective mechanism for alleviating or preventing unacceptable human suffering caused by internal conflicts and state collapse. ECOMOG's intervention, cast in terms of humanitarian intervention brings to the fore the wider debate on re-conceptualising humanitarian intervention in the post-Cold War period.[45]

Civil wars in West Africa have undermined the traditional norms of international society, in that ECOMOG interventions constrained the OAU and UN principles of non-intervention and political sovereignty. These principles have constrained the effectiveness of the OAU and the UN in the management and resolution of domestic conflicts. The threats posed by civil wars in West Africa have led to a fundamental rethinking of the norms of international society within the ECOWAS region. Fouad Ajami argues that:

> ...the cruel calculus of sovereignty versus misery has changed the way the international community thinks about foreign intervention and the rights of states.... In the face of an absolute doctrine of the rights of nations, there is now a tentative right to interfere. Man cannot eat sovereignty, we have learned; that order within nations is just as important as among them[46]

West African leaders, like the majority of those in Africa now recognise that non-intervention and political sovereignty are no longer sacrosanct when it comes to deadly internal conflicts. A fundamental shift in the international relations of African states in the recognition that 'internal human rights violations (and civil wars [sic]) is a threat to international peace and security warranting the attention of outside states'.[47] The OAU which has spent decades hiding behind the protection offered by the norms of international society had endorse ECOMOG's intervention in the West African conflicts. This paradigm shift in African inter-state relations means that states now have the responsibility to demonstrate not only the 'legal fiction' of juridical sovereignty, but also domestic sovereignty. ECOWAS interventions have been concerned not only with managing and resolving armed conflicts, but also with the reconstruction of collapsed states and halting humanitarian catastrophes. These kinds of 'reconstitutive interventions' have been regarded as permissible breaches of international law.[48]

The ECOWAS experiment in security regionalism has positively influenced other regional and sub-regional organisations. The West African example in Liberia served as the basis for the OAU's adoption of a security agenda in 1992 as a mechanism for the management of continental conflicts. It was followed by the adoption of the Mechanism for Conflict Prevention, Management and Resolution in 1993. The Southern African Development Community (SADC) in 1996 established an Organ for Politics, Defence and Security, which later organised and deployed an intervention force in the Democratic Republic of Congo. The ECOMOG peacekeeping and peace enforcement operations in West Africa have established a new co-operative security between the UN and ECOWAS in terms of task-sharing in the maintenance of international peace and security. ECOWAS security regionalism is to some extent emerging as the practical realisation of the OAU's 'try Africa first' approach to conflict management and resolution.

Conclusion

The ECOWAS experiment with security regionalism is a novel initiative, but the experience shows that developing a multinational force is the easiest part, sustaining the intervention and implementing an exit strategy are most times difficult. The ECOMOG interventions are also very expensive operations for the largely underdeveloped economies in the sub-region. The Nigerian government claims that by June 1995 it has spent an estimated US $4 billion on peacekeeping and enforcement in Liberia.[49] However, the ECOMOG experience demonstrates the need for the regional security organ to move beyond the traditional neutral inter-positionary approach to peacekeeping, and instead adopt a more comprehensive approach to regional security that embraces peacemaking, peacekeeping, peace enforcement, conflict management and conflict prevention.

ECOWAS security regionalism has re-defined the nature of future African inter-state relations. In contemporary international politics, ECOMOG, in spite of its limitations, is accepted as 'Africa's flagship in peace-making, peace-keeping and peace enforcement'.[50] ECOWAS as a nascent security community, is gradually establishing the norms of peaceful inter-state relations and the value of collective response to internal conflicts that threaten regional peace and stability. At the 22nd ECOWAS summit in 1999, the Nigerian President Olusegun Obasanjo stated that the 'time has come to draw the lessons from both good and bad from the ECOMOG experience . . . to establish a firm base for a peacekeeping force that can perform effectively on the principle of collective security'.[51]

Notes and References

[1] David J. Francis, 'The Fire Next Door: Regional Diplomacy and Conflict Management in West Africa', *African Review of Foreign Policy*, Vol. 2, No. 2, December 2000.

[2] David Francis, 'ECOMOG: A New Security Agenda in World Politics' in Bakut tswah Bakut & Sagarika Dutt (eds.) *Africa at the Millennium* London: Palgrave, 2000, pp. 177-202.

[3] George Klay Kieh, Jr., 'The Obstacles to the Peaceful Resolution of the Liberian Civil Conflict' *Studies in Conflict and Terrorism* Vol. 17, 1994, pp. 97-108.

[4] Leonard Brehun, *Liberia: The War of Horror* Accra: Adwinsa Publications, 1991, p. 24.

[5] *US State Department Report on Human Rights in Liberia* Washington, D. C., August 1990.
[6] *West Africa*, 6 December - 12 December 1999, p. 17.
[7] Ike Nwachukwu et al, *Nigeria and the ECOWAS since 1985: Towards a Dynamic Regional Integration* Fourth Dimension Publishing Co., Nigeria, 1991, p. 104.
[8] The Standing Mediation Committee was created at the Banjul ECOWAS summit in May 1990. It comprised The Gambia, Ghana, Mali, Togo and Nigeria, with the responsibility to implement the ECOWAS Peace plan for Liberia.
[9] ECOWAS Standing Mediation Committee, Decision A/DEC, Lagos: ECOWAS Secretariat, 1 August 1990.
[10] George Klay Kieh, Jr., 1994, *op. cit.*
[11] Robert Keohane & Joseph Nye, *Power and Interdependence* N.Y.: Harper Collins, 1989; Ben Soetendorp, *Foreign Policy in the European Union* London: Longman, 1999.
[12] Julius Okolo & Stephen Wright (eds.) *West African Regional Co-operation and Development* Boulder; Westview Press, 1990, p. 172.
[13] Chapter X, Articles 56 and 58 addressed the issues of both inter-state and intra-state conflicts, and recognised the need to 'establish a regional peace and security observation system and peacekeeping forces . . .' and also 'assistance in the observation of democratic elections'. *Economic Community of West African States (ECOWAS) Revised Treaty* Abuja; ECOWAS Secretariat, 1993, pp. 35-6.
[14] C. W. Kegley and E. R. Wittkopf, *World Politics: Trend and Transformation*, fifth edition, New York: St. Martin's Press, 1995.
[15] Muthiah Alagappa & Takashi Inoguchi (eds.) *International Security Management and the United Nations* Tokyo: UN University Press, 1999, p. 270.
[16] Boutros Boutros-Ghali *Agenda for Peace* New York; UN Publications, 1992.
[17] Alagappa & Takashi (eds.) *International Security Management and United Nations*, 1999, p. 317.
[18] For a discussion of the debate on mercenary intervention in African conflicts see: David Shearer *Private Armies and Military Intervention* Adelphi Paper 316 IISS, Oxford University Press, 1998; David Francis 'Mercenary intervention in Sierra Leone: providing national security or international exploitation?' *Third World Quarterly* Vol. 20, No. 2, 1999; Abdel-Fatau Musah & J. 'Kayiode Fayemi (eds.) *Mercenaries: An African Security Dilemma* London: Pluto Press, 2000.
[19] There are two plausible interpretations of the 'try Africa first' concept advocated by the OAU. On the one hand, it represents a genuine desire by the OAU to find new alternatives to African conflict management and resolution through local African initiatives. And on the other hand, it reflects the OAU desperation in its failure to resolve African conflicts, and its resentment with the role of extra-regional actors in African conflicts. As a concept, it has as its objective the exclusion of great powers from African conflicts. This is a rather unrealistic objective, given the history and nature of colonial and post-colonial linkages between Africa and the great powers. See Amadu Sesay, 'Peacekeeping by regional organisations: The OAU and ECOWAS Peacekeeping Forces in Comparative Perspective' in David Charters (ed.) *Peacekeeping and the Challenge of Civil Conflict Resolution* New Brunswick: Centre for Conflict Studies, University of New Brunswick, 1994.
[20] M. Alagappa, 'Regionalism and Conflict Management: A Framework for Analysis' *Review of International Studies* Vol. 21, No. 4, 1995, p. 276.
[21] Quoted in Yassin El-Ayoutu (ed.) *The Organization of African Unity: Thirty Years On* Westport, Praeger, 1994, p. 179.
[22] Francis Deng et al, *Sovereignty as Responsibility: Conflict Management in Africa* Washington, D. C.: The Brookings Institutions, 1996, p. 146.

[23] Quoted in Edmond Keller & Donald Rothchild (ed.) *Africa in the New International Order: Rethinking State Sovereignty and Regional Security* London: Lyne Rienner, 1996, p. 33.
[24] African Leadership Forum, *The Kampala Document: Towards a Conference on Security, Stability, Development and Co-operation* New York: African Leadership Forum, 1992, p. 9.
[25] E. John Inegbedion, 'ECOMOG in Comparative Perspective' in T. Shaw & J. Okolo (eds.) *The Political Economy of Foreign Policy in ECOWAS* New York: St. Martin's Press, 1994, p. 219.
[26] See: David Baldwin, 'The Concept of Security' *Review of International Studies* Vol. 23, No. 1, 1997, pp. 5 - 26; Caroline Thomas, *In Search of Security: The Third World in International Relations* Boulder: Lynne Rienner, 1987.
[27] Jennifer Morrison Taw & Andrew Grant-Thomas, 'US Support for Regional Complex Contingency Operations: Lessons from ECOMOG' *Studies in Conflict and Terrorism* Vol. 22, No. 1, 1999, p. 74.
[28] 'A no-nonsense commander' *West Africa* 24 - 30 March 1997, p. 466.
[29] *Presidential Address to the Parliament of the Republic of Sierra Leone* 22 May 1998, Sierra Leone web available at http://www.sierra-leone.org/slnews.html.
[30] CPLP comprise Guinea Bissau, Cape Verde, Portugal, Angola, Mozambique, Sao Tome and Brazil.
[31] Richard Falk perceives regionalism as a promising focus for both empirical and normative inquiry' and 'identifies emergent trends and structures and clarifies a distinct array of prescriptions and strategies'. *Predatory Globalization: A Critique* Cambridge: Polity Press, 1999, p. 65.
[32] Alagappa & Inoguchi, 1999, p. 270.
[33] Max A. Sesay, 'Collective Intervention or Collective Disaster? Regional Peacekeeping in West Africa, *Security Dialogue*, Vol. 26, No. 2, 1999, pp. 205-222.
[34] In the Casablanca Charter of 7 January 1961, the radical socialist-leaning African states such as Ghana, Guinea, Mali, Morocco, Libya, Egypt and Algeria, provided for a joint military command and an African common market. See: Alagappa & Inoguchi, 1999, p. 295.
[35] Collective security refers to a regional or global system in which aggression by any state will be deterred by a collective response. For example, Article 5 of the NATO Treaty spells out collective security thus: 'The Parties agree that an armed attack against one or more of them in Europe or North America shall be considered an attack against them all . . . .' *The North Atlantic Treaty* Washington, DC: 4 July 1949.
[36] Karl Deutsch et al, *Political Community and the North Atlantic Area: International Organization in the Light of Historical Experience* New Jersey: Princeton University Press, 1968; Bruce Russet *International Regions and the International System: A Study in Political Ecology* Chicago: Rand Mcnally, 1967.
[37] Groom & Heraclide (eds.) *International Relations Theory* London: Pinter, 1978.
[38] Clement Adibe, 'ECOWAS in Comparative Perspective' in Shaw & Okolo (eds.) 1994, p. 213.
[39] Karl Deutsch, *Political Community and the North Atlantic Area* Princeton University, 1957, p. 6.
[40] Emmanuel Adler & Michael Barnet (ed.) *Security Communities* Cambridge: Cambridge University Press, 1998.
[41] Amitav Acharya, 'Collective Identity and Conflict Management in Southeast Asia' in Adler & Barnet, 1998, p. 198.
[42] Ibid., p. 199.

[43] Adler & Barnet, 1998, p. 214.
[44] Shaw & Okolo, 1994, p. 218.
[45] For a discussion of both the restrictionists / realist and pluralist international society theorists and counter-restrictionists / solidarist international society theorists perspectives on humanitarian intervention see: Nicholas Wheeler, 'Humanitarian Intervention and World Politics' in J. Baylis & S. Smith (ed.) *The Globalization of World Politics* Oxford: Oxford University Press, 1997; Oliver Ramsbotham, 'Humanitarian Intervention: a need to re-conceptualise?' *Review of International Studies* Vol. 23, No. 4, 1997, pp. 445 - 468.
[46] F. Ajami, 'Somalis: The work of order and mercy' *US News and World Report* 21 December 1992, p. 25.
[47] Lori F. Damrosch (ed.) *Enforcing Restraint: Collective Intervention in Internal Conflicts* New York: Council of Foreign Relations, Inc., 1993, p. 160.
[48] I. William Zartman (ed.) *Collapsed States: The Disintegration and Restoration of Legitimate Authority* London: Lynne Rienner, 1995, p. 223.
[49] Alagappa & Inogochi, 1999, p. 319.
[50] Abass Bundu, 'Beyond Peace-keeping' *West Africa* 6 December - 12 December 1999, p. 14.
[51] Ibid.

3 ECOWAS and the New Regionalism

Introduction

The state-promoted economic regionalism in West Africa has not been oblivious to the transformation in the global political economy. ECOWAS expansion into security regionalism and the recognition of other actors in the regionalisation processes are part of two general responses to the imperatives of contemporary globalisation. The transformation within the ECOWAS community has been manifested in the economic, social and political dimensions of integration in the sub-region. This chapter therefore locates the restructuring in ECOWAS within the wider context of new regionalism and globalisation. By locating ECOWAS within the globalisation-regionalism nexus, it will illustrate the contradictory processes of simultaneous integration and fragmentation, and how ECOWAS is strategically repositioning itself to both exploit the benefits of globalisation, and at the same time limit the negative effects of the contemporary global restructuring.

From 'Old' Regionalism to 'New' Regionalism

ECOWAS emerged during the waning days of the 'old regionalism'; i.e. the phenomenon of regional integration between the 1950s and 1970s. It emerged within the historical context of Cold War bi-polar structure, with European Community (EC) integration serving as an attractive example. The theoretical interpretations of this 'old regionalism' project have been dominated by functionalism, neo-functionalism and classical economics theories. The ECOWAS trade liberation programmes and defence protocols are a manifestation of the 'old regionalisms' preoccupation with 'free trade arrangements and security alliances'.[1] To some extent, it could be regarded as hegemonic regionalism in that it was an elitist imposition, state-led, and largely copied the EC.

The 'new' regionalism emerged in the late 1980s as part of the responses to the end of the Cold War and the transformation of the global political economy. Björn Hettne and Fredrik Söderbaum see the latest waves and renewed trend as the 'new regionalism'. They define the new regionalism as:

> a comprehensive, multifaceted and multi-dimensional process, implying the change of a particular region from relative heterogeneity to increased homogeneity with regard to a number of dimensions, the most important being culture, security, economic policies and political regimes.[2]

Therefore, the new regionalism is a complex multi-dimensional and multi-level processes that are inextricably linked. The inter-regional dimension is important because the economic and political processes invariably affect other regions. The new regionalism is therefore a 'complex process of change taking place simultaneously at three levels: the structure of the world system as a whole; the level of inter-regional relations; and the internal pattern of the single region'.[3] The 'new regionalism' has been characterised as 'open regionalism' in that it is directed at the elimination of obstacles to intra-regional trade and the removal of external tariff barriers to world trade. The 'open regionalism' is therefore a reflection of the increasing economic and social interdependence and integration at national, regional and global levels in which 'new actors, new social complexes, and new forms of identity are emerging'.[4] The transition from 'old' to 'new' regionalism is an acknowledgement of the fact that 'regional interactions and organisations focus not only on states but on continuing linkages among a heterogeneous set of actors and realms, including states, economies/companies and societies/civil societies'.[5]

ECOWAS new regionalism of the 1990s has departed from the traditional statist integration and now embraces both the formal and informal actors such as commercial actors (companies and small traders), NGOs, new social movements and civil society organisations. ECOWAS new regionalism is about breaking out of the cocoon of the so-called collective self-reliance and protectionism to openness and inclusiveness in trade and market integration. But the real question is will further integration or incorporation of West African economies into the global economy promote economic development and generate welfare for the peoples? However, Fiona Butler asserts that 'The 'new regionalism' appears to be the 'only card game in town' for the political and economic survival of many developing states'.[6] Whilst this may have some ring of truth, ECOWAS new regionalism is not only about integration into the global economy via neo-liberal prescriptions, but is also geared towards taking advantage of the much neglected informal sector and trans-border regionalisation actors. ECOWAS new regionalism is therefore an attempt to provide understanding of the processes of regionalisation in West Africa within the wider context of globalisation. This understanding would include the monumental transformations in the global political economy as manifested in the increasing globalisation and regionalism processes; the increase in foreign direct investment and the free-flow of capital; the expansion of cross-border co-operation and alliances; the strategic management of TNCs which have resulted in global mergers; the globalisation of production and consumption; the liberalisation, privatisation and deregulation of markets; the increased inter-connectedness of the global economy; and the information technology revolution. All these developments pose considerable 'challenges to public authorities, economic agents and social actors in both developed and developing parts of the world'.[7]

Conceptually, four broad theoretical interpretations have been advanced to provide an understanding of the new regionalism. Institutionalist approaches underpinned by the old functionalist and neo-functionalist approaches, have been advanced to explain the new regionalism.[8] International political economy (IPE) approaches perceive the new regionalism as part of a wider process of world order transformation, especially the 'decline' of US hegemony and the end of the Cold War.[9] Edward Mansfield and Helen Milner focus on the domestic (political) factors and strategic trade theory to explain the renewed interest amongst policy makers in regionalism.[10] The new regionalism approach (NRA) has been advanced by Björn Hettne and colleagues at the World Institute for Development Economics Research at the United Nations University in Helsinki (WIDER/UNU) and the Department of Peace and Development Research (PADRIGU) at Gotenborg University. The NRA analysis regionalism, regionalisation and transnational cross-border flows and interdependencies in a global perspective through historical, multi-level and multi-dimensional perspectives.[11] The *Third World Quarterly* Special Issue edited by Marianne Marchand et al interprets the new regionalism as a multitude of overlapping (formal as well as informal), disjointed and often contradictory regionalisation processes. The authors therefore preferred to describe the processes as new regionalisms, instead of new regionalism, as a means of understanding contemporary practices and processes of regionalisation.[12]

ECOWAS New Regionalism and the Myth of Globalisation

Locating ECOWAS within the globalisation-regionalism dynamic invariably brings to the fore the contradictions inherent in globalisation; i.e. the simultaneous integration and fragmentation and the marginalisation of the South.

Globalisation and Regionalism: Mutually Re-inforcing or a Contradiction?

Exploring the relationship between globalisation and regionalism is important because the two phenomena bring together the economics and politics of contemporary global restructuring. The resurgence of regionalisms in North America (NAFTA), Latin America, Asia, Europe and Africa have been against the background of increasing globalisation. But what is globalisation? The term has become a common currency in the contemporary discussion of the transformation of the international order. Globalisation is described as a 'process of global restructuring of the political economy at all levels'.[13] The focus has been on the increased interconnectedness and interdependence of both states and societies, the global flow of the factors of production, knowledge, technology and ideas across national borders.[14] The increased international functional co-operation is made possible by technological developments, wherein the 'compression of 'time' and 'space' has led to the 'emergence of a global sense of accumulation, consumption, distribution and production, and equally important, differentiation'.[15] These global transformations have led to such popular phrases as 'one worldism', 'global village', 'a shrinking world', and the 'end of geography'. The popular image painted about globalisation is that of instantaneous telecommunications and modern transportation which transcend the national barriers between states and increase the range of interaction across international limits. In James Mittleman's view:

> The cliché is that people are exposed to the same global media and consumer products, that such flows are making borders less relevant, and that with foot-loose capital leap-frogging from one locale to another, employment patterns are changing rapidly, drawing vast numbers of immigrants from one country to another.[16]

Three broad definitions of globalisation highlight the main elements of the concept. Roland Robertson's sociological definition perceives globalisation in terms of 'world compression' and the corresponding intensification of 'global consciousness'.[17] David Harvey conceptualises globalisation in terms of the 'compression of space and time'.[18] However, Anthony Giddens perceives globalisation in terms of 'time-space distantiation', a global phenomenon made possible by technological progress, whereby the world is literally shrinking into a "global village"'.[19] Therefore, the popular myth often associated with globalisation is the tendency to 'reify globalisation' as an ineluctable trend, a juggernaut rolling into a new millennium'.[20]

The hyper-globalisation perspective is challenged by radical or sceptical globalists who contend that most of the claims advanced by hyper-globalists are rather unfounded.[21] Though sceptical globalists accept the obvious fact that radical expansionary and redistributive strategies of national economic management were no longer possible in the face of a variety of domestic and international constraints, they however argue that the highly internationalised economy is not unprecedented, and that it is one of a number of distinct conjunctures or states of the international economy that have existed since the 1860s.[22] Paul Hirst and Grahame Thompson argue that truly transnational companies (TNCs), the supposed primary agents of globalisation, are relatively rare. What seems to be the case is that most companies are nationally based and trade multinationally on the strength of a major national location of production and sales, and there seems to be no major tendency towards the growth of a genuinely international company. Hirst and Thompson further posit that capital mobility is not producing a massive shift of investment and employment from the advanced to the developing countries. Rather, foreign direct investment is highly concentrated among the advanced industrialised economies, mainly the triad (NAFTA, EU and Japan/Asian Tigers), because they provide better investment opportunities. The South therefore remains marginalised in both investment and trade, with a small percentage going to the newly industrialised countries. Even in the industrialised western societies there is the disparity between the 'haves' and 'have nots', i.e. the manifestation of what Caroline Thomas describes as the globalisation of the Third World.[23] Hirst and Thompson's version of economic globalisation is a 'myth that exaggerates the degree of our helplessness in the face of contemporary economic forces'.[24]

It becomes evident that both globalisation and regionalism are driven by two opposite forces, i.e. one centripetal and the other centrifugal. Some political analysts have argued that regionalism is a hindrance to globalisation and has the potential for conflicts in the sense of protective trading blocs, for example, the centripetal forces of regionalism. The potential of regionalism for protectionism and exclusiveness, and the often uncertain regional political dynamics have been cited as obstacles to globalisation. Inis Claude therefore argues that regionalism is sometimes regarded as a preferred alternative to globalisation, a 'superior substitute for the principle of universality'.[25] Though regionalism and globalisation could be regarded as contradictory processes, the same forces that drive globalisation could stimulate regionalism. In Louise Fawcett and Andrew Hurrell's view, the two processes are not necessarily antagonistic, and they could be mutually reinforcing.[26] Regionalism therefore provides the opportunity for large firms to operate as 'insiders' in other regions, thereby promoting globalisation. The dynamics of the global economy show that globalisation takes place through regionalisation. This is evident by the activities of most transnational corporations in the three core regions of North America, Europe and East Asia. Gary Gereffi reasons that:

> If Europe, North America, and Asia do indeed set up full-fledged trade blocs, closed to outsiders and open to insiders, regionally integrated TNCs are likely to capitalise on this trend by corporate strategies of globalisation through regionalisation.[27]

In a variety of ways, therefore, globalisation engenders regionalism, and vice versa. It is in this perspective that regionalism and globalisation could be regarded as two sides of the same coin.

Marginalisation of the South and the Myth of Globalisation

The impact of both globalisation and regionalism are uneven. The West African sub-region is used as an example to illustrate the wider marginalisation of the South in general, and the myth of globalisation. The perceived benefits of globalisation are not shared by all and the process itself has been regarded as a contributing factor for fuelling societal conflicts in Third World regions. According to James Mittleman, globalisation processes have:

> combined with local forces to consign at the end of millennium, 265 million people on one continent (Africa) to poverty, with little hope for escape in sight. The foremost contradiction of our time is the conflict between the zones of humanity integrated in the global division of labour and those excluded from it.[28]

The West African sub-region, like the majority of African regions, lacks the technological, economic, infrastructural and political capabilities to strategically exploit the benefits of globalisation. So where is the place of ECOWAS in this new international division of economic power? The restructuring of the global political economy marginalises ECOWAS and much of the South in the new international division of power and of labour. The globalisation of capitalism (investment and trade) in West Africa is reflected in brand-name consumer products such as Jumbo-Maggi, Coca Cola, mobile phones, pop music, shopping malls, hotel chains etc. However the benefits of this market globalisation are enjoyed by the privileged few who constitute the ruling and governing class in much of Africa; and those who have access to these benefits (e.g. internet facilities) and can afford to pay such as the business community and aspiring intellectuals. Therefore, even within the peripheral zone of the global economy, the paradox of globalisation is manifested in the disparity and inequality between the 'haves' and the 'have nots'. The processes of globalisation and regionalisation create both winners and losers, and the ECOWAS Community is located within the losers category because it is marginalised in both investment, trade, and technology. The majority of ECOWAS countries are exposed to the globalisation process from different starting points. Most of these countries are weak states, lacking institutional capacity and constrained by weak supply and demand capabilities. As such, their capacity to benefit from the opportunities and potential of globalisation are limited. In the majority of ECOWAS countries, it has led to increased impoverishment, less human security, society conflicts and the erosion of state power.[29]

West Africa in the global political economy is marginalised economically, politically, socially and technologically. Its position is one of vulnerability to external factors beyond its control in the international division of labour and of power. The increasing economic and technological polarisation between the North and South, as manifested in the ECOWAS example, is creating according to Maurice Strong a 'new Iron curtain separating the rich and poor'.[30] It is from this perspective that the ECOWAS Community could be regarded as a 'peripheral zone' which Hettne and Söderbaum portrays as continuing:

> ... to be politically turbulent and economically stagnant. War, domestic unrest, and underdevelopment constitute a vicious circle which will make them sink to the bottom of the system, creating a zone of war and starvation. Consequently, they will have to organise in order to arrest a threatening process of marginalisation and peripherisation.[31]

The further margination of the South as a result of globalisation is in Peter Wilkin's view the 'new mythology' because it reveals the deepening inequality which 'excludes those without the necessary social, economic and political power from either control or consumption of the very products that capitalism is able to generate'.[32] In the same vein, the so-called global accumulation of capital, technology, military, etc. creates a considerable political and ideological power for a particular group of people. According to Caroline Thomas, it privileges a particular value system; i.e. the Western liberal social and political values, and in turn, 'undermines the value of local diversity and legitimises the dominant liberal agenda, presenting it as universal, 'natural' and common. Yet it is rooted in a local essentially Western, capitalism worldview.'[33]

ECOWAS and Responses to the New Regionalism

Far from replicating Hettne and Söderbaum's 'zone of war and starvation', the ECOWAS Community has managed to respond to the challenges and marginalisation of globalisation. The responses to the transformation of the global political economy simultaneously occurred in economic, political and security areas. ECOWAS Community as a security complex, i.e. a conflict-prone region, has been forced in the 1990s to transform its traditional political and security preoccupations. The new politico-security thinking focuses on the interface between economic development, democratisation, regional security and stability. This new thinking led to the expansion into the domain of security regionalism, with the formation of ECOMOG. The ECOWAS Community also adopted a Declaration of Political Principles in 1991, which reaffirmed the Community's commitment to the observance of democratic principles and respect for human rights and the rule of law. The 'wind of democratisation' that swept across Africa saw the exit or transformation of some authoritarian regimes and military dictatorships, and the emergence of multi-party politics and participatory democracy. Even the outdated ECOWAS Treaty of 1975 could no longer cope with the challenges of contemporary world politics and the restructuring of the global political economy. In 1993, a Revised ECOWAS Treaty was adopted which made regional foreign, political and security co-operation a permanent feature of ECOWAS regionalism. All these are regional responses to create the conducive environment for attaining the goals of economic regionalism.

The expansion of ECOWAS into the security domain reflects the challenges of the new regionalism - globalisation nexus. It is a realisation of the inability of Community members to unilaterally address national and regional problems, and the recognition that such problems may be better handled through constructive and sustained pooling of sovereignty at regional level. The political and security responses of ECOWAS are in fulfilment of its normative origins. At the heart of ECOWAS regionalism lies the desire to establish the conditions for peace and avoidance of war, i.e. how regional co-operation can sustain peace, security and development. The expansion into the security domain, as part of the wider response to the new regionalism reflects the diversity and multi-dimensionality of contemporary regionalisms. For whilst the security regionalism compliments the ECOWAS integration, it also conflicts with the economic regionalism objectives. If Hettne and Söderbaum's definition of 'regionness'[34] is anything to go by, the expansion into concrete political and security domains is a manifest transformation of the ECOWAS Community from a passive object of international politics, to a subject with capacity to articulate its interests. These processes have led to the evolution of a regional identity, for example, ECOMOG is synonymous with West Africa and collective security. ECOWAS regionalism has provided some form of 'regional convergence and coherence' on issues relating to economics, politics, security and development.[35] ECOWAS is playing a central role in the sub-region's international relations with the rest of the world, and has demonstrated the potential to serve as the framework for negotiations with other regions on trade and investment issues.

In the 1990s, ECOWAS had to make the transition from its exclusive, protectionist, inward-oriented regionalism to an outward and open integration into the global economy. At the July 1996 ECOWAS Summit, the 25 per cent domestic equity regulation for investment in the ECOWAS region was scrapped. This removed investment restrictions within the Community, and served as a means to open up the region to foreign direct investment and to further integrate the sub-region into the global economy. It was a regional attempt to integrate the national economic policies and structural adjustments adopted by member states. The removal of restrictions on community investment was also an attempt to attract trade, investment and technological development on which the Community members depend for national and regional development.

Under the auspices of the ECOWAS-ACP-EU Sectoral Industrial Forum, there is a growing partnership between West Africa and European economic operators. The main objectives of the Forum include, promoting enterprise and the private sector; attracting foreign investment needed to develop the industrial sector, and to strengthen the capacity of regional economies with potential for large business markets. However, ECOWAS openness entails costs. Given the peripheral role of ECOWAS in the global economy and the underdeveloped nature of most of its economies, it is doubtful whether further openness will generate economic development and welfare. In fact, foreign companies and the small group of ruling and governing elites in West Africa are the main beneficiaries of this market globalisation and incorporation. Further openness, to a very large extent, only heightens the vulnerabilities of the region. However, the dilemma is that the nature of contemporary global political economy is such that no region can afford to be an island, mainly due to the globalisation of trade, finance, production and technology.

ECOWAS regionalism had traditionally focused on the official, intergovernmental-directed structures and economic actors, whilst neglecting the informal sector and civil societies economic interactions and interdependence. ECOWAS countries have been the main actors in the regionalisation process. But in the 1990s, other crucial actors, both formal and informal, have been recognised within the 'realm of the state-society-economy triangle'.[36] ECOWAS' economic response to the new regionalism is to take cognisance of the invaluable role and interplay of the formal and informal state-society-economy processes and activities, i.e. a recognition of what Marchand et al describes as the 'political economy of regionalisation from below'.[37] The situation of ECOWAS is not peculiar. African regional integration projects, like the majority of regionalisms in the South, have often neglected the potential contribution of the informal sector to the attainment of economic integration objectives. The informal economy which includes diverse a range of actors and entrepreneurs often provides the sustainable basis for most economies.

The new focus of ECOWAS regionalism therefore incorporates not only the traditional statist and realist preoccupations but also 'regional practices in the informal border politics of small trade, of smuggling and crime, and the network and associations involved in these practices'.[38] The ECOWAS recognition of the informal border economies within the sub-region is a strategic attempt to tap into their economic potential and opportunities. The reality is that the small-scale regional traders, cross-border smugglers who criss-cross sub-regional borders such as Sema (that brings together traders from Nigeria, Benin and Togo) and Koindu (Sierra Leone, Liberia and Guinea), rely on informal routes and networks to facilitate the movement of goods and services. In fact, the actors involved in the informal border economies and politics have usually refused to be directed by state apparatus and state-led regionalisation processes. They have deliberately created an informal space outside the officialdom of ECOWAS integration, but at the same time exploit the official economic integration objectives such as ECOWAS citizenship, free movement of people and the removal of customs duties. Even with the freeing of trade, not only TNCs and foreign investors will benefit, but also the small-scale traders and smugglers who operate the informal economy. The advantage is that they have direct impact on border communities in that the economic benefits of their activities are immediately reaped by the people; for example the availability of cheap-imported consumer goods, and scarce commodities. Therefore, ECOWAS' new inclusive (formal and informal) and region-wide economic regionalism manifests the response of the Community to the new regionalism.

ECOWAS' response to the new regionalism is part of a wider trend in contemporary world politics. For example, in Southern Africa, the transformation of SADCC into SADC has led to the rejection of its traditional sectoral and aid co-ordination approach to market integration, the expansion of the Community membership and even establishing a defence and security organ.[39]

Conclusion

ECOWAS response to the new regionalism is an attempt to take advantage of the potential and opportunities of globalisation. It is also an attempt to attain an economic, political and security order in West Africa as a means of limiting the disadvantages of its peripheral role in the global political economy. Far from being a passive victim of marginalisation in the international division of labour and of power, ECOWAS has responded, albeit limitedly, by taking the necessary economic and security initiatives. The recognition and formalistion of the informal border economy and politics is a radical departure from the official ECOWAS regionalism approach. Henceforth, ECOWAS is in a position to exploit the state-society-economy, both formal and informal regionalisation processes, with the hope that it will generate welfare and development for the peoples of the Community.

The analysis of ECOWAS within the context of the globalisation-regionalism dynamics brings to the fore the simultaneous process of incorporation and marginalisation of globalisation, well as the paradox between those with the capacities to enjoy the benefits of globalisation and those without. ECOWAS peripheral status in the global political economy, and weak capabilities, are always bound to work against its strategic re-positioning.

Notes and References

[1] Björn Hettne, and Fredrik, Söderbaum, 'The New Regionalism Approach', *Politeia*, Vol. 17, No. 3, 1998, p. 7.

[2] Ibid.

[3] Björn Hettne, Andras Inotai, and Osvaldo Sunkel (eds.), *The New Regionalism: Implications for Global Development and International Security*, 1994 cited in Marianne Marchand, Morten Böas and Timothy Shaw, 'The Political Economy of New Regionalisms', *Third World Quarterly*, Vol. 20, No. 5, 1999, p. 902.

[4] Louise Fawett and Andrew Hurrell (eds), *Regionalism in World Politics: Regional Organization and International Order*, Oxford: Oxford University Press, 1995, p. 324.

[5] M. Marchand, M. Böas and T. Shaw, 'The Political Economy of New Regionalisms', *Third World Quarterly*, Vol. 20, No. 5, 1999, p. 897.

[6] Fiona Butler, 'Regionalism and Integration', in John Baylis and Steve Smith (eds.), *Globalization of World Politics: An Introduction to International Relations*, 1997, p. 418.

[7] Mariane Marchand et al, 'The Political Economy of New Regionalisms', *Third World Quarterly*, Vol. 20, No. 5, 1999, p. 898.

[8] Andrew Moravcsik, 'Preferences and Power in the European Community: A Liberal Intergovernmentalist Approach', *Journal of Common Market Studies*, Vol. 31, No. 4, 1993, pp. 474-480.

[9] Anthony Payne and Andrew Gamble (eds.), *Regionalism and World Order*, New York: St. Martin's Press, 1996.

[10] Edmond Mansfield and Helen Milner (eds.), *The Political Economy of Regionalism*, New York: Columbia University Press, 1998.

[11] Marchand et al, op. cit., 1999, p. 902. See also: B. Hettne, A. Inotai and S. Osvaldo (eds.), *Studies in the New Regionalism Volumes I-V*, London: Macmillan, 1998 and 1999.

[12] M. Marchand et al, op. cit., 1999.

[13] Ibid., p. 898.

[14] James Mittleman (ed.), *Globalization: A Critical Reflection*, Boulder: Lynne Rienner, 1996.

[15] Marchand et al, op. cit., p. 898.

[16] James Mittleman (ed.), *Globalisation*, 1996, p. 229.

[17] Roland Robertson, *Globalisation*, London: Sage, 1992.

[18] David Harvey, *The Condition of Post-Modernity*, Oxford: Blackwell, 1989.

[19] Anthony Gibbens, *The Consequences of Modernity*, Cambridge: Polity Press, 1990.

[20] James Mittleman (ed.), *Globalization*, op. cit.; Hirst and Thompson, *Globalization in Question*, op. cit.

[21] Paul Hirst and Grahame Thompson, *Globalisation in Question*, London: Polity Press, 1996. James Mittleman (ed.) *Globalization*, op. cit.; Hirst and Thompson, *Globalization in Question*, op. cit.

[22] Ibid.

[23] Caroline Thomas, 'Where is the Third World Now?' *Review of International Studies*, Vol. 25, December 1999, pp. 225-243.

[24] Hirst and Thompson, *Globalisation in Question*, 1996, pp. 1-3.

[25] Inis Claude, *Swords into Ploughshares: The Problems and Progress of International Organisation*, London: London University Press, 1965.

[26] Louise Fawcett and Andrew Hurrell (eds.), *Regionalism in World Politics*, Oxford: Oxford University Press, 1995.
[27] In James Mittleman, op. cit., 1996, p. 76.
[28] Ibid., p. 18.
[29] For further discussion see: UNRISD, *States of Disarray: The Social Effects of Globalisation*, Geneva: United Nations, Ankie Hoogvelt, *Globalisation and the Postcolonial World*, London: Macmillan, 1997, pp. 162-181.
[30] Maurice Strong, 'The 'New South', *The World Today*, November 1995, p. 216.
[31] Björn Hettne and Fredrik Söderbaum, op. cit., 1998, p. 19.
[32] Peter Wilkin, 'New Myths for the South: Globalisation and the Conflict between Private Power and Freedom', *Third World Quarterly*, Vol. 17, No. 2, 1996, p. 227.
[33] Caroline Thomas, 'International Institutions and Social Economic and Cultural Rights: An Exploration', in Tony Evans (ed.), *Human Rights fifty Years On*, Manchester: Manchester University Press, 1998, pp. 161-187.
[34] 'Region-ness' is defined as the process whereby a geographical region is transformed from a passive object to a subject with capacity to articulate the interests of the emerging region, Hettne and Söderbaum, op. cit., p. 9.
[35] Louis Fawcett and Andrew Hurrell (eds.), *Regionalism in World Politics*, 1995, p. 44.
[36] Marchand et al, op. cit., p. 900.
[37] Ibid., p. 906.
[38] Ibid.
[39] Fredrik Söderbaum, 'The New Regionalism in Southern Africa', *Politeia*, Vol. 17, No. 3, 1998, pp. 75-94.

4   Sierra Leone in ECOWAS

Introduction

In order to establish a basis for the analysis of Sierra Leone's ECOWAS regionalism, the country's political economy, characterisation of the state and politics of underdevelopment, and the provision of institutional structures for ECOWAS integration will be first looked at. This will establish a background understanding for evaluating Sierra Leone's ECOWAS regionalism and how the peculiar circumstances of the country limit or enhance the opportunities for the politics of economic regionalism and co-operation.

Regionalism and co-operation are a multi-sectoral processes that covers such areas as finance, trade, economics, development, agriculture, industry, transport and communication, customs and excise, immigration, police, state security, army, foreign and national planning. Hence, co-ordination and linkages between and amongst Community and national institutions becomes an imperative. The interface between the realm of domestic and international politics is a crucial factor in economic regionalism. It is the shared responsibility of member states and ECOWAS institutions to implement the protocols, decisions and programmes formulated by the Community. Putting into place an effective national institutional structure to supervise and monitor the implementation of the ECOWAS protocols, decisions and programmes is a necessary prerequisite for member states if they want to share in the benefits of regionalism. There is the expectation of rewards and gains from regionalism. Often the expectations that accompany the integration process are immediate, tangible, absolute and differential between member states. But such rewards can only be reaped if the appropriate policies are adopted and structures put in place.

This chapter will therefore evaluate the political economy of Sierra Leone, its rationale for joining the economic community and the institutional provisions for ECOWAS activities. It will also examine the issue of Sierra Leone's financial and infrastructural contribution to ECOWAS, the level of popular participation in the integration process and the link between the politics of regionalism and national development.

Political Economy of Sierra Leone

Sierra Leone is one of Africa's smaller countries, with an estimated population of 4.9 million (1998) and an area of approximately 72.000 square miles, about the size of Scotland. Sierra Leone is bounded on the north-east by Guinea, on the south-east by Liberia and on the south by the Atlantic Ocean. Sierra Leone has one of the longest 'modern histories' of any West African nation, and has the oldest modern state in the sub-region, with a constitutional history that dates back to 1787.

The American slave trade was effectively started at the watering station of King Jimmy market in Freetown by Sir John Hawkins in the 1560s.[1] The name Sierra Leone came from a Portuguese trader, Pedro Da Cintra, who in 1462 arrived off the peninsula of present day Freetown. He was fascinated by its mountainous terrain that resembled lions and thus called it *Serra Lyoa (Leo)* (Lion mountain). The transatlantic slave trade is of vital importance to understand the history and political development of the country. The High Court ruling of Lord Chief Justice Mansfield in 1772 abolished slavery in England. Following this ruling, the 'black poor', i.e., thousands of freed slaves, found themselves roaming the streets of Britain. They posed a social problem for the British government. The Sierra Leone settlement in what is modern day Freetown, was established by British philanthropists and missionary societies in 1787 to serve as a re-settlement in Africa for the freed slaves. British altruism only went as far as making atonement for the injustice they believed Europeans had done to Africans for centuries of slave labour. In reality, it was a means of getting rid of a potentially difficult social problem in England. However, the motivations of Christian missionaries, abolitionists, and philanthropists like Granville Sharpe, William Wilberforce, and Thomas Clarkson could not be faulted. It was envisaged that the repatriated Africans would engage in agriculture and commerce. Akintola Wyse argues that the colony was also meant to serve as an experiment in social engineering; 'The founders hoped that by creating the right conditions, an opportunity would be given to emancipated Africans ... to evolve a free and self-governing black community patterned on western civilisation.[2]

However, the history of Sierra Leone pre-dates the slave trade era. Modern Sierra Leone has been continuously inhabited by indigenous Africans of diverse ethnic groups. Historical accounts, mainly by European visitors around the sixteenth century reported the existence of kingdoms in this part of the world. There were the Sapes, a confederation of coastal peoples with a substantial level of civilisation.[3] The Mane invasions of the sixteenth century and immigration in the eighteenth century are notable influences. The Manes in particular, established strong political and social institutions which did not survive the constant invasions and migrations of other ethnic groups. This illustrates the point that pre-colonial Sierra Leone had fairly well-established political and socio-economic institutions. The 'Province of Freedom' became a British Crown Colony in 1808. Much later, at the height of the scramble for African territories in the, a British protectorate was declared over the hinterland of Sierra Leone in 1896, thereby establishing effective colonial administration over the colony and protectorate. The 'wind of change' generated by agitation for self-determination of subject territories and the 'end of empire' led to independence from British rule on 27 April 1961.

The political administration of post independence Sierra Leone has been managed by both civilian and military governments, with five civil and four military regimes. The Sierra Leone Peoples Party (SLPP) led by Dr. Milton Margai formed the first democratic government in 1961. The Westminster model of politics bequeathed by the British was shattered in 1967 with the first military intervention into democratic politics led by the Army Force Commander Brigadier David Lansana. Lansana was replaced by Colonel Juxon-Smith, whose ruling junta was later ousted by a counter coup in April 1968. Parliamentary democracy was restored with the swearing in of Siaka Stevens as Prime Minister in charge of the All Peoples Congress (APC) party-led coalition government. Under Siaka Stevens the political landscape of the country was transformed. It became first a republic in 1971 and then a one-party state in 1978. President Stevens handed power to his Army Chief, Brigadier Momoh, as the sole presidential candidate in 1985. The APC governed Sierra Leone from 1968 until it was overthrown in 1992 by a coup led by the 27 year old Captain Valentine Strasser. Captain Strasser was replaced in a palace coup, by his deputy, Brigadier Maada Bio. The NPRC junta was forced to hold democratic elections in 1996 which were won by the SLPP led by Ahmed Tejan Kabbah. The government of President Kabbah was briefly overthrown by the Armed Forces Revolutionary Council (AFRC), but was re-instated by ECOWAS in 1998. The dominant parties in the post-independence political history have been SLPP and APC.

Sierra Leone has a predominantly agro-based economy. Agriculture provides employment for the majority of the rural population. The main agricultural exports include palm oil, coffee, cocoa, timber, palm kernels, Ndama cattle, fish and piassava. The excessive focus on mining industries as the primary source of earning foreign exchange has serious repercussions on agricultural development. The country, which was self-sufficient in rice production (the country's staple food) and even exported rice to neighbouring countries, has now become a major importer of this product. The agricultural sector was already in difficulties by the 1980s owing largely to neglect, low producer prices and problems in transporting commodities. According to the UN Food and Agricultural Organisation (FAO), the food situation in the country reached a 'crisis point' in 1992 and the government estimated that it would have to import about 70 per cent of the country's basic food requirements.

The main mineral resources of the country include diamond, bauxite, iron ore, rutile (titanium dioxide), alluvial gold, platinum, chromium, zinc, lead, silver and rock salt. In the early 1970s, diamond, bauxite and iron ore represented about 80 per cent of the country's total export trade. Diamonds have been Sierra Leone's major foreign exchange earner until briefly overtaken by rutile. The country is the tenth largest producer of diamonds and until, 1995, the second largest producer of rutile. Diamond exports for the following years demonstrates the heavy dependence on the mineral industry: 1992—328,000 carats; 1993—198,000; 1994—174,000; 1995—266,000; 1996—327,000.[4] It is important to note that this is only the official export statistics. It is estimated that the unofficial export and smuggling of Sierra Leone's diamonds far exceeds the official figures. The principal exports for 1995/96 were diamonds, rutile, fish and shrimps, and cocoa.

The manufacturing sector in Sierra Leone is still relatively underdeveloped. Despite attempts since independence to develop this through import substitution, it contributed only 5 per cent of GDP in 1996 and accounted for 12 per cent of formal employment.[5] The main industrial products include cement, shoes, nails, cigarettes, tobacco, beer and confectionery, plastics, clothing, chemicals, tuna and vegetable oil. In 1996 the following sectors contributed to GDP: agriculture 52 per cent; minerals 23 per cent; primary industry 16 per cent; manufacturing 5 per cent; and services 32 per cent, mainly from occupational and sectoral services such as banking, business services, industry, hotels, transport, clerical, administrative/managerial, professional/technical.[6]

At independence in 1961, Sierra Leone had a promising economy.[7] Even in colonial times, there was a rigorous market in both capital and goods. The opening of the interior to trade began a period of close urban and rural interaction. Agriculture developed and rice was exported. The diamond and gold boom made Sierra Leone a powerful magnet for immigrants from West Africa and other countries. By 1980, the developing economy gradually deteriorated as a result of domestic and external factors. Accumulated debt, mismanagement, institutionalised corruption, massive smuggling and a neglected agriculture had taken their toll. Between 1980-

1990, Sierra Leone suffered a negative per capita income growth rate. Sierra Leone's GNP per capita real growth rate from 1970 to 1994 is as follows: 1970-1980 1.1 per cent; 1980-1990 -1.5 per cent; 1985-1994 -1.9 per cent.[8] The total external debt of Sierra Leone in 1998 was estimated at US $1,150 billion. By 1998, external debt service as a percentage of the exports of goods and services of Sierra Leone was 33 per cent. This high level of debt service, against the background of poor economic performance, seriously constrained the capability of the state to provide social services and welfare, and put further pressure on scarce foreign exchange resources. Debt repayment far exceeds the government budget for health, education and poverty alleviation. Diverting meagre resources to debt servicing makes it difficult to undertake meaningful and sustainable development. The export of capital in the cause of debt service constrains national development programmes. In 1992, the Paris Club group of official creditors announced the cancellation of 50 per cent of debt-service obligations on non-concessional lending and re-scheduled the other 50 per cent over 26 years.

Analysis shows that the 1980 OAU Summit in Freetown at an estimated cost of US $100 million started the economic decline of Sierra Leone.[9] The increasing economic difficulties and the declining government revenue in the 1980s and 1990s jeopardised the capacity of both the Stevens and Momoh regimes to effectively manage the state. This forced them to turn to the IMF/World Bank SAPs. The late 1980s and early 1990s saw the full implementation of the IMF Structural Adjustment Programmes. The IMF/World Bank stabilisation and adjustment policies further aggravated the economic and political difficulties faced by the country. The austerity measures imposed by SAPs such as de-regulation, removal of government subsidies, devaluation and streamlining of government bureaucracies invariably led to unemployment, escalating inflation, a balance of payment crisis, and a further drop in the real income for the majority of the citizenry. The measures that targeted efficient management of the state directly affected the human security of ordinary Sierra Leoneans in such areas as health care delivery, education, social services and infrastructural development. It marginalised those already below the poverty line and also excluded and impoverished the middle class and petty bourgeoisie. The negative effects of SAPs led to the expansion of the informal economy, whilst the state's economic policies further impoverished the peasant producers. The consequences of SAPs intensified political unrest and generated a wave of popular political actions by trade union workers, students and teachers. In this situation, the conception of government became an abstract and remote group of small and excessively corrupt ruling and governing class. By the early 1990s, the state's extrative and allocative capacity had considerably reduced. The country's international reserves dropped to a meagre $5 million during the Momoh regime. Between 1990 and 1995, growth in the economic sector came to a virtual standstill. This was largely due to the civil war which started in 1991.

The civil war led by the Revolutionary United Front (RUF) is a product of socio-economic and political factors. It unleashed devastating economic and political consequences in the country. The RUF armed insurrection ensured the virtual closure of the economically viable mineral sector. This considerably affected government revenue and its allocative capacity. The cost of reconstruction, rehabilitation and socio-economic development of a country crippled not only by civil war but by decades of political mismanagement and economic decline is phenomenal.

Successive governments have formulated a comprehensive private sector development strategy within which the privatisation and deregulation of the economy is perceived as part of a wider sub-regional market. Despite the economic orientation towards private enterprise, much of the Sierra Leonean participation had been via parastatals. There is substantial Lebanese and Indian community, who collectively control the economy of the country, backed by the political class. The Lebanese economic stranglehold is part of the patron-clientelist political system. The late President Stevens is noted to have remarked that 'people say I have sold the country to the Lebanese ... (and) that the economy of Sierra Leone is controlled by the Lebanese. But this is not the only part of the world where the economy is controlled by foreigners.'[10] The cumulative effect of this patrimonial politics has been to paralyse local indigenous business people and industry and create monopolies in favour of influential Lebanese and Indian competitors. Sierra Leone's position today is a net exporter of raw materials and an import-dependent country. The extra-regional dependent nature of the economy points to the fact that developments in these western industrialised countries almost always bring additional problems for both the domestic politics and economics of the country.

Sierra Leone, like the majority of sub-Saharan African states, is a periphery economy, considerably marginalised by the structure of the global economy. According to the UN Human Development Report for 1991 and 1992, Sierra Leone was classified on the Human Development Index (HDI) as the world's least developed and second least developed nation, respectively. Per capita income of the average Sierra Leonean is US $150 (1996), which is far below the poverty line. Sierra Leone has no reason to be categorised as the world's poorest nation because of its rich natural and human resources. It has the oldest educational centre in sub-Saharan Africa, Fourah Bay College, founded in 1827. This University became the locus of educational enterprise in West Africa and has often been referred to as the 'Athens of West Africa'.[11] But a combination of factors both internal and external have all connived to make the country an economic disaster area. Sierra Leone has not suffered from the devastation of famine, drought and desertification that has bedeviled other African states. The exceptional wealth of the country has not been translated into meaningful development and better standard of living. There is a Sierra Leonean joke that, when God created West Africa, He endowed the country with such wealth of natural resources that the angels protested at the unfairness of His distribution. 'Oh that's nothing' God replied. 'Just wait till you see the people I put there'. The seriousness of this joke becomes apparent when one analyses the nature of domestic politics and the patrimonial underdevelopment in post-colonial Sierra Leone.

Characterisation of State and the Politics of Decline in Sierra Leone

The political economy of Sierra Leone provides the basis for the characterisation of the state and analysis of the politics of underdevelopment. Evaluation of Sierra Leone's ECOWAS regionalism necessarily begins with an assessment of the nature of the domestic political culture and patrimonial decline.

The analyses of the political economy of state recession in Sierra Leone suggest the extent to which the state is able to reap the benefits or maximise the opportunities of economic regionalism and co-operation. The historicity of Sierra Leonean society and the dynamics of domestic politics helps to explain Sierra Leone's ECOWAS regionalism.

Dependency and underdevclopment theorists such as Andre Gunder Frank and Samir Amin assume that the underdevelopment of countries such as Sierra Leone can largely be attributed to the conditions of dependency on the capitalist West. However, the characterisation of state and politics in Sierra Leone demonstrates the inadequacy of the underdevelopment perspective. Political clientelism and patrimonial interpretations provide a plausible alternative understanding of the nature of the political economy of state fragmentation in Sierra Leone. Clientelism and patrimonial politics established by the post-independent leaders worsened the crisis of legitimacy of the state and had often led to the retrenchment of democracy. The patron-clientelist system, first established under the SLPP government of the Margais (1961-1967), and consolidated under the Stevens and Momoh one party rule (1968-1991), was based on a web of informal networks through which state resources were appropriated to supporters and followers. Christopher Clapham describes this nature of domestic politics as political clientelism, in that it is a:

> mechanism of exchange: by recognising private interests and using the machinery of the state to purvey private benefits to groups and individuals, in the process giving them vested - and purely instrumental-interest in the maintenance of the state itself.[12]

This clientelistic relationship ensured that access to state resources in the form of jobs, government contracts, development loans, opportunities for illegal gains and access to resources not directly controlled by the state but subject to its regulation such as import and export permits (diamond and gold) and business licenses emanated from State House, namely the Stevens, Momoh, Strasser, and their followers. It also ensured the personal loyalty of the army and the police force to the government in power, on which these regimes relied for their survival.[13]

Linked to the politics of clientelism is that of patrimonalism and neo-patrimonialism, which is an extension of the patron-clientelistic relationship and political patronage. It focuses on the lack of distinction between public and private relationships and the general privatisation and informalisation of political life. Jean Francois Medard's definition of neo-patrimonalism aptly describes this post-independent politics of underdevelopment in that 'public authority has been made an object of appropriation by the formal office holders, functionaries, politicians, and military personnel, who based their strategies of individual ascendancy or family ascendancy on a private usage of the *res publica*'.[14] The clientelistic and neo-patrimonial politics produced immobility, inefficiency, unbridled corruption, illegitimacy and exploitation. The privatisation and informalisation of the state progressively weakened the legal, political and economic institutions of the 'official' state or, at least, were converted to serve the private interests of the small ruling and governing class.

Prebendal politics in Sierra Leone converted the state into a 'market' where office holders competed for the acquisition of material benefits.[15] Jimmy Kandeh aptly captured the predatory and patrimonial nature of the state in Sierra Leone:

> Conversion of state offices and public resources into sources of private wealth has been the primary mode of accumulation among Sierra Leone's political elites since independence in 1961. Stevens ... turned over the entire diamond and fishing industry to Jamil Sahid Mohamed, his Afro-

Lebanese crony and business partner, who also at the time operated his own bank in addition to marketing, insurance and light manufacturing ventures. Under Stevens, Mohamed attended cabinet meetings (although he was not a minister or official member of government), occasionally vetoed ministerial decisions and routinely violated government foreign exchange regulations.[16]

At the height of APC patrimonialism, Siaka Stevens' popular Krio saying 'usai u go tie cow nah dae e for eat' (meaning where a cow is tethered there it grazes), became the 'abiding principle of the decaying polity'.[17] The APC patrimonialism was predicated on a tribute mode of accumulation which permeated all stratas of the government bureaucracy and parastatals. Bogus contracts were signed by government functionaries and salaries of non-existent workers or 'ghost workers' were routinely diverted to private use by bureaucrats and politicians. The Sierra Leone press became awash with headlines such as 'squandergate', 'contractgate'; 'vouchergate' and 'die-man racket'. The nature of APC patrimonialism is what has been described by Coleman and Rosberg as 'Fuherism', and 'sultanism' by Weber, whereby Stevens and Momoh behaved as if they owned the 'state', or that it was their private property.[18]

Brigadier Joseph Momoh, in his capacity of Chief of the Army, was selected by the ageing Stevens to replace him in 1985. President Momoh therefore inherited a prebendal politics rooted in corruption, opportunism, cronyism and sycophancy.[19] Momoh's singular contribution to this patrimonial decline was to elevate the ethnic Limba-based socio-political and economic organisation, the *Ekutay*, into a ruling cabal, who were locally known as the Binkolo Mafia (Binkolo is Momoh's home town).[20] To develop a power base, Momoh resorted to 'ethnic corporatism' in order to prop up his 'new order regime'. Momoh was generally regarded as an 'imposed presidential candidate', an 'ethnic upstart, and a weak leader who never really had the total support of the APC ruling class'. Momoh's regime further polarised and heightened the ethnic divide and tensions between the north and south-east of the country.

The excessive external-dependent nature of the political economy of Sierra Leone, in particular the mining sector, illustrates that in several respects Sierra Leone is a rentier state. The corrosive effects of both external rent (from MNCs, IFIs and Western donors), and the dynamics of internal development (such as the emergence of a rentier mentality and rentier class) are clear.[21] The mining sector has played a significant role in the politics of decline in Sierra Leone. Strategic minerals like diamonds, have been regarded by some as a blessing in that they provide the financial resources needed to accelerate economic and social development. Others, however, perceive such resources as a curse that has retarded economic development and stultified political change. The diamond booms of the 1950s and 1960s and their depletion in the 1970s and 1980s have considerably shaped the political discourse on democratic governance and development in the country.[22] The crucial question that requires explanation is why, in spite of the extraordinary resources generated by the mining sector, the economic and social progress of the country have remained so underdeveloped.

The rentier nature of the economy and the 'allocation state' has totally failed to formulate any sustainable economic policies. State resources had been appropriated to sustain the patrimonial politics in which personal aggrandisement became the prerogative for political power. The SLPP, APC, and NPRC regimes promoted neither growth nor welfare but were preoccupied with the enrichment of the elites who controlled the state apparatus. The rentier mentality therefore created in Sierra Leone a situation whereby 'the welfare and propriety imported from abroad pre-empts some of the urgency for change and rapid growth and may in fact coincide with socio-political stagnation and inertia'.[23] The primary consideration for the rentier elite, in whose hands political power is concentrated, is to defend the status quo at all cost. Allocation of state resources therefore becomes the channel of purchasing consent of the governed. Jimmy Kandeh argues that state patrimonialism in Sierra Leone has deprived public institutions and agencies of the resources and autonomy to respond to societal needs, interests and aspirations. The 'state' within the Sierra Leonean context, according to Kandeh, is a 'soft', fragile, incoherent and disarticulated entity.[24]

By the 1980s, Sierra Leone was nothing more than a 'collapsing state' that could hardly respond to the basic imperatives of statehood such as control over its territory, both domestic and external sovereignty, security for its citizens, institutions of rule and a legal order. The parasitism that developed between the state bourgeoisie, compradors and metropolitan interests sustained the patrimonial politics. It therefore produced 'widespread impoverishment, shrinking social services, dilapidated infrastructure, a rapidly deteriorating educational system, and a grossly managed economy'.[25] The privatisation and informalisation of the legitimate political order eventually laid the foundation for state collapse, the marginalisation and exclusion of the majority of the populace from the economic and political processes in the country. The widespread political and socio-economic discontent provided the breeding ground for armed insurrection. Governance and state legitimisation were therefore based not on credible and popular representative institutions, but on the 'reinforcement of the oppressive state apparatus'.[26]

Paul Richards posits that the politics of decline and state recession is not a recent phenomenon, but a product of how 'long-term patterns of 'primitive accumulation' of forest and mineral resources in Sierra Leone have fed a modern politics dominated by patrimonial redistribution'.[27] The SLPP, APC and NPRC regimes demonstrated that political support of the ruling elite was based on redistributing state resources to followers and clients - a distribution hardly based on bureaucratic rationality or accountability. William Reno argues that the 'personal fortunes' of patrimonial leaders are political resources which had been used to fund the working of the 'shadow state'. In Reno's view, the 'shadow state' is the substance of patrimonial politics that has come to represent the private face of the post-colonial 'modern state'.[28] In the Sierra Leone situation, the 'official' visible state has been propped up by patrimonial appropriations. It is important to note that Sierra Leone reflects the wider patrimonial authoritarianism experienced by the majority of post-colonial African states.

Patrimonialism in Sierra Leone suffered a crisis of legitimacy in the 1980s and 1990s because of a combination of complex factors. The global economic recession had serious effects on the prices of mineral and raw materials. Diamond resources were in considerable decline in Sierra Leone. The end of the Cold War resulted in a virtual drying up of the channels of aid money. The withdrawal of transnational diamond mining interests in the 1980s and replacement by small-scale tributors and widespread smuggling starved the government of much needed revenue for the formal state to fund public sector services such as education and public health. Therefore, with less resources to maintain 'the crumbling facade of the 'official state''[29] state fragmentation was set in motion both physically and sociologically. Thus, the socio-economic and political exclusion of the majority of the citizenry and the fragmentation of state apparatus became apparent.

Patrimonialism in Sierra Leone widened the gap in the political economy between the capital Freetown and the isolated rural districts, and between the mining sector of the economy and the stagnant semi-subsistence agriculture. Heavy dependency on the diamond mining industry diverted attention from agricultural development and the cultivation of rice. The patrimonial state therefore had to intervene to ensure cheap rice supplies from overseas. Paul Richards argues that 'Allocating licences to sell government-imported rice (mainly APC government ministers and supporters) provided further scope for patrimonialism .... The APC government became locked within a cycle of dependency on diamonds and white rice'.[30] According to A. Zack-Williams, Sierra Leone's social formation in terms of relations to means of production and mode of appropriation has produced two distinct classes: the 'ruling class' (which formally controls the state apparatus); and the 'governing class" (which controls the economic lifeline of the state).[31] Political clientelism and patrimonialism produced in Sierra Leone a large constituency of underprivileged, impoverished, socio-economically and politically excluded citizenry. This disgruntled constituency was held in check or coerced into silence by the oppressive state security apparatus, most notably, the APC paramilitary force, the Special Security Division (SSD), pejoratively referred to by the people as 'Special Siaka Dogs'. In effect, the civil war of 1991 shows the extent of the 'protracted post-colonial crisis of patrimonialism'.

Sierra Leone's ECOWAS regionalism was therefore an extension of the patrimonial strategy of the 'shadow state' to tap rentier resources and opportunities from economic regionalism and co-operation, in order to complement national development, and to further support the patronage and clientelistic networks. Herein lies the reason why the politics of economic regionalism had become important to successive regimes in Sierra Leone.

Sierra Leone's Foreign Policy Approach to ECOWAS Regionalism

Sierra Leone has been a periphery actor in the regional and international division of labour and of power because of its small size, population, economic and technological capabilities. It has, however, played constructive roles in intra-Africa relations through the hosting of the OAU and ECOWAS summits. Its strategic resource endowment and natural harbour have sometimes accorded Sierra Leone a relatively important role in international affairs.

Sierra Leone's foreign policy has been primarily traditional and state-centric with a 'focus on influences or determinants of policy, objectives, interests of the state, and formal policy towards global actors, as well as on traditional objectives of defence and development'.[32] It has been traditionally influenced by the following factors: colonial legacy, resource endowment, intergovernmental relations, and centralised decision making. The colonial inheritance has pre-determined and shaped the conservative, Western-oriented foreign policy approach of post-colonial Sierra Leone. British influence remains dominant in the country's politics and development. Sierra Leone's strategic resource endowment has also played a crucial role in its international relations with major powers. Its diamond diplomacy has often given the small country a significant leverage in international political and economic affairs. However, the nature of the politics of underdevelopment has denied the country the economic capability to project a meaningful foreign policy in international affairs, in comparison to the diamond diplomacy of Botswana or Nigeria's oil diplomacy. In contrast Botswana, a small diamond-rich country, which has succeeded in establishing a credible 'global network of trusted diplomatic connections enabling it to aspire to a participatory role in virtually any African issue or conflict, at times extending even beyond Africa'.[33]

To overcome the disadvantages of small size and population, Sierra Leone has made membership of intergovernmental organisations an important foreign policy approach. This approach provides the advantages of collective solidarity and a political and economic bargaining bloc in pushing for African issues at the global level. This foreign policy approach has led to membership of the UN, OAU, Commonwealth, ECOWAS, MRU, Non-aligned Movement, Organisation of Islamic States and others. Therefore, Sierra Leone's ECOWAS regionalism is a manifestation of the country's intra-African foreign policy and diplomacy. Stephen Wright argues that, through co-ordination within IGOs and pooling of sovereignties, states such as Sierra Leone are 'able to project a presence quite beyond their individual capabilities'.[34]

During the Cold War, Sierra Leone's membership of the Non-Aligned Movement (NAM) provided a foreign policy strategy to play off the East and West against each other in order to reap economic, political, military and other strategic benefits. The rhetoric of non-alignment saw Stevens maintaining strong diplomatic links with communist China, Cuba and Soviet Union as well as the capitalist west. The case of Sierra Leone is however not unique because the instrumental utility of non-alignment has been exploited by developing states to secure foreign aid and military assistance.

The post-independence foreign policy of Sierra Leone emphasised political sovereignty and territorial integrity. This approach is predicated on the notion of sovereign equality of members of the international system, and has also been used, according to political realists, to ensure the security and survival of the state in the 'anarchical' international system. Sierra Leone therefore advocated decolonisation in Africa through the OAU platform. Sierra Leone added its political and diplomatic support for the independence of Guinea Bissau, Zimbabwe and Namibia, and also campaigned against apartheid South Africa through co-operation with the Front-Line States. Pan-Africanism motivated the campaign against apartheid and decolonisation under the auspices of the OAU and

ECOWAS. However, the rhetoric of Pan-Africanism has been responsible for some of the contradictory positions adopted on African issues. The Pan-Africanist umbrella of ECOWAS therefore provided an opportunity to overcome foreign policy predicaments on international issues.

Post-independence foreign policies have also focused on economic development generally predicated on modernisation. The country's foreign economic policies have led to bilateral and multilateral trading, and economic agreements and co-operations, such as the ACP-EEC relations/Lomé Convention, and membership of economic and financial organisations such as WTO, IMF and World Bank. Sierra Leone's ECOWAS regionalism is a solid plank in the foreign economic policy approach of the country because it is expected that the economic objectives of ECOWAS would provide direct and indirect economic dividends.

Although Sierra Leone's foreign policy has been broadly non-aligned during the Cold War period, the country had been generally more aligned with the West. Sierra Leone even sent a medical unit to join the allied forces during the Gulf War of 1990-91, though the country's hospitals were in dire need of doctors and nurses. The new thinking in the foreign policy of the post-Cold War era is to strengthen existing bilateral and multilateral relations, with a new emphasis on regionalism. The conference of High Commissioners and Ambassadors in 1988 was an attempt to formulate a rational approach in the pursuit of the national interest, a departure from what has been regarded as a 'whimsical conduct of foreign policy'.[35] Two fundamental principles have been the basis of Sierra Leone's foreign policy: political autonomy and economic development. The participation of the country in intergovernmental organisations and economic regionalism and co-operation schemes has been in pursuit of these two goals. President Stevens in his speech during the establishment of ECOWAS in May 1975 stated that 'following our political independence and its concomitant separatist tendencies, many states of Africa have come to realise that their future lies in co-operating with their neighbours'.[36] As far as the President was concerned, political and economic considerations seem to have been the primary motivations for Sierra Leone's membership of ECOWAS. Siaka Stevens described ECOWAS as a Community set up to add the economic ingredient to political independence in West Africa, 'for economic prosperity in the sub-region lies in our grouping together'. The personalised rule of Stevens during this period meant that his personal inclinations constituted the foreign policy of the state. According to the former Foreign Affairs Minister, Abdul Karim Koroma, 'The repository of decision-making is vested in the president whose vision the minister articulates'.[37] Stevens was a conservative pan-Africanist who favoured South-South co-operation and collective self-reliance through regional integration and co-operation. It was this ideological persuasion that led to the creation of the Mano River Union in 1973. Steven's approach also manifest a centralised foreign policy decision making. However, the nature of domestic politics and the peripheral status of Sierra Leone in the international division of power considerably constrained the achievement of the two fundamental principles of the country's foreign policy.

Sierra Leone's ECOWAS regionalism was perceived not in the sense of integration as an end in itself, but as a means to an end: the end being the attainment of the traditional goals of politics, i.e. power, prestige and influence; and for economic development. It was seen as a complement to national development strategies. It was not a long-range integration for its own sake, but for immediate economic and political gains. The economic problems faced by the country, and the constraints on resources available, pre-disposed Stevens to turn to economic regionalism to seek immediate and dramatic gains from integration. He came to believe that the country could not develop by national efforts alone, considering its small size and relatively small population, and hence the best option available was developmental regionalism. The accelerated rate of development envisaged was expected to come from increased trade, investment, industrial productivity from a large-scale economy and equitable distribution of the benefits of economic regionalism. It was envisaged that Sierra Leone's ECOWAS regionalism would lead to national specialisation in the production of particular products for which the country offered comparative advantages, thereby reducing the costs of production, and the availability of cheaper regional goods.

It was assumed that there were tangible political and economic benefits to be achieved by being a member of a club of West African allies. The view was that it would be in the country's interest to attach its predominantly agro-based economy to more advanced ones. It was further expected that ECOWAS regionalism would provide access to IFIs and international organisations that might offer attractive opportunities to Sierra Leone in the post-1973 oil crisis period. The fear of 'exclusion' in the international relations of the sub-region also played a decisive factor. It was thought Sierra Leone could not afford to be left out of the evolving regional economic and political co-operation manifested in South-South relations. It was considered that membership of ECOWAS would maximise the influence of the economic community in international affairs through a single coherent West African approach. It was therefore assumed that the ECOWAS member states would benefit from their collective bargaining power with other economic blocs. The mere existence of the Community served as an instrument of foreign policy for the member states. The Sierra Leone government was eager to join ECOWAS because it was seen as an international asset and a means of strengthening its position in the international system. Sierra Leone as such was only building on the 'integrative habit' inculcated in the formation of the Mano River Union. It is from these perspectives that President Stevens expressed great optimism that Sierra Leone would be a potential beneficiary of ECOWAS regionalism.

A combination of economic and political factors both domestic and external were the motivation for joining ECOWAS. Sierra Leone's national goals with respect to ECOWAS could be summarised as follows. The economic goals generally included economic development and growth, strengthening technological capability, the reduction of unemployment, co-operation among industry and universities, equilibrium in external trade and balance of payments, self-sufficiency or security of raw materials, mineral resources and environmental protection. The political goals included political autonomy and territorial integrity, political co-operation in West Africa, regional peace and security, human rights and democratic governance, and development of West African and continental unity. The social goals included social integration in West Africa to bridge the colonial divide, improvement of the quality of life, medical health and social well-being, education and training, preservation of national and ethnic identities, religious tolerance, preservation of cultural heritage and regional cultural contacts.

Broadly speaking, therefore, the changed international environment of the post-Cold War era have considerably affected the capability of Sierra Leone, like the majority of developing countries, to pursue influential foreign policies. The economic and political conditionalities of liberalisation and democratisation of the 1990s have further shifted economic and fiscal decision making away from the government to IFIs such as the IMF and World Bank. The foreign policy predicaments and challenges faced by countries such as Sierra Leone are that the limited relevance of strategic resources and the growing significance of global financial and high-tech resources means these states have to compete with MNCs, IFIs and other regional economic blocs. The overall effect of the changed international environment is that Sierra Leone's contemporary foreign policy, though largely underpinned by conservative continuity, reflects the challenges of global society, in that it has moved from its traditional state-centric focus to an incorporation of non-state actors such as NGOs, civil society organisations, IGOs, and warlords. In the 1990s,

ECOWAS regionalism has emerged as the most dominant foreign and security policy approach for Sierra Leone largely due to the role of ECOWAS and ECOMOG in peacekeeping / enforcement, and the civil war peace settlement in Sierra Leone. Stephen Wright therefore observes that regionalism probably provides the most realistic alternative for African foreign policy,[38] a regionalism that shifts away from the formal and 'old' regionalism to a 'new regionalism' that 'recognises informal economies and encourage informal polities; civil societies at regional level'.[39]

Sierra Leone's Institutional Structure for ECOWAS Responsibilities

The Ministry of Economic Planning and Development is officially responsible for Sierra Leone's ECOWAS activities. The Minister has supervisory responsibility for ECOWAS and reports to the cabinet and parliament on all issues relating to Sierra Leone's ECOWAS regionalism. The Development Secretary is the administrative head responsible for Sierra Leone's ECOWAS affairs at the ministry. In comparative terms, Senegal, Guinea and Burkina Faso are the only ECOWAS member states that have a specific African Economic Integration Ministry.

In 1992, this aspect of international co-operation was added to the Ministry of Foreign Affairs in order to enhance the co-ordination of ECOWAS activities between the Economic Planning and Development Ministry and that of the Foreign Ministry. The intervention of ECOMOG and its implications for national security means that the Ministry of Defence and Internal Security have been brought to the centre stage of Sierra Leone's ECOWAS regionalism. Due to the multi-sectoral nature of the regionalism process, Sierra Leone's ECOWAS responsibility is shared among other ministries depending on the specific issues: the Finance Ministry deals with fiscal matters and the Central Bank co-ordinates regional monetary co-operation; the Ministry of Foreign Affairs deals with regional political and security co-operation, whilst the Ministry of Defence handles matters relating to military and security issues; the Ministries of Trade and Industry and Internal Security jointly deals with trade, customs and immigration matters. Co-ordination among the ministries is intended to enable the country to maximise the opportunities of economic regionalism and co-operation. It has been acknowledged that economic regionalism is an important aspect of national and regional development, and that economic diplomacy underpins the politics of regionalism. Sierra Leone's institutional provision is a reflection of what is happening at Community level. It is a manifestation of the multi-sectoral nature of the integration process, hence the variety of ministries responsible for ECOWAS activities.

A decision of the ECOWAS Authority in December 1983 mandated the establishment of ECOWAS National Units to monitor the implementation of ECOWAS protocols and decisions. Sierra Leone's ECOWAS National Unit was established in 1983 and had been playing a vital role in facilitating the participation, co-ordination and involvement of the country more effectively in the integration process. The National Unit ensured the proper co-ordination, and implementation of ECOWAS decisions, protocols and conventions at national level. It holds meetings with 'shared line' ministries, i.e. ministries with shared responsibility for ECOWAS activities; parastatals, governmental departments and NGOs. At the 20th ECOWAS summit in 1997, the National Units were given a special mandate to ensure the removal of obstacles impeding regional integration and to revitalise ECOWAS.[40] Enhanced co-operation between the Community institutions and the National Units is clearly essential for the realisation of ECOWAS' integration objectives. ECOWAS National Units are an essential element in the institutional arrangement for promoting economic regionalism in West Africa. Although ECOWAS institutions are responsible for initiating and developing economic regionalism and co-operation programmes, actual implementation is the responsibility of the member governments. National institutional structures and monitoring provisions are an imperative for sharing in the benefits of regionalism. Studies conducted have confirmed that some member states including Sierra Leone have not taken adequate political and official steps to secure the smooth operation of the National Units. Political considerations have in most cases affected the operationalisation of the National Units and even the implementations of protocols and decisions.

In addition to the National Unit, a National ECOWAS Co-ordination Committee has been established in Sierra Leone. The Committee brings together and oversees all sectors that have something to do with the integration process. The Co-ordination Committee is headed by the Developmet Secretary. It comprises representatives from ministries including Finance, Foreign Affairs, Trade and Industry, Agriculture, Immigration, Internal Security, Transport and selected private sector organisations like the Chambers of Commerce and the Sierra Leone Export Development and Investment Corporation (SLEDIC). Furthermore, Sierra Leone has established permanent ECOWAS committees to promote, monitor and ensure the implementation of Sierra Leone's ECOWAS regionalism. These committees include:

i. Technical Committee of Experts: This includes experts from various ministries such as Finance, Development, Central Bank, Customs, Immigration, Central Statistics and others.
ii. Committee on Land Transport: The committee monitors implementation of protocols on the inter-state road transit of goods. The committee is headed by the Minister of Transport and comprises the Permanent Secretary of the Transport and Communications Ministry; Chief Immigration Officer; Inspector General of Police; Controller of Customs; President of the Drivers Association and the Executive Secretary of the Chamber of Commerce.
iii. National Economic Committee: Chaired by the Deputy Minister of Finance and comprising the Governor of the Central Bank; Financial Secretary; Development Secretary; Trade and Research Department; and the Economic Policy and Research Unit (EPRU) of the Finance and Justice ministries.

An important omission in the institutional arrangement is the informal sector which accounts for over 60 per cent of Sierra Leone's intra-regional trade. The many trade associations which represent the informal sector could make an important contribution especially by drawing the attention of the Community to the difficulties experienced by their members in conducting trade with other ECOWAS countries.

The contention has been made that the institutional arrangement for Sierra Leone's ECOWAS responsibility is inadequate. In spite of the fact that there officially exists a National Unit, National Co-ordination Committee and Permanent Committees, these do not really amount to a proper monitoring and supervisory mechanisms. The charge is often levied by officials at the Sierra Leone ECOWAS secretariat that the administrative and political heads are more interested in attending international conferences and claiming their per diems. There is also a contentious relationship between the administrative heads and technical experts in terms of conference attendance. In the words of the ECOWAS Director of Transport and Communications, 'While the Community is moving on, Sierra Leone has not, because it has not established the adequate structures and mechanisms that would enable the country to benefit from the integration arrangement'.[41]

The Sierra Leone government's understanding of the issues of economic regionalism has also been brought into question. It is argued that in spite of the fact that there exists an inadequate structural arrangement for the supervision of ECOWAS activities, there is also a lack of comprehensive and defined objectives of what Sierra Leone's regionalism objectives are and what the administrators are expected to achieve from the regionalisation process. The apparent lack of official direction, apart from the general economic assumptions about integration, probably accounts for the absence of sustained political and official commitment, except when it serves the political and security interests of the ruling elite.

The absence of a comprehensive national focal point for matters of economic regionalism in many countries explains many features on the West African scene in the field of economic integration. It explains why most countries rarely evaluate the costs and benefits of membership of organisations concerned with economic regionalism and co-operation. The point that should be emphasised is that the establishment of a meaningful institutional structure is not an assurance of effective implementation of protocols and decisions. What is needed is sustained political commitment and sufficient political leverage, but this is largely determined by the political exigencies and imperatives of the government in power.

The co-ordination and liaison role of the National Units with Community institutions has been fraught with problems. Part of the problem has been the flow of information between the ECOWAS National Co-ordination Committee and the Community Institutions. To improve this situation, the Community Computer Centre is studying ways of equipping National Units to 'log on to' ECOWAS internet facilities such as electronic mail. The ineffective performance of National Units is also largely due to lack of material and financial resources. If member states are to participate effectively in the activities of the Community and monitor its regional programmes regularly, there should be closer co-ordination of the National Units, the sector ministries, the political leadership and economic operators.

In view of the important role the ECOWAS National Units are meant to play, they have been required to attend all ECOWAS technical meetings in order to enable them to play their role more effectively in the regionalisation process. This however opens another avenue for potential problems. In member states with inadequate institutional structures and lack of clear domestic regional integration objectives like Sierra Leone, the personal interest of the administrators in the ministry responsible for ECOWAS activities ensures they take the opportunity to attend every technical committee even when they might not be the competent experts required to participate. There is no doubt that Sierra Leone's ECOWAS institutional structure is ineffective and as such creates the situation wherein utilising the opportunities of regionalism and sharing in the benefits of economic co-operation becomes difficult. There is room for improvement in terms of structural provisions. The worthy examples of some Community members in establishing a specific government ministry for African regionalism, should be emulated with some national modifications to suit the domestic realities. Moving beyond the rhetoric of regionalism is the first step towards the proper functioning of the National Units and the eventual implementation of ECOWAS protocols and decisions.

The Politics of Ratification of ECOWAS Protocols and Decisions

The ratification of ECOWAS protocols and decisions by member states is a recurrent problem highlighted at summit meetings. ECOWAS has an impressive array of signed protocols but an equally poor record of protocols and decisions not yet ratified by member states.[42] It is here that the gap between the realities and rhetoric of regionalism becomes apparent. The ratification of protocols is the first step towards implementation. The next step is to translate the content of the protocols into the language of domestic law or administrative action. It normally takes a great deal of time to accomplish this, which probably accounts for the states' poor record of ratification. Ratification remains 'the pitiable aspect of the unfinished business in ECOWAS'.[43] The impressive or poor record of ratification of protocols has not to do with the size or economic status of the member states. Size of the country has been used as an important argument to justify the poor record of ratification on the grounds that small countries have limited economic and political interests at stake and as such can afford to ratify all protocols and decisions.

Of the 34 protocols and Conventions signed since 1978, Sierra Leone has ratified a total of 26 as of March 1997. Ghana has the highest number of ratifications with 32, followed by Senegal at 31, Mali and Guinea at 30 respectively.[44] This effectively counters the argument that only small countries are more inclined to ratify protocols, because Ghana and Senegal are among the ECOWAS 'big four' and if anything, have major interests at stake. Sierra Leone is the seventh highest member in the Community in terms of status of ratification. By 1992, Sierra Leone had ratified a total of 23 out of the 28 ECOWAS protocols. The high level of ratification has to do with the politics of regionalism at that time. During this period, the young military leaders of the NPRC junta in Sierra Leone, lacked legitimacy and international recognition. They became convinced of the political and diplomatic relevance of ECOWAS regionalism, and thus took the lead in the ratification of protocols. This was an attempt by the military regime, unhindered by parliamentary scrutiny and oversight, to play an influential role in ECOWAS regionalism, and by so doing achieve some measure of international credibility and legitimacy. It could be argued that the politics of ratification of protocols and decisions also accounts for the half-hearted attempt in terms of implementation. This point should however not be stretched too far because ratification, albeit for political considerations, is far better than non-ratification.

There is a persistent tendency for states to weigh more carefully the implications of adopting protocols on their economies and the domestic political scene before their ratification and implementation at national level. It clearly reflects the position of Sierra Leone after the formal adoption of the ECOWAS Treaty. Sierra Leone was not among the first wave of the nine countries that ratified the Treaty even though the country had been meaningfully involved in the deliberations leading to the formation of the economic community. Sierra Leone is noted to have made some preliminary reservations about some aspects of the Treaty particularly with regard to free movement of persons.

Ratification is not an end in itself. This is to give the legal instrument for the implementation of the protocols. The issue of non-ratification is a prevalent problem among Community members. The so-called big powers in ECOWAS, Nigeria and Côte d'Ivoire, have ratified only 29 and 25 protocols respectively. The case of Mauritania, which is more Arab North Africa oriented, is a peculiar one and it is not surprising that it has ratified only 3 protocols. The basic problem with the ratification of protocols is mainly the fact that these have to be adopted into domestic law before they can be applied in the local jurisdiction of member states. The Revised Treaty makes provision for supranationality in that it confers full power on the Authority to take decisions which would be binding on community institutions as well as member states after ninety days. The practical application of this principle still leaves a lot to be desired.

Financial and Infrastructural Obligation to ECOWAS

The issue of member states' financial contribution to the Community's institutions has been a perennial problem. Sierra Leone, like most Community members, has been tardy in its contribution to the organisation.[45] The rather poor economic and financial situation of the member states over the years has posed a major hindrance in honouring their financial obligations. Some member states do not even make national budgetary appropriations for regional organisations. This is the position that Sierra Leone found itself in, in the late 1980s. The Community therefore has to rely on external funding for its operations.

Sierra Leone's financial obligations cover such areas as budgetary contributions to the ECOWAS Secretariat, the Fund's capital, the Compensation budget, and the construction of Community institutions such as the ECOWAS headquarters, the Fund's headquarters and WAMA headquarters. Other financial contributions cover such areas as regional security, i.e. ECOMOG's military and logistical needs.

Sierra Leone's financial obligation could best be illustrated in its contributions to the Fund. The Fund as a development finance institution derives its main source of revenue from member states' contributions. The authorised capital of the Fund was fixed in July 1977 at US $500 million, the equivalent of 426,825. 104 West Africa units of account (UA). The sum of US $100 million (85, 365,021 UA) or 20 per cent of the authorised capital was called up for payment in two equal tranches, the first of which was declared for immediate subscription in 1977, while the second tranche became due for payment in 1987. This called-up capital was meant to serve as first-tier capital of the Fund which would provide the basis for its relative strength of participation in capital markets, its rating, and capacity in project financing.[46] Sierra Leone's contribution to the first tranche called up in 1977, which has been fully paid, amounts to 1,878.030 UA, i.e., approximately US $2,629,242 million. As of September 1997, Sierra Leone has only partially contributed to the second tranche called-up in 1987. The total amount of the country's assessed contribution is 1, 726,601 UA. The amount partially paid is 164,291 UA, i.e., approximately US $230,007. The amount outstanding is 1.562,310, i.e., approximately US $2.187,234 million. For the second tranche, only Benin, Burkina Faso and Guinea have fully paid up. The Gambia, Mali, Nigeria, Sierra Leone and Togo constitute the category of partially paid up members. As of October 1993, Liberia, Guinea Bissau, Mauritania, Niger and Senegal had not made any payment. In addition, Sierra Leone also has contributed to the construction of the headquarters. The total amount contributed as of December 1995 was 1,082,245 UA, i.e. approximately US $1,515,143 million.[47]

The criteria for member states financial contribution are based on their economic position, size, population and other variables. The percentage of Sierra Leone's contribution is 4.4 per cent. Nigeria with 32.8 per cent, Côte d'Ivoire 13 per cent and Ghana 12.9 per cent are the highest contributors. Countries in the same category as Sierra Leone are supposed to make the following contributions: Togo - 3.6 per cent; Burkina Faso - 2.6 per cent; Guinea - 1.5 per cent; Liberia - 6.7 per cent; and Mali - 1.9 per cent. Senegal which is one of the ECOWAS 'big four' contributes only 5.4

per cent. Sierra Leone is the sixth largest contributor to the ECOWAS Fund. However, the economic realities of these countries belie their contribution percentage. Sierra Leone and Guinea who have been categorised as the world's poorest nations in 1991 and 1992 respectively are the sixth and ninth largest contributors to the Fund. Liberia, the fifth largest contributor with a percentage of 6.7 per cent belies current economic realities resulting from a destructive civil war. Senegal with a 5.4 per cent contribution, was the only ECOWAS country in the middle-level category of the UN Human Development ranking for 1996. The point is that these criteria were agreed at a time when the economies of the member states were relatively stable. The slow and late payment of contributions by member states is therefore not surprising.

Sierra Leone's rather tardy financial contribution to the Fund reflects the general problem of the Community members the majority of which are fragile and underdeveloped economies. To address this problem, the Authority resolved that punitive actions were to be taken against any member state that is in default of their budgetary contribution to the Community. Such actions include prohibiting member states from filling statutory posts allocated to them and even the removal of member states' staff from Community positions. This was an incentive for Sierra Leone partially to honour its budgetary payment because the politically relevant post of Executive Secretary was held by the country. The approach of Abass Bundu, the then Executive Secretary, was to threaten to resign if Sierra Leone's contribution was not paid. A combination of national political considerations and personal interests forced the government to pay its contribution. It became a constant source of embarrassment for the Executive Secretary whose country was constantly in arrears to the Community he heads. It would have also meant that the holder of the office would be out of a job if the resolution was put into effect.

In analytical terms, one would like to know whether the diversion of millions of dollars from national development programmes such as health services, schools, domestic infrastructures, food production is worth the benefits of economic regionalism. It is clear that Sierra Leone expected to achieve something tangible or intangible in return for the value of its financial contributions to the Community.

Sierra Leone's infrastructural obligation takes the form of hosting the Secretariat of the West Africa Monetary Agency. The WAMA headquarters is located in the capital city, Freetown. The country provided not only a financial contribution towards the construction of the headquarters, but also valuable land for the construction of the Secretariat and accommodation for senior executives of the monetary agency. From a realist perspective, the establishment of WAMA headquarters in Sierra Leone was in pursuit of the traditional ends of politics. The location gives the host government the opportunity to conduct its economic and monetary relations in a familiar environment that is favourable to the pursuit of its goals. The provision of the headquarters provides a context in which leadership at this monetary level might be sought. In hosting the WAMA secretariat, the government sought to exercise influence among other ECOWAS members. In general, the setting up of regional institutional secretariats is a rational political calculation, for example, the EU in Brussels, the Commonwealth Secretariat in London, SADC in Zimbabwe, and former EAC in Kenya. Through shrewd political leadership, Sierra Leone could generate maximum political influence in ECOWAS for least cost.

Level of Popular Participation in ECOWAS Regionalism

The formation of regional integration groupings is to a very large extent an elitist pre-occupation. The initiative to join a regional grouping normally comes from the government with the support of interest groups. The political elite has been in the vanguard of promoting the creation of regional projects because it served their political and socio-economic interests. This top-down approach is a common feature of integration schemes in both developed and developing regions. In comparative terms, the EEC/EU debate has always provoked party-political divisions and popular agitation as in the referendum on membership and the single currency. This has not been the case in West Africa largely due to the official and governmental approach to regionalism. Integration in West Africa is ostensibly for and with the people. Practical realities however show that it is more 'for' but 'without the people'. The participation of the people is important because it determines the extent to which the impact of regionalism is perceived and the extent to which the costs and benefits among member states and for a particular state is appreciated.

In an effort to reach the people, the Community mandated all member states to name a street in their respective capital cities 'ECOWAS Street'. This initiative is one positive attempt by the Community to bring ECOWAS to the people, to get them involved and to identify their social interactions with the ECOWAS regionalism process. A prominent commercial street in the heart of the city of Freetown, Charlotte Street, has been renamed 'ECOWAS Street'. It will take some time for people to get used to the change of name, but it is generally regarded by officials as a positive effort by government to identify the regionalisation process with the people.

The awareness of the efforts of economic regionalism in West Africa is very low among the general population. Some amusingly interpret ECOWAS as a department of government, a football team, an intervention force, or an organ of the OAU based in Nigeria. This shows that the efforts at economic regionalism should go beyond the mere affairs of government. After all, it is the people through their socio-economic activities that transcends existing national boundaries who would give real meaning to ECOWAS regionalism. The people should therefore be closely associated with the thinking of the government on issues of economic regionalism and co-operation.

After the ratification of the ECOWAS Treaty in 1975, Ghana, in an effort to spread the message of ECOWAS, organised a week-long public education campaign through symposia and the media, explaining the treaty to the people and its benefits to the country. The Commissioner for Economic Planning Col. Roger Felli stated that 'You can begin today to regard our brothers and sisters from member countries not as foreigners, but as community citizens'.[48] Ghana is one of the few Community members that tried to involve and bring economic regionalism to the people. It might well be that the politics of regionalism was the deciding factor. As a military government, the political leaders were only using this popular involvement of the people in regional co-operation as a means to secure some semblance of political credibility and legitimacy. However, the fact that the people were considered as a major stimulus in the regionalism process is in itself important. By contrast, in Sierra Leone the majority of the people were not involved and did not know exactly what they stood to gain from ECOWAS regionalism. The general perception was that it was a shrewd design by President Stevens to carve out an international image for himself by bringing the country into ECOWAS.

The involvement of people in the integration process begins with the recognition of their relevance to economic regionalism and co-operation and establishing adequate structures that will facilitate the popular participation of people. In Sierra Leone, this recognition and the necessary structures remain elusive. Raising awareness about ECOWAS priority programmes amongst economic operators and the general populace is a necessary means of encouraging popular participation. However, community institutions and member states do not make sustained efforts or commit enough resources for the implementation of programmes designed to publicise the Community. For instance, with regard to the programme, 'ECOWAS Air Time', not all member states have broadcast programmes and presented reports on ECOWAS regionalism. In Sierra Leone's case, the participation of the country in the ECOWAS Trade Fair in Dakar and Accra, through the involvement of the private sector, brought considerable state television coverage of integration activities. However, television is a privilege restricted to those few who can afford it, mainly elite and the business class. Inadequate electricity power supply makes it an unreliable means of information dissemination. Radio, which is cheap and available in almost every household, becomes the only alternative means of information dissemination. What is lacking in the case of Sierra Leone is a sustained public awareness campaign to bring the populace on board the ECOWAS regionalisation process, especially popularising the benefits that the country can derive from integration.

People can only give their support to ECOWAS (or any integration scheme for that matter), if they are informed about what ECOWAS regionalism is all about and the supposed benefits to be derived from it. The lack of an adequate and sustained information campaign in Sierra Leone has made the people perceive the regionalisation process as a government or quasi-governmental function that has nothing to do with them. Prior to the involvement of ECOWAS and ECOMOG in the Liberian and Sierra Leone crises, knowledge about ECOWAS amongst the populace was scanty. Even in the post-ECOMOG intervention period in both countries, only the military and security aspects of ECOWAS seem to have gained popular knowledge amongst the people. This is understandable because the presence of a multinational force which usually attracts the sex trade; and the bombing raids by ECOMOG Alpha jets could not go unnoticed by the people who bore bear the brunt of these military activities in 'blood and money'.

Some general views about ECOWAS regionalism ranges from the positive to the negative. To Sierra Leonean students, ECOWAS, and in particular ECOMOG, is a projection of pax-Nigeriana in West Africa, while others perceive it as a political club for West African leaders that has not achieved much. An itinerant Sierra Leonean business woman who has been repatriated from The Gambia sees ECOWAS as a backward looking organisation threatening the existence of law abiding Sierra Leoneans. She considers the protocol guaranteeing free movement an aberration.[49] *West Africa* reports an instructive encountrer between a Sierra Leonean Immigration Officer and a 'West African citizen'. An immigration officer at Lungi international airport requested a Malian passenger who had just disembarked from an aircraft for a visa. 'But I don't require one to enter Sierra Leone' replied the visitor. 'Mali and Sierra Leone belong to ECOWAS, and I am assured I don't need a visa to enter the country. I am here for just one month.' 'ECOWAS or no ECOWAS stand aside. You must have your documents in order', the officer commanded. 'You people come here and talk about ECOWAS and before we know it you are in the diamond area.'[50] Such incidents are not peculiar to Sierra Leone. Travellers at several airports and border crossings in the region have had similar experiences, emphasising the point that ratifying a protocol does not guarantee its implementation. To ask the ordinary people in the street what they think about ECOWAS in the pre-1990 days was to be met with a blank stare and even government officials would tell you that ECOWAS was a matter for the experts and had no bearing on everyday life.[51]

The recognition of popular participation of the people in the integration process is gradually gaining momentum, against the background of the resurgence of the regionalism in the sub-region in the 1990s. The involvement of people in Community integration has been identified as one of ECOWAS' priority programmes. Such public enlightenment programmes include the institutionalisation of an 'ECOWAS National Week' and the celebration of 'ECOWAS Day'. Member states are encouraged to make the participation of the people a reality. However, the gap between the official, governmental approach and the popular participation of the people still remains difficult to bridge. It is therefore important to map out strategies which incorporate the people factor as a means of strengthening the popular base of regionalism. As has been pointed out, there is little public support for ECOWAS regionalism not because the people do not want it, but simply because they are isolated from the process.

The Sierra Leone situation is a reflection of what obtains at the Community level as a whole. Very little systematic effort has been made to explain to the people why links between West African countries are needed and how these links would benefit them. In the absence of such efforts, they have tended to look to relationships with the western world as the source of economic progress and have failed to appreciate the value of links within Africa. It must be emphasised that unless the people themselves are at the heart of the integration process, and are interested in, and enthusiastic to make an effort, all the fine paper schemes outlined in the integration treaty and protocols may come to nothing.[52] Without citizen participation, a true 'Community citizen' is difficult to evolve. The effective mobilisation of public support should be regarded as a crucial ingredient for the success of the ECOWAS regionalisation process. A corollary to this is the compelling need to create a constituency of active supporters of the Community amongst the political parties, professional and business associations, grassroots and non-governmental organisations. They should be kept regularly informed, encouraged and assisted to interact directly with their counterparts in other member states. The need to improve information flows within the Community in order to enlighten public opinion therefore becomes an imperative.

Conclusion

Sierra Leone's ECOWAS regionalism falls within the functional approach to nation building and the politics of economic development in developing countries. The country, though not a major power within the Community has endeavoured to carve out an area of political and diplomatic influence for itself. It is evident that successive governments have not established effective institutional structures to enhance Sierra Leone's ECOWAS activities, and there seems to be a lack of clear objective of what is to be achieved from the regionalisation process or what is expected of the administrative heads of the institutions. The nature of the domestic political culture and patrimonial decline largely accounts for the inadequate institutional provisions and lack of sustained political commitment to Sierra Leone's ECOWAS regionalism. The civil war and subsequent ECOMOG military intervention has made the politics of ECOWAS regionalism all the more relevant to political elites and successive governments.

The existing institutional framework for Sierra Leone's ECOWAS regionalism should be strengthened and given the much needed political and official commitment if the country is to share in the benefits of regionalism. The recognition of the private sector and the valuable role of the people in economic regionalism and co-operation are vital to the overall integration objectives of Sierra Leone in ECOWAS.

Notes and References

[1] Joe A. D. Alie, *A New History of Sierra Leone*, London: Macmillan, 1990.
[2] A. J. G. Wyse- *The Krios of Sierra Leone: An Interpretative History* (Freetown, 1989, p.1).
[3] Max Sesay, *Interdependence and Dependency in the Political Economy of Sierra Leone* (unpublished PhD. thesis, Southampton University, 1993).
[4] *Economic Intelligence Unit Country Report 1st Quarter 1997*- EIU Ltd. 1997, p. 22.
[5] *Economist Intelligence Unit Country Report, 4 Quarter* 1999, London, p. 22.
[6] Ibid.
[7] A. K. Koroma, *Sierra Leone: The Agony of a Nation*, London: Andromedra Publications, 1996.

[8] *Trade Liberalisation in the Economic Community of West African States: An Assessment*-Report Prepared by the Commonwealth Secretariat, London, May 1997, p. 54.
[9] A. K. Koroma, op. Cit., 1996.
[10] *West Africa*- 4 March 1985.
[11] A. K. Koroma, op. cit., 1996.
[12] C. Clapham, *Private Patronage and Public Power: Political Clientelism and the Modern State*, London: Frances Pinter, 1982, pp. 22.
[13] See Georg Sorensen's discussion of patrimonialism and the personal loyalty generated by the 'Strongman', in *Democracy and Democratization: Processes and Prospect in a Changing World*, Oxford: Westview Press, 1993, pp. 51-2.
[14] Quoted in Douglas A. Yates, *The Rentier State in Africa: Oil Rent Dependency and Neocolonialism in the Republic of Gabon*, Trenton, N.J., 1996, p. 5.
[15] René Lemarchand, 'The State, the Parallel Economy, and the Changing Structure of Patronage System', in Donald Rothchild and Naomi Chazan (eds.), *The Precarious Balance: State-Society in Africa*, London: Westview Press, 1988, p. 154. Prebend is a concept introduced by Max Weber to describe personal benefits acquired from the appropriation of public office. Max Weber, 'Wirtschaftund Gesellschaft', in H. H. Gerth and C. Wright Mills (eds.), *From Max Weber: Essays in Sociology*, New York: Oxford University Press, 1958.
[16] Jimmy Kandeh, 'Ransoming the State: Elite Origins of Subaltern Terror in Sierra Leone', *Review of African Political Economy*, No. 81, 1999, p. 351.
[17] D. Francis, 'The Economic Community of West African States', *Democratization*, 1999, p. 146.
[18] J. S. Coleman and C. G. Rosberg, *Political Parties and National Integration in Tropical Africa*, Berkeley, Ca.: University of California Press, 1966; Max Weber, op. cit.
[19] Jimmy Kandeh, op. cit., p. 352.
[20] Kandeh describes Ekutay as an organisation of Limba politicians, cultural entrepreneurs and influence peddlers, whose membership became bloated by opportunistic non-Limba elites, Ibid.
[21] Ibid., p. 6. The theory of the rentier state according to Douglas Yates concerns the patterns of development and the nature of states in economies dominated by external rent, particularly oil and diamond rent (p.11). Hossein Mahdavy who postulated the 'rentier state' theory sees these countries as those that receive on a regular basis substantial amounts of external economic rent. H. Mahdavy, 'The Pattern and problems of Economic Development in Rentier States: The case of Iran, in *Studies in the Economic History of the Middle East* M. A. Cook (ed.). (Oxford, OUP, 1970), p. 428.
[22] A. K. Koroma, op. cit., 1996.
[23] Ibid, p. 21.
[24] Jimmy A. Kandeh, Sierra Leone: Contradictory Class Functionality of the 'Soft' State' *Review of African Political Economy* No. 55; 1992, p. 30-31.
[25] Ibid., p. 42.
[26] A. Zack-Williams, 'Sierra Leone: The Political Economy of Civil War, 1991-98', *Third World Quarterly*, Vol. 20, No. 1, 1999, p. 144.
[27] Paul Richards, *Fighting of the Rain Forest: War, Youth and Forest Resources in Sierra Leone* James Curey, Oxford, 1996), p. xviii.
[28] William Reno, *Corruption and State Politics in Sierra Leone* Cambridge University Press, Cambridge, 1995.

[29] Paul Richards, 1995, p. 36.
[30] Ibid., p. 51.
[31] Alfred Zack-Williams, *Tributors, Supporters and Merchant Capital: Mining and Underdevelopment in Sierra Leone*, Avebury, Aldershot, 1995, p. 6.
[32] Stephen Wright (ed.), *African Foreign Policies*, Boulder: Westview Press, 1999, p. 2; Olajide Aluko (ed.), *The Foreign Policies of African States*, London: Hodder & Stoughton, 1977; T. Shaw & O. Aluko (eds.), *The Political Economy of African Foreign Policy*, New York: St. Martin's Press, 1984.
[33] James Zaffiro, 'Exceptionality in External Affairs: Botswana in the African and Global Arenas' in S. Wright, 1999, p. 74.
[34] S. Wright, p. 3.
[35] Abdul A. Koroma, *Sierra Leone: A Nation in Agony* Andoramera Publications, London, 1996, p. 99.
[36] *West Africa-* 30 June 1975, p. 756.
[37] Interview- London, 19 November 1996.
[38] S. Wright, p. 16.
[39] T. Shaw, 'The South in the 'New World (Dis) Order': Towards a Political Economy of Third World Foreign Policy in the 1990s', *Third World Quarterly*, Vol. 15, No. 1, 1994, p. 21.
[40] Interview with Director of Economic Research, Frank Ofei, Lagos, 30 October 1997.
[41] Interview, Lagos, Nigeria, 30 October 1997.
[42] *ECOWAS: Achievements, Challenges and Future Prospects*, ECOWAS Publication, Lagos, n. d.
[43] Ibid.
[44] *Memorandum on the Status of Ratification of the Revised Treaty, Protocols and Conventions as at 15 March 1997* Executive Secretariat, Lagos/ECWW/AFC/XX/4 August 1997, p. 2.
[45] *ECOWAS: Achievements, Challenges and Future Prospects*, op. cit.
[46] *ECOWAS Fund: Report and Audited Accounts, 1995*, Lomé, ECOWAS Publication, 1995.
[47] ECOWAS Publications, *ECOWAS Fund: Report and Audited Accounts, 1995*.
[48] *West Africa-* 28 July 1975, p. 877.
[49] 'What is this ECOWAS?' *West Africa* 27 May 1985, p. 1062.
[50] Ibid.
[51] Ibid.
[52] Commonwealth Secretariat, *Trade Liberalisation in the Economic Community of West African States. An Assessment* London: Economic Affairs Division, Commonwealth Secretariat, 1997. See also, ECA, *Proposals for Strengthening Economic Integration in West Africa* Addis Ababa: 1985.

5 Civil War in Sierra Leone: Interpretations

Introduction

Civil wars in Africa have generally been interpreted by some media commentators and political analysts as ethnic or tribal wars, such as the wars in Somalia, Rwanda, DRC, Burundi, and Liberia. The ethnic description and labelling of these civil wars and intra-communal violence have been used to replace analysis of the fundamental economic and socio-political factors responsible for the outbreak of civil wars in Africa. The outbreak of civil war in Sierra Leone in 1991 has led to a variety of interpretations of the plausible causes of the war, state implosion and the horrifying acts of violence for which the civil war has become internationally infamous. As a resource-based war, the civil war represents the changing nature of warfare in contemporary world politics, i.e. from inter-state to intra-state, domestic, low-/high intensity warfare with capacity for massive disruption. The war is a classic example of the interface between strategic minerals and low-intensity conflicts in Africa. This chapter will therefore explore how strategic policy failures and the use of Sierra Leone's territory as a military base for ECOMOG's peacekeeping operations in Liberia provided the spark that ignited the fundamental causes of the outbreak of the civil war.

Civil War in Sierra Leone

The guns of the Revolutionary United Front (RUF) rebellion led by Corporal Foday Sankoh were first heard at Bomaru, eastern Sierra Leone on 23 March 1991. The RUF launched another flank in the southern region, Pujehun District, by using the Mano River bridge that links Liberia and Sierra Leone. The RUF strategy was to stretch the capacity of the unprepared, poorly armed and conventional Sierra Leone Army (SLA). The initial RUF fighters comprised Sierra Leonean exiles, Burkinabe and Liberian mercenaries.[1] The RUF announced through the BBC 'Focus on Africa' Programme in April 1991 that its objective was to overthrow the corrupt APC one-party regime of President Momoh and restore multi-party democracy in Sierra Leone. The RUF insurgency was dismissed by the Momoh government as a spillover of the Liberian civil war. The official view was that the RUF rebellion was a Charles Taylor sponsored rebel incursion.

The RUF invasion of Sierra Leone was covertly supported by Taylor's Liberia, Blaise Compaore's Burkina Faso and Gaddafi's Libya. A variety of reasons have been advanced to explain the support for the RUF insurgency in Sierra Leone. Charles Taylor's support for the RUF, according to intelligence reports, dates back to the fact that both had been trained at the Benghazi military camp in Libya. Col. Gaddafi promoted the ideology of 'revolutionising' Africa by providing military training for African dissidents at Benghazi. These so-called revolutionaries, indoctrinated in Gaddafi's *Green Book* ideology had the mission to overthrow authoritarian and dictatorial regimes in their respective countries. Gaddafi's support for dissidents and some African governments was an attempt to create a sphere of political influence sympathetic to the Libyan cause and sharing the Muslim 'revolutionary' ideals. It was a political strategy to overcome Libya's international isolation and pariah status. Taylor and Sankoh were therefore ploys in Gaddafi's *realpolitik* calculations.

Charles Taylor himself had been part of Doe's regime and served as Director-General of the General Services Agency. Accusations of embezzlement against Taylor forced him into exile. Taylor escaped from a United States prison whilst awaiting extradition hearings. He returned to West Africa, received training in Libya and then mobilised West African dissidents to overthrow the Doe regime. The understanding was that Sankoh would support Taylor to launch his rebellion against Doe, which could later serve as a launching pad and support base for Sankoh to organise his armed insurgency against the APC regime in Sierra Leone. Before launching his rebellion, Taylor was refused permission by the Momoh government to use the territory of Sierra Leone as a launch pad to invade Liberia. Dubious politicians swindled huge sums of money from Taylor as a pretext for conceding to his request, but then plotted his arrest and imprisonment in Sierra Leone.[2] Another element encouraging Taylor's support for Sankoh's rebellion was the motive of revenge against Sierra Leone government officials who had swindled and imprisoned him.

Burkina Faso and Côte d'Ivoire covertly supported the RUF insurgency largely through the Charles Taylor-Liberia connection, and the motivation to exploit the diamond resources. The relational and personal context explains the Taylor-RUF support. It was common knowledge in

West Africa that there was no love lost between President Houphouet-Boigny of Côte d'Ivoire and Samuel Doe of Liberia. Doe, during his 1980 military coup, summarily executed Liberian government officials including the brother of the President, A. B. Tolbert. Tolbert's widow, Daise Tolbert happened to be Houphouet-Boigny's God daughter. Daise Tolbert, later married Blaise Compaore, President of Burkina Faso. It is alleged, according to intelligence reports, that Houphouet-Boigny covertly supported the military coup led by Compaore which overthrew Captain Thomas Sankara in 1983. This relational context explains why Houphouet-Boigny and Compaore supported Taylor's rebellion against Doe, and later the RUF insurgency. In fact, Taylor launched his armed insurgency from Côte d'Ivoire's territory.

The RUF drew its military capacity largely from youth conscription, mostly forced or voluntary. These conscripts and sympathisers were drawn from unemployed youths, the Lumpen proletariat and declassé elements of society, and those intellectuals and political opportunists excluded from the economic and political processes in the country. The initial support for the RUF was largely drawn from the marginalised, excluded and unemployed rural population who had been impoverished by the corrupt APC system and the socio-economic crisis in the country. However, the carnage and destruction, terror and looting perpetuated against the civilian population in the eastern and southern regions considerably diminished any initial enthusiasm and sympathy for the RUF insurgency.

In April 1992, a mutiny by junior military officers over pay and conditions at the war front was converted into a coup d'etat which led to the overthrow of President Momoh, who then fled to Guinea. The junior officers established the National Provisional Ruling Council (NPRC) with Captain Valentine Strasser as head of the ruling junta. The NPRC junta which comprised civilian technocrats and experts, banned all political activities and suspended the constitution. It announced that its primary objectives were to bring the war to a speedy conclusion, reform the economy and return the country to civilian democracy. The NPRC military intervention was initially applauded by the majority of Sierra Leoneons who perceived it as a 'rescue mission' from the APC's manipulations to perpetuate itself in power. However, the objectives of the NPRC were compromised by the economic and political opportunities provided by the war, whereby the constitutional army became involved in the criminal exploitation of the diamond resources.

By 1995, the RUF controlled the strategic diamond territories in eastern Sierra Leone, and the bauxite and rutile mining regions in the south.

The cash-strapped IMF/World Bank propped up NPRC regime, was therefore deprived of much needed revenue and foreign exchange. *This led to the privatisation of security in Sierra Leone and the involvement of private military companies such as the Gurhka Security Ltd., the South African-based Executive Outcomes (EO) and the London-based Sandline International.* The Strasser regime was overthrown in a palace coup by his deputy Brigadier Julius Maada Bio in January 1996.

The strategic military impact effected by EO and the pro-government civil militias, the kamajors,[3] saw the retreat of the RUF from its objective of overrunning the Freetown. The pro-democracy determination of the people, and the general perception that the army was using the war as a pretext to hold on to power, forced the Bio regime to organise parliamentary and presidential elections in February-March 1996. The elections, held against the backdrop of intimidation, political violence and civil war, were won by the Sierra Leone Peoples Party (SLPP) led by Ahmed Tejah Kabbah. The electoral victory of the SLPP marked a return to pluralistic political competition after being absent for two and half decades. However, the 15 month old civilian government of President Kabbah was overthrown on 25 May 1997 by a coalition of the national army and the RUF, who established the Armed Forces Revolutionary Council (AFRC) led by Major Johnny Paul Koroma. The AFRC junta, which lacked international recognition and domestic support, was overthrown by the Nigerian-led ECOMOG force, with the support of Sandline International, in February 1998. The constitutional government of President Tejan Kabbah was then restored in March 1998, under the auspices of ECOWAS with the Nigerian Head of State, General Sani Abacha, playing a dominant role.[4]

Since the outbreak of the civil war, three civil war peace settlements have been signed, namely, the Abidjan Peace Accord of 1996; the Conakry Accord of 1997; and the Lomé Peace Accord of 1999.[5] The Lomé Peace agreement formally ended the war between the RUF and the government of Sierra Leone. It established a power-sharing government between the RUF and the Kabbah regime, blanket amnesty for all parties to the conflict, and the deployment of a UN peacekeeping force, the United Nations mission in Sierra Leone (UNAMSIL). This was an attempt to do a Mozambican-style war-to-peace transition in Sierra Leone. However, the power-sharing transitional government broke down in May 2000, after the RUF broke the terms of the Lomé accord by abducting 500 UN peacekeepers and killing four others. The RUF leader has been arrested and imprisoned, to be tried for treason and war crimes. A new leader of RUF was appointed in August 2000 in the person of 'General' Issa Sesay, a former military Commander. 'General' Sesay is perceived as someone the Kabbah government, ECOWAS and the international community can do business with in bringing peace and security to war-torn Sierra Leone, but this is yet to be seen in reality. The civil war peace settlement of the nine-year old war had been made possible by the co-operation of the domestic civil society and the international community through ECOWAS, OAU, UN, Commonwealth, international NGOs, and Western governments such as Britain and America.

ECOMOG Military Base in Sierra Leone: An Obstacle to Charles Taylor's Presidential Ambition

ECOMOG has been 'blamed' for indirectly bringing Liberia's rebel war into Sierra Leone. In the early 1990s this assumption brought Sierra Leone's ECOWAS membership into question. ECOMOG's connection with the civil war has to do with the use of Sierra Leone's territory to facilitate the military operations of the peacekeeping force in Liberia. The decision to use Sierra Leone as a base to facilitate the operations of ECOMOG in Liberia was taken by the ECOWAS Heads of State following the advice of regional military Chiefs of Staff in Banjul in August 1990.[6] This decision was based on strategic considerations in view of the fact that Sierra Leone has a long stretch of land border with Liberia providing the best location for sea, air and land operations.

By 1991, the only obstacle between Taylor and the Liberian Presidency, was the capture of Monrovia and the military obstacles posed by ECOMOG. This provided the excuse for Taylor to threaten to attack Sierra Leone for allowing its territory to be used by ECOMOG; thereby hindering his grand ambition of becoming president of Liberia. In an interview with Robin White on the BBC 'Focus on Africa' on 1 November 1990, Charles Taylor categorically warned that he would take the war into Sierra Leone. The following extract from the interview makes clear Taylor's threat:

> Robin White: You have been talking about ECOMOG planes bombing your area, just what has been going on?
> Charles Taylor: They are bombing, they are killing people. The destruction is visible and there is no moral justification for Nigeria doing this and I am not sure of how long I can continue to accept Nigerian air planes taking off out of Sierra Leone. I may just have to put a stop to it.
> Robin White: How would you do that?
> Charles Taylor: Well, its anybody's guess, but I have had enough of the

Sierra Leone government permitting Nigerian aircrafts to come out and kill my people. I am saying that planes are taking off from bases at the international airport in Freetown at the end of the runway, that leave and come and blow Liberian babies, women and old people away and my patience has run out with Momoh permitting this to happen from his territory.
Robin White: But how exactly do you propose to stop it?
Charles Taylor: Is anybody's guess. Maybe Momoh doesn't know but he will soon find out.
Robin White : Are you suggesting that you will go and attack Sierra Leone yourself?
Charles Taylor: That's not what I am saying. But it's for Momoh to determine.[7]

Taylor's interview provided justification for some Sierra Leoneans to conclude that the immediate cause of the war was the decision by the Momoh government to facilitate the use of its territory as an assembling point for ECOMOG's intervention in Liberia. Some critics point out that the government of President Momoh should have foreseen the possibility of an attack by NPFL for thwarting its Liberian presidential enterprise. Abdul Karim Koroma argues that:

> Indeed military and political logic, if not plain common sense, would have made it evident that an intervention in the civil conflict of a contiguous nation with whom relations were at best frail, was in a way bound to generate a hostile response. Furthermore, given the history of relations between Sierra Leone and Taylor, it made such a response inevitable. This should have been anticipated and necessary defensive measures taken.[8]

However, Koroma's analysis is instructive because he was the Foreign Affairs Minister when the decision was taken. The government at that time believed it was taking a 'rational' decision in the interests of national security and territorial integrity. But as Niccoló Machiavelli had earlier warned, 'No state should ever think it can always make secure decisions. On the contrary, it should consider all decisions it takes as risks, because it is in the nature of things that in seeking to avoid one difficulty you run into another'.[9] In the case of Sierra Leone, the risks were apparent, but against the background of the politics of decline, no significant strategic response was undertaken to forestall this potential problem. The general thinking among government policy makers was that the provision of Sierra Leone's territory for ECOMOG's operation was only a fulfilment of the country's international obligation to ECOWAS. The crucial failure was that no corresponding measure or agreement was concluded with ECOWAS in the event of problems associated with this decision. It becomes evident that, with one stroke of the pen, Sierra Leone effectively ceded its national sovereignty and territorial integrity to ECOWAS without tacit assurance of protection. Military planes and naval ships of the Nigerian-led ECOMOG forces therefore used Sierra Leone's territory without authorisation or clearance from the constituted government of the country. Even the bilateral military agreement between Nigeria and Sierra Leone, the Status of Forces Agreement (SOFA), did not amount to free access to the country's territory. In fact, the Nigerian contingent assigned was under the command of the Nigerian ECOMOG Field Commander, then based in Liberia.

In general, the threats posed by the NPFL rebel group were dismissed with contempt by Sierra Leone government officials as lacking capacity to pose any serious threat to the security of the state. The prevailing attitude amongst the military establishment was that the Liberian army was an inept and poorly structured establishment, largely inferior to the Sierra Leone military in combat and professional experience. However, the NPFL proved to be a highly trained guerilla force with strong external support. Part of the problem causing the lack of strategic response to the NPFL threat was the fact that the nature of the NPFL insurgency warfare was unfamiliar to both the conventional army and people of Sierra Leone. It is therefore not surprising that the Taylor-supported RUF insurgency was persistently presented by the Momoh regime as external aggression. The external assistance for the RUF rebellion could be seen in combat support and arms supply route originating in Burkina Faso through Côte d'Ivoire into NPFL territory in Liberia. The Momoh regime capitalised on the external dimension of the RUF insurgency to secure international assistance, knowing that most countries are reluctant to give military assistance to an exclusively internal conflict. At the outbreak of the war, President Momoh appealed to ECOWAS for assistance since the external nature of the rebel invasion made it justifiable for military assistance under the terms of the 1981 Defence Protocol. Financial difficulties constrained the ability of ECOMOG to create and supervise a buffer security zone between Liberia and Sierra Leone which could have prevented arms and supplies reaching the RUF from Liberia.

However, it is argued that with or without Taylor's threat to attack Sierra Leone, it was a foregone conclusion that the country would be invaded by Sierra Leonean dissidents who wanted to overthrow the corrupt APC patrimonial regime. The domestic public opinion concerning ECOWAS' role in 'bringing' the rebel war into Sierra Leone is without analytical foundation. The initial public revulsion is understandable in terms of finding a 'scapegoat', and also the fact that they had to bear the brunt of the war in 'blood and money'. This meant that the people would react negatively to anything remotely responsible for their plight. The civil war in Sierra Leone is a product of fundamental political, economic, social and governance problems.

Civil War and its Interpretations

The civil war in Sierra Leone has become infamous for its 'mindless' and horrifying acts of brutality and violence. The world community has been shocked by the savagery and brutality of the war which was graphically portrayed in a documentary by a Sierra Leonean journalist Sorous Samora titled: *Out of Africa*. The civil war has been notorious for its gross violations of human rights, war crimes and lack of respect for all recognised international norms and laws relating to the conduct of war. It is difficult to give an accurate estimate of war casualties, internally displaced persons and refugees. According to recent estimates, there are about one and a half million internally displaced persons, more than 75,000 people killed, hundreds more have their limbs, hands and ears hacked off, and has resulted in more than half a million refugees.[10] Robert Kaplan described Sierra Leone as 'a microcosm of what is occurring in West Africa and much of the underdeveloped world: the withering away of central governments, the rise of tribal and regional domains, the unchecked spread of disease, and the growing pervasiveness of war'.[11] Despite Kaplan's highly exaggerated and rather apocalyptic portrayal of West Africa, the carnage and brutality of the civil war in Sierra Leone forces one to attempt an analytical understanding of the unfolding tragedy.

The civil war in Sierra Leone has been interpreted as caused by the failure of patrimonial and clientelistic systems of successive governments in post-colonial Sierra Leone. According to Paul Richard, the war 'is a product of this protracted, post-colonial crisis of patrimonialism'.[12] However, some analysts, whilst recognising the contribution of the privatisation and informalisation of the official state, cannot explain why similar problems elsewhere have not led to state implosion and the banalisation of violence denied of ideology, political support and ethnic identity.[13] Ian Smillie et al. argue that the economic opportunity presented by the breakdown of law and order became the driving force to sustain the violence in what has become a highly criminalised war economy. They posit that 'The point of the war may not actually have been to win it, but to engage in profitable crime under the cover of warfare'.[14]

New Barbarism versus Political Economy of Violence

The brutal violence in civil wars such as Sierra Leone, Liberia, Rwanda and Somalia have been interpreted by some analysts as 'new barbarism' i.e. 'violence driven by environmental and cultural imperatives'. Robert Kaplan sees the war in Sierra Leone as a manifestation of the new barbarism.[15] Paul Richards outlines three ideas central to the new barbarism thesis in Africa. Firstly, that cultural identity or identity based competitions are the factors for some of these wars. This so-called 'clash of civilisations' transcends Africa to include other regions such as Eastern Europe.[16] Secondly, the changing nature of warfare in the post-Cold War era has led to the emergence of diverse groups, making use of the light, cheap and widely available assault rifles such as AK47 and Kalashnikov, to contest state hegemony.[17] Thirdly, the culture clashes, resource competition and environmental breakdowns provoke a variety of low-intensity conflicts with regional and international implications, some of which are apolitical, but most of which have the propensity for criminal violence.[18] Drawing from Martin van Creveld's analysis, Robert Kaplan argues that in situations such as Sierra Leone where there has been 'mass poverty, people find liberation in violence'.[19] This is a fundamentally flawed argument that can not be used to interpret the war in Sierra Leone. The war in Sierra Leone lacks any Cold War ideological, religious or ethnic dimensions. Furthermore, Sierra Leone is hardly the place to look for major environmental collapse or population pressures that could create violent competition for scarce resources. The war is largely the product of economic and political failures. Paul Richards refutes the application of the new barbarism thesis to Sierra Leone, and instead sees the war as a product of social exclusion.

But what explains the horrifying acts of brutality and 'mindless' violence against defenseless civilians? Under the influence of crack cocaine, these brutalities have been committed by all the factions including child soldiers. The 'mindless' violence have been widely interpreted as proof of African savagery and barbarism.[20] However, these terroristic methods deployed have been explained as 'rational madness', a rational violence used to achieve economic, military and political ends. This explanation is not in anyway a justification for unspeakable acts of brutality. This systematic terrorisation, according to Paul Richard, is a tactic that has 'been fully effective in disorienting, traumatizing and demoralizing victims of violence. In short, they are devilishly well-calculated'.[21] But do these terroristic tactics justify the cutting off the hands, limbs and arms of two to four year old children? What conceivable political and economic advantages could be secured by such acts of brutality? Can the rationalisation of these brutalities not be interpreted as an attempt to provide justification or explanation for violence from the comfort of academic offices at western universities?

It is reasonable to argue that economic motivation has been the driving force for the war. This economic interpretation conflicts with Paul Richards claim that:

> The war in Sierra Leone drags on essentially because there are social factors feeding the conflict, and because the main rebel group feels it has not yet had the chance to get its political point of view across, and that it needs to do so to honour activists who died in its cause.[22]

Richards has since changed his 1996 position, but this raises the question of propriety of so-called African experts whose advice has been fed into the international policy processes on Africa. The violence therefore becomes the strategy for 'primitive accumulations'. However, Yusuf Bangura is critical of the crisis of patrimonialism analysis in that political violence 'does not have only one logic, but several: there is obviously the logic of political violence ... but this competes, co-exists and interacts with the logics of banditry, hedonism and brutality'.[23] Therefore Bangura's economic interpretation is fiscal in nature in that it is linked to 'the informalisation of key industries like diamonds...'.[24] In support of the political economy of violence interpretation, Paul Collier's investigation of large-scale civil conflict since 1965 failed to find a positive correlation between ethnic grievances and the incidence of conflict. Instead, economic agendas seem to be the primary factor for understanding why civil wars start.[25] Paul Collier identifies primary export commodities as serving not only as a proxy for 'lootable' resources, but also as a powerful source of attractions for recruits, most of whom are young, unemployed and uneducated.[26] The war therefore becomes an 'income-earning opportunity', an alternative to poverty and unemployment. For all the parties to the conflict, i.e. the RUF, soldiers, civil militias, and even some politicians and ordinary Sierra Leoneans, the war has become a lucrative income-earning opportunity, hence creating an instrumental interest in sustaining the war. For these groups and interests, peace and security in war-torn societies are detrimental to their economic accumulation and income-earning opportunities. Collier's conclusion is that since 'civil wars create economic opportunities for a majority of actors even as they destroy them for the majority, economic agendas therefore ignite and sustain these wars.[27] In this same vien, David Keen asserts that civil wars are better understood as the continuation of 'economics' by other means.[28] The 'greed' and economic based interpretation of the civil war has found support at national level. According to the Finance Minister James Jonah:

> It is now an internationally accepted view that the prolonged nature of the war in Sierra Leone is driven by greed .... In other words, the war in Sierra Leone is simply about diamonds.[29]

Whilst the argument relating to the contribution of the diamond resources in fuelling and prolonging the war in Sierra Leone cannot be denied, to simply interpret the war as one based on 'greed' would be missing the point. It is argued that resources as catalysts for war can only be a short- and medium-term strategy for financing the war in order to attain the ultimate goal, i.e. political power. In other words, 'greed' and economic motivations are not the end in themselves, but the means to an end, i.e. the attainment of state power. For instance, the war in Liberia has not only been about 'primitive accumulation'. The economic exploitation of the war has been used by Charles Taylor to terrorise and pay his way into the Executive Mansion in Liberia. The economic wealth generated by the vicious exploitation of the war economy have been used by Taylor to consolidate his grip on power and repress political opponents. The same argument can be advanced for Sankoh's exploitation of the war economy in Sierra Leone and Savimbi in Angola. This analysis explains why Sankoh, in spite of his huge personal fortune accumulated by exploiting the diamond resources, still remained unsatisfied and hence attempted to secure political power through force of arms in June 2000.

The World Bank and some western governments have been instrumental in promoting the 'greed', and resource-based, economic interpretation of civil wars. Mats Berdal and David Malone's edited book *Greed and Grievance: Economic Agendas in Civil War* (2000), has set the tone of the debate in contemporary political analysis of civil war. But the crucial question is that, in countries such as Sierra Leone, why is it the case that though diamonds had been discovered in the 1930s, the country did not degenerate into violent civil war in the pre-1990s era? Does this not undermine the economic exploitation, resource-based interpretation of civil wars as the primary cause? What becomes obvious is that this kind of interpretation moves the debate from the usual 'pigeon-holing' of African conflicts as ethnic and tribal wars.

The causes of the civil war in Sierra Leone can be traced back to long-standing grievances. Poor political management of the post-colonial system, which became entrenched during the APC regimes, led to widespread and deep-seated grievances amongst the population. The corrupt one-party system economically and politically excluded the educated elite and disillusioned employed youths. The progressive economic deterioration pauperised the majority of the citizenry. The neglect and marginalisation of the rural population by successive governments who 'over centralised' all opportunities in Freetown, further entrenched the polarisation and grievances between the rural and urban population. In effect, the causes of the civil war in Sierra Leone are a product of long-standing and deep-seated grievances, which cannot be simplified as merely a struggle for the control of diamond resources.

'Falamakata' Sociology of Violence

There is a plausible deep-seated sociological interpretation for the horrifying acts of brutality within the context of Sierra Leone. Sierra Leoneans are not generally predisposed to violence and brutality and there are social norms that target the exclusion of such behaviours. There is also the lack of a culture of revenge as in Somalia. However, the majority of Sierra Leoneans have a social predispositon for imitation, described in the lingua franca as 'falamakata'. This 'falamakata' phenomenon is geared towards the imitation of anything 'foreign' that has a social appeal, i.e. unique social phenomenon. Secondly, it is driven by the desire for perfection, i.e. to supercede the feat or expertise of the 'originator'. 'Falamakata' itself is supposed to be good. For example, the former RUF Field Commander, Sam Bockarie, alias 'General Maskita', as a night club or 'disco dancer' in the 1980s in eastern Sierra Leone, was often seen on stage imitating the dance routine and antics of the American pop star Michael Jackson or the reggae musician Bob Marley.

But what is the 'falamakata' sociology of violence? The majority of the initial RUF forces had fought alongside NPFL soldiers in Liberia where the terror tactics of horrifying brutality were first practised. The Liberian mercenaries who fought alongside the RUF deployed these terror tactics in Sierra Leone, which 'became a nightmarish experience for our civil population'.[30] These terroristic methods have similarities with RENAMO's tactics in Mozambique.[31] The RUF first introduced the terror tactics of slitting throats, and hacking limbs, ears, hands and fingers, apparently copied from the Liberian civil war. The SLA and civil defence forces were later to 'falamakata' these RUF terror tactics, the rationale being to give the rebels a 'taste of their own medicine'. At the height of these horrifying acts of brutality, the warring factions in their attempt to refute accusations of acts of violence, would justify their complicity or lack of it, by making the macabre distinction that the Kamajors cut off hands from the elbow.

Some analysts argue that some of these terror tactics may have been improvised spontaneously by child soldiers under the influence of crack cocaine.[32] Other observers see it as a dramaturgy of the Hollywood 'Rambo' war culture.[33] What becomes relevant is that whether these horrifying acts are spontaneous improvisation or the dramaturgy of Hollywood war films, they seem to fit the 'falamakata' phenomenon in Sierra Leone. It becomes easy to understand how the warring factions, having grown up in a social culture of 'falamakata' and under the influence of hard drugs, who could perform such acts of brutality that defy decent human imaginations.

RUF as a Political Alternative

It has been claimed that the RUF rebellion was an attempt to present a credible alternative political system to the corrupt and discredited APC regime. Paul Richards' claim that the RUF leadership had a 'clear political' vision of a reformed and accountable state, is difficult to substantiate. According to Richards, 'the war has a clear political context, and the belligerents have perfectly rational political aims, however difficult it may be to justify the levels of violence they employed in pursuit of these aims'.[34] This assumption shows a fundamental misunderstanding of what the RUF war is really about. The comments by RUF rebels that they 'took up arms to fight for multi-party democracy and against state corruption' could be interpreted as nothing more than rhetoric and a useful instrument for the indoctrination of the majority of RUF 'Lumpen' fighters and declassé elements. A child soldier, carrying an AK47 rifle 'longer' than him, commented in an interview in 1998 that 'he was fighting for his country' though it was patently obvious that he had no conception of what he was talking about. The claim of providing a political alternative by the RUF 'Lumpen' and declassé elements could be interpreted as a manipulation of their sense of grievance against the corrupt APC regime, and hence served as a means for the organisation to be able to secure additional recruits more cheaply.[35]

The only claim of the RUF to represent a political alternative or political platform was between 1991 and 1993. The original RUF comprised student radicals and marginalised intellectuals who shared a variety of neo-Marxist ideology, Gaddafi's *Green Book* ideas, Toffler's futurology, and radical Pan-Africanism.[36] The politically-oriented RUF members were eliminated by Sankoh who controlled the declassé majority of the movement.[37] After this period, the RUF progressively degenerated into a war of economic exploitation. Discarding the rhetoric and pronouncements of the RUF, one can reasonably infer from the pattern of behaviour of the movement that a political alternative was never the real driving force. Instead, the desire to secure political power and control over the state remains the driving force. The RUF leadership under Sankoh used the rhetoric of politics when it suited their strategic and economic motivations. The RUF has demonstrated that it was not about establishing an alternative political system in Sierra Leone, for example, the coalition with the AFRC regime in 1997, but fundamentally about having a share of the economic and mineral resources of the state, resources from which they have been excluded for decades. For the majority of the RUF fighters, the war therefore provided a form of employment whereby they used criminal violence to achieve economic benefits. It was neither about political alternative nor violence for the sake of it, as Bradshaw and Luttwak assumed,[38] but violence directed economic accumulation, for the ultimate goal of political power for the sake of 'power', not for constructive regime change and efficient political and economic management of the state.

Conclusion

The civil war in Sierra Leone is a product of fundamental political and socio-economic failures. As such, no single interpretation or variable sufficiently explains or provides an understanding of the civil war. Though clearly an economic based war, other factors such as the failure of patrimonialism and political clientelism were contributing factors. The economic and income earning opportunities provided by the 'criminalised' war economy partly explains the continuation of the war because of the disparate domestic and international interests involved in sustaining the war. The new barbarism thesis and the crisis of patrimonialism have proved inadequate in explaining the horrifying acts of violence perpetuated by the warring factions. 'Mindless' violence has become a 'rational' economic and political weapon, but the aim is not the ultimate goal of political power, but economic exploitation and personal aggrandisement of the political actors and warlords. The political economy of violence and the 'falamakata' sociology to some extent provide an understanding of the irrationality of the horrifying acts of brutality for which the civil war in Sierra Leone has become internationally infamous.

Notes and References

[1] Paul Richards, *Fighting for the Rain Forest: War* Oxford: James Curey, 1996, p. 5.

[2] A. K. Koroma, op. cit. 1996, for further explanation of this account.

[3] The Kamajors are local hunters traditionally from the Mende land in eastern Sierra Leone. They are part of the civil defence forces organised to fight alongside the national army and ECOMOG forces. Other civil defence forces include: Donsos, Tamaboros and Kapras.

[4] For an analysis of ECOWAS democratic intervention in Sierra Leone, see: David J. Francis, 'The Economic Community of West African States, the Defence of Democracy in Sierra Leone and Future Prospects' *Democratization,* Vol. 6, No. 4, 1999, p. 142.

[5] See, David Francis, 'Torturous Path to Peace: The Lomé Peace Agreement and Post-War Peacebuilding in Sierra Leone', *Security Dialogue,* vol. 30, no. 3, 2000, pp. 357-373.

[6] Interview with Major General Tarawalli, former Force Commander, Republic of Sierra Leone Military Forces, (RSLMF), London, 26 October 1997.

[7] Cited in David J. Francis, *Sierra Leone in ECOWAS: Political and Economic Implications,* unpublished Ph.D.. Thesis, University of Southampton, 1998.

[8] A. K. Koroma, *Sierra Leone: The Agony of a Nation,* London: Andromeda Publications, 1996, p. 207.

[9] Niccoló Machiavelli, *The Prince,* translated by Stephen J. Miller, Phoenix Papaerback, 1995, p. 42.

[10] UNAMSIL, Report on Sierra Leone 1999.

[11] Robert Kaplan, 'The Coming Anarchy', 1994, p. 48.

[12] Paul Richards, *Fighting for the Rain Forest,* Oxford: James Curey, 1996, p. xviii. See also: William Reno, *Corruption and State Politics in Sierra Leone* Cambridge: Cambridge University Press, 1995; Jimmy Kandeh, 'Ransoming the State: Elite Origins of Subaltern Terror in Sierra Leone', *Review of African Political Economy* No. 81, 1999, pp. 349-366.

[13] Ian Smillie, Lansana Gberie and Ralph Hazelton, *The Heart of the Matter: Sierra Leone, Diamonds & Human Security* Ottawa: Partnership Africa Canada, January 2000, p. 1, available at http://www.sierra-leone.org/heartmatter.html.

[14] Ibid.

[15] Robert Kaplan, op.cit. 1994.

[16] Samuel Huntington, 'The Clash of Civilisation?', *Foreign Affairs,* vol. 72, 1993.

[17] For an analysis of the transformation of war see, Martin van Creweld, *On Future of War* London: Brasseys, 1992.

[18] Paul Richards, op. cit. 1996, p. XIV.

[19] Robert Kaplan, op. cit. 1996, p. XIV.

[20] 'Hopeless Continent', *The Economist* 13 May 2000.

[21] Paul Richards, op. cit. p. XVI.

[22] Ibid., p. XVII.

[23] Yusuf Bangura, 'Understanding the Political and Cultural Dynamics of the Sierra Leone War. A Critique of Paul Richards Fighting for the Rain Forest' *Africa Development,* XXII, 3/4, 1997, p. 130.

[24] Ibid.

[25] Paul Collier, 'Doing Well out of War: An Economic Perspective' in Mats Berdal and David Malone (eds) *Greed and Grievance: Economic Agendas in Civil War* London: Lynne Rienner, 2000, p. 21.

[26] Ibid. p. 94.

[27] Ibid. p. 91.
[28] David Keen, 'The Economic Functions of Violence in Civil War', *Adelphi Paper 320*, Oxford, Oxford University Press, for the IISS, 1998, pp. 1-88.
[29] James Jonah, 'Economic Dimensions of the Conflict in Sierra Leone', *Paper presented at the International Policy Dialogue on Development and Disarmament*, German Foundation for International Development, Bonn, 1 November 2000, p. 3.
[30] The RUF blames the terror tactics on the 'veterans of the Liberian Civil War' as reported in *Footpath to Democracy: Towards a New Sierra Leone* The Revolutionary United Front of Sierra Leone, 1995.
[31] K. B. Wilson, 'Cults of Violence and Counter-Violence in Mozambique' *Journal of Southern African Studies* Vol. 18, No. 3, 1992, pp. 527-582.
[32] L. Brehun, *Liberia: the War of Horror* Adwinsa Publications, 1991.
[33] Paul Richards, 1996.
[34] Ibid. p. XVII.
[35] Berda and Malone, op. cit. 2000, p. 92.
[36] M. Gaddaffi, *The Green Book* Benghazi, n. d: A Toffler and H. Toffler, *War and Anti-War: Survival at the dawn of the 21st Century* London: Little, Brown & Co., 1994.
[37] Ibrahim Abdullah, 'Bushpath to Destruction - The Origin and Character of the Revolutionary United Front/Sierra Leone' *Journal of Modern African Studies*, Vol. 36, No. 2, 1998, pp. 207-213.
[38] S. Bradshaw, 'The Coming Chaos?' *Moving Pictures Bulletin* Issue 25, Feb. 1996, pp. 18-19: E. N. Luttwak, 'Great-powerless days' *Times Literary Supplement* 16 June 1995, p. 9.

6 Political Economy of Diamonds and Trans-border Regionalisation

Introduction

The civil war in Sierra Leone establishes the link between conflict diamonds, trans-border regionalisation and the opportunities of contemporary economic globalisation. Diamonds are fuelling wars in Africa because the proceeds from conflict diamonds are used to purchase arms, drugs, uniforms and even cultivate strategic alliances domestically, regionally and internationally. The domestic and international exploitation of conflict diamonds has further established the link between 'war diamonds', the privatisation of security, arms trade, drug trafficking and money laundering. In effect, the exploitation of conflict diamonds has led to the complicity of the international diamond industry and trading centres such as Antwerp, London, Tel Aviv, and political elites, regional leaders, warlords and MNCs, all of whom are taking advantage of opportunities of economic globalisation. Diamonds, arms smuggling and drug trafficking illustrates the regional and international dimension of the civil war in Sierra Leone. The case of Sierra Leone is not peculiar. From Angola to DRC to Sudan, strategic minerals such as diamonds, oil, gold and copper are fuelling conflicts in Africa. The human security costs for these weak and war-torn polities are enormous. This chapter therefore provides an understanding of the dynamics and complexity of the political economy of diamonds and how this phenomenon is aided by trans-border regionalisation and economic globalisation.

Diamonds and the Politics of Underdevelopment

Diamonds have been the 'fire' that is fuelling the civil war in Sierra Leone and have torn the country apart. Diamond resources in countries such as Botswana, Namibia and South Africa have been a blessing; in Sierra Leone they have been a curse. The well-known expression that 'Diamonds are forever', has taken a new meaning in Africa of the 1990s, i.e. 'Diamonds are forever bloody'.

History of Diamonds in Sierra Leone

Diamonds were discovered in Sierra Leone in 1930, and shortly afterwards, other minerals such as gold, platinum, iron ore and chromites were discovered. In 1934, the colonial TNC, the Consolidated African Selection Trust (CAST) took over control of the country's diamond deposits through its private subsidiary company, the Sierra Leone Selection Trust (SLST). CAST, which was already operating diamond mines in the then Gold Coast, was a corporation controlled by the Selection Trust Group of London, with other shares held by the South African-based De Beers Consolidated Mines Limited.[1] In 1935 the SLST was granted the monopoly to prospect and mine diamonds in Sierra Leone for a period of 99 years. Alfred Zack-Williams explains that this monopoly was maintained until 1956 when the Alluvial Diamond Mining Scheme (ADMS) was established. The ADMS empowered private individuals to undertake alluvial mining activities in the marginally diamondiferous areas demarcated by the company.[2] The alluvial diamond scheme provided for two types of mining activities: the individual licensed mining and 'native firms'. 'Native firms' mining welcomed a 49 per cent share capital investment from non-Sierra Leoneans. The 'native firm' scheme was an acknowledgement of the dominance of non-Sierra Leoneans in the mining industry, especially the Lebanese who owned much of the investment in the non-SLST sector. The scheme was not only an attempt to protect SLST's lease, but also to allow local participation in diamond mining.[3] The scheme therefore legalised individuals to operate as private 'alluvial diamond dealers'. Kono district, in eastern Sierra Leone, is the heart of the diamond mining operations. The diamond fields became the 'wild west of West Africa' for fortune hunters of all nationalities.[4]

In 1970, the APC government of Siaka Stevens took over 51 percent of SLST's shares and formed a new company, the National Diamond Mining Company (NDMC) of Sierra Leone. With the virtual 'nationalisation' of SLST by Stevens, its remaining share was sold in 1984 to the Afro-Lebanese Jamil Sahid Mohammed, a strong commercial ally of Stevens. Jamil Sahid established the Precious Metal Mining Company (PMMC).

The star of Sierra Leone, a 969 carat diamond, was discovered in the Koidu area, Kono district. According to estimates by Ian Smillie et al, 'by 1937 Sierra Leone was mining one million carats annually, reaching a peak of 2 million carats in 1960. From 1930 to 1998, approximately 55 million carats were mined (officially) in Sierra Leone'.[5] By 1968, earnings from diamonds accounted for 70% of government foreign exchange, but by 1988 recorded official exports had dropped to a paltry US $22,000.[6]

Zack-Williams observed that 'the diamond industry from its inception has provided both governments and mining interests with a mechanism for building support and alliances, among the chiefs and other members of the elites'.[7] To illustrate this diamond politics, the SLST as early as 1935 signed an agreement with the chiefs and tribal authorities in the main diamondiferous chiefdoms whereby the company paid a stipend of £30 to each Paramount Chief. In return, they were to prohibit any further settlement of 'strangers'. Also in 1959, SLST established a Contract Mining Scheme (CMS) which handed over certain areas of the company's Yengema lease in Kono district to miners in Kono who were obliged to sell their products to the company. This was a strategic business response by SLST to win support of the chiefs in its battle against DeBeers over prices of rough diamonds sold to the Central Selling Organisation.[8] These mining contracts were to be awarded only to persons nominated by the Paramount Chiefs of the chiefdoms.[9] The Paramount Chiefs in these diamondiferous chiefdoms, as a result of their traditional claim as custodians of the land, therefore became powerful political and economic instruments in the politics of diamond mining in Sierra Leone. When Siaka Stevens came to power in 1968, he purged those pro-SLPP chiefs and officials who refused to support his 'shadow state'.

The privatisation of the state during Stevens' one-party regime, and the unchecked smuggling were largely responsible for the reduction in official diamond exports. Ian Smillie et al explains that the Stevens-Momoh patrimonial edifice established informal networks that linked political leaders with 'big men' such as Jamil Sahid Mohamed who had connections to the European and North American markets and with access to international credit facilities. With the exit of DeBeers and the emergence of Momoh, the Lebanese dominance of the diamond mining was eclipsed by 'Israeli investors' such as Shaptai Kalamanowitch of LIAT and Mir Guaz of SCIPA, who had close connections to Russian and American crime families, and ties to the Antwerp diamond trade.[10] However, this Israeli dominance of the Sierra Leone diamond industry was short-lived.

Patrimonial Politics and Diamond Smuggling

Smuggling has always been associated with diamond mining, and in the process embraced the domestic politics of the country. Diamond smuggling dates back to the colonial era which institutionalised smuggling. This phenomenon continued into the post-colonial period with little or no attempt to realistically address the problem. By the time Sierra Leone attained independence in 1961, there were already well-defined diamond smuggling routes that linked the diamond fields with markets in Liberia, Beirut and Antwerp.[11] Graham Greene's novel *The Heart of the Matter* (1948), portrays the scale of diamond smuggling in Sierra Leone.

The Madingos and Lebanese, mostly naturalised Sierra Leoneans, populated the buying and smuggling of diamonds. Colonial restrictions tightening security in the mining areas forced the Lebanese smugglers to transit their goods through Liberia. Liberia therefore became an attractive transit route that linked Lebanese smugglers with diamond merchants in Antwerp and Israel. To counter this phenomenon DeBeers opened a buying office in Monrovia in 1954 in an attempt to control the rough diamond trade. The Lebanese were able to establish their dominance of the diamond smuggling trade by taking advantage of CMS which granted mining and buying licences to indigenous miners. The dominance of the Lebanese in the exploitation. of the Sierra Leone diamond resource made the Lebanese community a key financier of the 1970s civil war in Lebanon. For instance, the leader of the Amal faction, Nabih Berri, was born in Sierra Leone and was a close friend of the diamond magnet, Jamil Sahid.[12] The link between Sierra Leone's diamonds and Lebanese civil war became a critical issue for the Israeli intelligence services.

In the politics of decline in Sierra Leone, diamond resources became the mainstay for oiling the patrimonial system. In an attempt to build an economically and politically viable patronage system in the diamond industry, Stevens established the Co-operative Contract Mining Scheme (CCMS) whereby land formerly owned by the state-controlled NDMC in the eastern region was leased to private individuals for re-mining. The CCMS provided an important source of private capital accumulation for chiefs, politicians and APC salwarts. Diamond smuggling was therefore covertly supported by the ruling and governing elites whose clients controlled the transit routes and even served as couriers. William Reno observed that:

> By 1987, the diamonds that passed through formal taxable channels were valued only $100,000. Stevens and several associates ... had appropriated much of the rest. They also diverted profits and assets from other state enterprises, most notably from oil and rice marketing. In so doing they destroyed the effectiveness of most institutions, starving them of formal resources of revenue and turning them into extensions of their private patronage networks.[13]

It therefore becomes obvious that the diamond industry had never been fully under the control of the state. The diamond fields were controlled by rival economic operators supported by politicians and international financiers, often with dubious credentials. Momoh's attempt to bring some sanity to the diamond industry by deploying the military in 1989 to rid the diamond fields of illegal miners directly alienated these miners and disrupted the commercial networks of his political rivals. This was to create a supportive constituency for the RUF insurgence. The majority of the unemployed youths locally known as 'sansan boys' had flocked to the mining areas, and were now being thrown out, could not help but sympathise with the RUF, whom they assumed were fighting their cause.[14] William Reno's view is that Momoh's assertive strategy which seemed appropriate to centralise state control over resources, instead widened the gap between the state's authority in the capital and its capacity to control the mine fields. Illicit miners who fled from the mining areas lost their source of income. Many had become miners out of desperation to find an income as job opportunities in the civil service and the formal economy disappeared.[15]

'Operation Pay Yourself': Incentive for Exploitation of War Economy

The economic and income-earning opportunities created by the war converted the national army into a freelance insurgency group exploiting the criminalised war economy. With the overthrow of the APC regime, the NPRC junta became the privileged economic and political group whilst the bulk of the underprivileged soldiers who did not have access to state power and its resources, were forced to find new strategies of benefiting from the war. Instead of fighting the rebels, the soldiers plundered diamonds and agricultural resources such as cocoa, coffee, palm oil and household properties. They were performing the same acts the rebels were accused of and it became popular knowledge that the government security forces were carrying out most of the looting and armed robberies in the war-affected areas. Hence, the pejorative description of the army as 'sobel', i.e. bandit soldiers; a coinage from 'soldier' and 'rebel'. According to C. Magbaile Fyle, 'These soldiers thereby began acquiring wealth in a few months which they realised they would never have obtained in a whole working life as regularly paid soldiers'.[16] The exploitation of the war by soldiers largely through plundering of settlements, led to the defection of government soldiers to the rebel faction. The neglect of the lower echelons of the army, and the mutual interest with the rebels to exploit the 'profitable' material resources of the war were some of the reasons for defection. There were allegations of government soldiers trading ammunition and uniforms with rebels. The neglect of the lower echelons and some sections of the officer corp of the army by the ruling NPRC junta led to the informal launching of 'Operation Pay Yourself'.[17]

Military officers organised recruited soldiers into gangs of diggers to mine diamonds. There were also allegations that ECOMOG soldiers were involved in diamond mining. A leaked report by UNAMSIL Commander Major-General Vijay Kumar Jetley on the crisis in Sierra Leone accused the Nigerian-led ECOMOG forces of complicity with the RUF in the exploitation of conflict diamonds. The report states that:

> Nigerian Army was interested in staying in Sierra Leone due to the massive benefits they were getting from illegal diamond mining. Brig. Gen. Maxwell Khobe was commonly known as the 'Ten Million Man', it is alleged that he received up to 10 million dollars to permit the activities of RUF. The ECOMOG Force Commander Maj. Gen. Kpamber was also involved in the illegal diamond mining in connivance with RUF leader Foday Sankoh.[18]

'Operation Pay Yourself' therefore provided economic incentives for the war to continue.

It is important to note that many of the soldiers recruited by the Momoh government and NPRC regime to increase the numerical strength of the government forces were hoodlums, urban and rural drifters, petty thieves and thugs. These underprivileged and declassé elements 'drafted' into the army, together with unemployed university graduates, discovered the economic and political power of the gun. The gun therefore provided economic empowerment, a phenomenon William Reno describes as the 'Kalasnikov business advantage'.[19] Jimmy Kandeh observes that:

> By heavily recruiting thugs, criminals and rural drifters into national security apparatuses, incumbent political elites sowed the seeds of their own political demise and as well as that of the state. Socially uprooted and politically alienated, lumpenised youth are inherently prone to criminal adventurism and when enlisted in the army are more likely to become 'sobels' or renegade soldiers.[20]

Kandeh further argues that the 'sobelisation' of the national army made the rebel war unwinnable. This phenomenon effectively de-professionalised the army, shattered rank discipline and contradicted the raison d'être of the military as a state institution.[21]

However, the experience of exploiting the war economy dates back to the participation of the Sierra Leone contingent in the ECOMOG force deployed in Liberia. Sierra Leonean soldiers returning from 'duty' brought back looted properties such as cars, which became a powerful economic and material attraction for the majority of the underprivileged soldiers. Some civilian Sierra Leoneans even became involved in exploiting the war economy of war-torn Liberia.

Conflict Diamonds, Privatisation of Security and Globalisation

Conflict diamonds[22] are diamonds produced in war-torn countries and illicitly sold on the international market. These conflict diamonds are fuelling wars in Africa by providing the resources to fund rebel armies in countries such as Sierra Leone, DRC, and Angola. In the process, conflict diamonds have forged an unusual criminal network of warlords, drug and arms traffickers, gangsters, government officials, regional leaders and international firms, all of whom strive on the opportunities of globalisation. The *Partnership Africa Canada* (PAC) report *The Heart of the Matter: Sierra Leone, Diamonds and Human Security* contributed tremendously to raise awareness and focus international attention on how diamonds are fuelling the brutal civil war in Sierra Leone. Also, the Fowler[23] Report of March 1999 focused international attention on the link between civil wars in Africa, conflict diamonds and arms trafficking, with a special reference to the Angolan civil war. The Fowler report implicated African leaders who have helped to fuel the war in Angola by supplying arms and fuel in return for payment in diamonds. The report named leaders such as Togo's Eyadama, Burkina Faso's Compaore, late Mobutu Sese Seko of Zaire, and former President Pascal Lissouba of Congo. For these leaders, the imposition of the UN arms embargo in 1993 and the UN ban on the purchase of UNITA diamonds in June 1998 meant virtually nothing. Profit from conflict diamonds meant more than the lives of thousands of Africans killed. Conflict diamonds are therefore changing the face of the diamond as a symbol of love, beauty and purity, into a symbol of blood, killing and brutality.

However, diamonds as a currency of war is nothing new. The wars in Angola and former Zaire have been about the domestic and international exploitation of strategic minerals, albeit with an East-West ideological underpinning. In the 1990s, international attention had been focused on illicit diamonds as an integral part of Africa's crisis. As Robert Neild argues:

> The whole nexus of rich natural deposits, arms, war and corruption was veiled during the Cold War, but there can be no doubt that competition between the two superpowers for command of natural resources was a significant factor shaping diplomacy in the Third World and also covert and overt military operations.[24]

The issue of conflict diamonds has only now become internationally prominent because of the security vacuum created by the absence of superpower rivalry. This vacuum has been filled by warlords, drugs and arms traffickers and rogue states, exploiting the economic opportunities of globalisation.

Conflict diamonds have generated huge personal fortunes for warlords, rebel movements and their regional and international clients. The RUF's sale of conflict diamonds in 1999 was estimated to be US $70 million which the rebel group used to purchase weapons from European arms dealers.[25] In effect, Sierra Leone's high demand crystal diamonds have been used to bankroll the RUF war. According to De Beers' estimate in 1999, about US $150 million worth of rough diamonds were mined in UNITA controlled territories. In the DRC, approximately US $35 million worth of diamonds were produced in rebel-held territories.[26] Warlords such as Foday Sankoh, Charles Taylor and Jonas Savimbi have established trans-continental smuggling and commercial networks that link them to the global financial market. For example, Charles Taylor, as warlord between 1991 to 1997 supplied a third of France's tropical hardwood requirements through French companies.[27] Duffield argues that:

> a high level of complicity among international companies, offshore banking facilities, and Northern governments has assisted the development of war economies. There is a growing symbiotic relationship between zones of stability and instability within the global political economy.[28]

However, according to De Beers' estimate, conflict diamonds account for only around 4 per cent of world production but this figure is contradicted by NGOs campaigning for the boycott of conflict diamonds who put the figure at 20 per cent. The table below illustrates the estimate of conflict diamonds against total world production estimate.

Table 2: Conflict Diamonds – Estimate Against Total World Production, 1999 (US$ Million)

Country	Conflict	Non-Conflict	Total
Botswana	-	1782	1782
Russia	-	1625	1625
South Africa	-	776	776
Angola	150	468	618
Namibia	-	430	430
Canada	-	405	405
D.R.C.	35	361	396
Australia	-	367	367
Venezuela	-	120	120
Sierra Leone	70	-	70
C.A.R.	-	67	67
Brazil	-	54	54
Guinea	-	40	40
Tanzania	-	24	24
Ivory Coast	-	20	20
Guyana	-	14	14
China	-	14	14
Ghana	-	12	12
Liberia	-	10	10
India	-	8	8
Lesotho	-	3	3
Indonesia	-	2	2
Total World Production	255	6602	6857
Conflict production as % of worldwide production			3.70%

Source: De Beers cited in *West Africa* 26 June - 2 July 2000, p. 10.

Ian Smillie et al in their report lay the blame squarely at the threshold of the international diamond industry in that: 'De Beers is part of the problem. In its efforts to control as much of the international diamond market as possible, it is no doubt purchasing diamonds from a wide variety of dubious sources, either wittingly or unwittingly'.[29]

The South African-based De Beers conglomerate has dominated the world diamond industry since the 1930s. It now controls 60 per cent of the US $7 billion a year world market for uncut diamonds. De Beers controls the supply and demand for rough diamonds on the world market through its London-based Central Selling Organisation (CSO). In 1980, De Beers reduced its mining involvement in Sierra Leone, but maintained an off-shore mining concession and an office in Freetown. It opened diamond buying offices in Conakry, Guinea and Liberia. De Beers' policy of global dominance of the diamond market included buying conflict diamonds from Africa. For example, the company purchased an estimated $14 million worth of diamonds from unlicensed operators in 1992, whilst the peace negotiation was in progress between the government and UNITA rebels.[30]

At the heart of the diamond industry is Antwerp, the world centre for rough diamonds. The formal trading of diamonds in Belgium is structured around the Hoge Raad voor Diamant (HRD - the Diamond High Command). The HRD protects Antwerp's position as the world centre for diamonds and serves as the mouth-piece for the entire Belgian diamond industry.[31] Ian Smillie et al in their report launched a scathing attack on the HRD and the Belgian government for their lack of policies to regulate diamond smuggling. To illustrate this, Smillie et al show the vast disparity between West African diamond export figures with those of Belgian imports:

> - while the Government of Sierra Leone recorded exports of only 8,500 carats in 1998, the HRD recorded imports of 770,000 carats.
> - Liberia's diamond mining capacity is between 100,000 and 150,000 carats annually, but the HRD records Liberian imports into Belgium of over 31 million carats between 1994 and 1998 - an average of over six million carats a year.
> - Ivory Coast, whose small diamond industry was closed in the 1980s, exported an average of more than 1.5 million carats to Belgium between 1995 and 1997.

However, one has to be cautious because Belgian diamond dealers, in an attempt to circumvent the 0.3 per cent import levy charged by the Belgian government on non-African goods, have used Liberia as a cover for diamonds possibly coming from Russia. Smillie et al conclude that the lack of regulation of the diamond industry by both the Belgian government and HRD is a 'violation of almost any definition of neutrality, and is an invitation to corruption'.[32] This position was supported by the Fowler report which also attacked the lax regulatory system of the HRD in that it 'facilitates and encourages illegal trading activity'. The report was critical of the HRD's dual role as regulator and promoter of the diamond industry. The greed and corruption in the international diamond industry is largely responsible for turning a blind eye to conflict diamonds and the purchase of large amounts of diamonds even from countries with a negligible production base or from conflict zones. Antwerp therefore provides the nerve centre of the network for the exchange of conflict diamonds for arms.

Global Witness, a London-based NGO, in coalition with other governments such as Britain, Canada and America, and the UN, are leading the campaign to conscientise consumers of the role played by war diamonds in fuelling Africa's bloody conflicts. These campaigns led to a UN diamond ban on Sierra Leone in July 2000. De Beers, in response to fears about possible consumer backlash, has opted for self-regulation and refused to trade in conflict diamonds. De Beers has committed itself to some form of monitoring mechanism that will ensure that its sale of uncut diamonds did not include any 'which come from any area of Africa controlled by forces rebelling against the legitimate and internationally recognised government of the relevant country'.[33] In an attempt to improve its international credibility, De Beers has closed down its buying offices in West and Central Africa. De Beers has also appointed a Desk Officer for conflict diamonds at its London Office. Some analysts however argue that De Beers volte-face commitment is a strategic attempt to position itself as producer and distributor of 'clean' or legitimate diamonds. The *Financial Times* suggested the formulation and implementation of a global certification scheme supported by import controls, as a way of regulating the diamond industry. This would include a certificate of origin of diamonds.[34]

The international debate generated by conflict diamonds and the complicity of the diamond industry has re-ignited the dilemma between the protection of legitimate diamond trade and how to stop diamonds financing war. The diamond industry's attempt at self-regulation includes championing the debate on conflict diamonds. There is the general fear that, if the diamond industry is not pro-active against war diamonds, it will potentially be destroyed as happened in the case of the fur trade. A series of international conferences was organised including the South African 'Kimberley Process'; the World Diamond Congress meeting in Tel Aviv in July 2000; the World Diamond Council Meeting in September 2000; and the London 'Conflict Diamond' conference in October 2000. These conferences brought together the primary stakeholders such as producing, processing and importing countries, and the key players in the diamond industry. The objective was to address the issue of conflict diamonds by building a consensus on the need for an international certificate scheme for rough diamonds.

However, the global verification of diamonds is fraught with many practical difficulties because such a certificate would possibly only show where diamonds were bought, not where mined. Furthermore, gems are too small, portable and easy to hide, and the porous nature of African borders would create serious difficulties in terms of implementation. Also, some countries in the diamond industry would be reluctant to see a global certificate, and it could be problematic to balance the economic interests of the diamond producing and diamond importing countries. The Sierra Leone government has established a Diamond Certificate Scheme for the export of its diamond resources. The new diamond certificate plan is designed to deny export of RUF diamonds on to the world market. The successful implementation of this scheme remains to be seen.

Trans-border Regionalisation of Conflict Diamonds and Arms Trafficking: The Taylor-Sankoh Axis

The creation of Sankoh's RUF was a strategic move by Taylor to have access to the country's diamond resources and a military ally in next door Sierra Leone. As stated earlier, Taylor and Sankoh met in Libya at the Benghazi military camp in Libya. Sankoh helped Taylor launch his rebellion in 1989 and, in return, Taylor helped create the RUF and sponsored the RUF incursion in 1991 under Liberian field commanders. William Reno argues that the Taylor-sponsored Sankoh invasion was an expansion of Taylor's warlord political economy. Having declared himself president of 'Greater Liberia', i.e. those territories under his control, with Gbanga as the seat of his 'government', he then appointed Sankoh as 'Governor of Sierra Leone', i.e. those territories under RUF control, primarily the strategic mineral territories in eastern and southern Sierra Leone. Therefore, exploiting the political economy of warlordism led to the informal re-drawing of the territorial boundaries of both Liberia and Sierra Leone, whereby Liberian territory became informally extended to include eastern and southern Sierra Leone.[35] This phenomenon is replicated in the Central Africa region where the involvements of Museveni's Uganda and Kagame's Rwanda in the civil war in DRC have led to the informal 'expansion' of both countries' territories to include the strategic diamond regions of DRC under rebel control.

The military and strategic support of President Taylor for the RUF is internationally recognised. Taylor's Liberia provides the main conduit for the sale of RUF diamonds in return for arms from the global network of arms traffickers from eastern Europe and the Middle East. At the UN Security Council hearing on the diamond industry in Sierra Leone held on 30 June - 1 July 2000, there was unanimous agreement about the role

Liberia and Burkina Faso are playing in fuelling the war in Sierra Leone. Experts and diplomats at the hearing explained how Taylor's Liberia and Compaore's Burkina Faso are exporting illicit diamonds mined in RUF held territories, the proceeds from which are used to purchase arms and other logistics. Intelligence reports allege that Taylor holds regular meetings with the RUF leadership in Monrovia or Ouagadougou, Burkina Faso to arrange the sale of diamonds, purchase of arms and formation of RUF military strategy.[36] Intelligence experts claim that Taylor has established a company, the Liberian Investment Corporation, with a branch in Burkina Faso, to handle conflict diamonds and logistical support to the RUF.[37] Liberia is used as a base to stockpile RUF weapons.

Blaise Compaore for his part, has armed, trained and provided combatants for Taylor's NPFL. The relational context of Compaore's assistance to Taylor was extended to Sankoh. Burkina Faso has been used as the transit point for arms originating from Eastern Europe and destined for Taylor's NPFL, Sankoh's RUF and UNITA in Angola. Burkina Faso utilised its end-user certificates to import arms for its rebel allies. Blaise Compaore has also used the arms network established between the former President of Zaire, Mobute and UNITA. The Fowler Report states that:

> ...arms destined for Burkina Faso have been unlawfully diverted to other end-users .... In the context of the relationship between Burkina Faso and UNITA ... it is highly likely that arms legally sold and transported to Burkina Faso have been diverted by Burkinabe authorities ....[38]

Due to Taylor's support for the RUF, British pressure led to the suspension of US $43 million EU aid to Liberia in June 2000. Taylor and Sankoh are both militarily indistinguishable in terms of the exploitation of conflict diamonds. Though Sankoh was the de facto political leader of the RUF, the real military capability lay with Taylor. Taylor had deployed former NPFL fighters, Liberian 'volunteers', Burkinabe and Ukrainian mercenaries, Libyan and South African military advisers to support the RUF's control of the diamond territories, especially the Konu district. Even with the signing of the Lomé peace agreement and his self-styled image as peace maker, Taylor's military support for the RUF continued. Taylor used the conflict diamonds to enrich himself and to consolidate his autocratic regime in Liberia.

Since 1992, Taylor has done everything he could to protect the diamond fields under RUF control. He has been assisted by the former RUF Field Commander, Sam Bockarie, alias 'General Maskita', who had split up with the RUF political leadership and nominally heads his own independent RUF faction based in Liberia. Bockarie himself was an urban drifter, a failed night-club dancer, hairdresser and motor mechanic in Sierra Leone, who migrated to Liberia in search of economic opportunities. The ruthless military exploits of Bockarie during the Liberian and Sierra Leone wars, and his support within the RUF have provided strategic opportunities for Taylor. Taylor has manipulated Bockarie to his military and economic advantage. Bockarie now serves as an unofficial security adviser to Taylor. Those militias who 'fled' to Liberia with him have been incorporated into Taylor's dreaded Anti-Terrorist Unit. This therefore clearly establishes the fact that Taylor's security apparatus and that of the RUF are inseparable.

Taylor's motive in playing an influential role in the Lomé peace agreement, and pressuring the RUF to release the UN peacekeepers held hostage in May 2000, was primarily a strategic calculation geared towards forging a political settlement which ensured that the RUF continued to retain control of the diamond territories. Documents found in Sankoh's villa, after being stormed by pro-democracy demonstrators on 8 May 2000, directly implicated Liberia and Burkina Faso in exploiting conflict diamonds and supplying arms. According to the *Sunday Telegraph:*

> Liberia is now the hub of the diamond-for-arms trade that is driving the Sierra Leone civil war and has dragged British troops into the region. In a world of shadowy South African, Israeli, and Ukrainian businessmen who pass through Monrovia, gems flow out of Sierra Leone through Liberia, eastern European weapons bought with the proceeds make the reverse journey.[39]

Apart from the exploitation of Sierra Leone's diamond resources, it is argued that Taylor's political survival in Liberia is directly linked to the ability of the RUF to control eastern Sierra Leone, which shares a common border with Liberia. Armed factions such as ULIMO and LPC who had fought Taylor are always waiting in the wings poised to launch military attacks and destabilise his regime. Taylor's fears were confirmed when an armed faction attacked Lofa County from the Guinean border. Also, Taylor who fought and maintained a fractious relationship with ECOMOG, does not favour the deployment of Nigerian troops near Liberian borders. Taylor's military fear is that if the Sierra Leone government and UNAMSIL regain control of eastern Sierra Leone, it would provide a gateway for dissidents to attack Liberia. Furthermore, the defeat of the RUF may lead to the return of large numbers of former NPFL fighters and RUF combatants into Liberia. These largely 'impoverished, discontented ex-combatants already pose a danger to Taylor at home, and the arrival of more would likely heighten the peril'.[40]

In the exploitation of conflict diamonds, the RUF relies on the shifting informal patterns of regional trans-border and international commercial linkages to market its diamonds and secure arms and other war-fighting logistics. The trans-border economic linkages and networks are therefore vital to the survival of RUF. In addition, given the limited competence of these collapsing states to exercise control over their territories, we see the emergence of a criminalised trans-border trade.[41] The violence associated with the exploitation of war economies within the MRU regionalisation context, has in turn provided the ruling and governing elites in these countries with an alternative politico-economic strategies of survival. Mark Duffield therefore argues that 'market liberalisation has encouraged the deepening and expansion of all forms of transborder activity', hence the link between the exploitation of conflict diamonds and neo-Liberal globalisation.[42] Taylor's involvement in the Sierra Leone civil war is a classic illustration of this link in that 'By the end of the 1990s, Liberia had become a major centre for massive diamond-related criminal activity, with connections to guns, drugs and money laundering throughout Africa and considerably afield'.[43] The trans-border nature of war economies and their dependence on Northern commercial complicity is at the heart of the difficulties associated with the resolution of conflicts such as in Sierra Leone.

Diamonds and the Privatisation of Security in Sierra Leone

By 1995, the RUF, with the support of foreign mercenaries, had taken control of the diamond territories and other strategic economic areas such as the rutile and Bauxite mines in southern Sierra Leone. The level of state collapse, and the inability of NPRC regime and the Nigeria-led ECOMOG to end the civil war led to the privatisation of state security and the eventual mortgaging of the mineral resources of the country. The privatisation of security in Sierra Leone led to the emergence of a new kind of 'concession for protection' racket fronted by international security conglomerates.[44] However, the hiring of private security firms to police mining operations dates back to the colonial period. The SLST established a Diamond Protection Force and other mining operators made their own private security arrangements to protect the diamond fields.

The UK-based Gurhka Security Guards Ltd. was the first on the security market. Its inability to provide combat support, rather than military assistance and training, led to the termination of its contract with the NPRC government.[45] Three international conglomerates operating in Sierra Leone have firmly established the link between the 'diamond concession for protection' phenomenon. The Antwerp-based Rex Diamond have mining concessions in southern (Zimmi) and eastern (Tongo) regions of Sierra Leone. In 1991, after the shooting down of the government's only combat helicopter, the management of Rex Diamond was implicated in a deal with the Kabbah government to supply military equipment and ammunition worth US$ 3.8 million.[46] The Toronto-based AmCan minerals, which holds exploration licenses in Sierra Leone, has not been able to operate effectively due to general insecurity. AmCan has recently acquired the South African-owned Amsec International (SL) firm, with connections to both the diamond and the private security industries. Ian Smillie et al point out that AmCan's legal adviser in Sierra Leone also chairs the Government Gold and Diamond Office (GGDO), the body with oversight for monitoring, valuation and taxation of the diamond industry.

The London-based DiamondWorks which has mining concessions in Sierra Leone, has raised a lot of controversy because of its alleged association with private military companies (PMCs). Branch Energy Ltd. which also had mineral concessions in Sierra Leone, was acquired by DiamondWorks in 1995. Both DiamondWorks and Branch Energy have alleged links with PMCs such as Executive Outcomes (EO) and Sandline International. After the termination of the contract of Gurhka Security Ltd, EO was hired. EO was able to effect a strategic military impact on the war and forced the RUF to the negotiating table and led to the signing of the Abidjan Peace Agreement in November 1996. However, the huge financial burden of EO military operations on the cash-strapped Kabbah government led to the termination of EO's contract, but not before Branch Energy was granted a lucrative 25 years mining concession from the Kabbah regime. The new national mining code declared by the Kabbah regime in July 1998 exempted Branch Energy from the new mining policy, which stipulates that 'foreigners will only be granted licenses if they have a Sierra Leonean partner holding at least a 25 per cent stake in the project'.[47]

Sandline International, which is alleged to have close ties with EO, was hired by the overthrown Kabbah regime. Sandline was instrumental in the overthrow of the AFRC military junta in 1998, and the re-instatement of the Kabbah government. The involvement of Sandline in the Sierra Leone conflict led to a political controversy in Britain wherein the Blair government was criticised for covertly supporting mercenary intervention in a foreign country, and for breach of UN arms embargo on Sierra Leone.[48]

What becomes apparent is the fact that these mining companies were introduced into Sierra Leone during the context of state collapse and civil war. Smillie et al conclude that in such a situation 'beleaguered and legitimate governments find little formal international protection against internal predators, and are forced into Faustian bargains in order to survive'.[49]

After the collapse of the Lomé agreement and the inability of the Kabbah government to regain control of the diamond territories from the RUF, the government has expressed its intention to hire foreign private military companies. According to Presidential spokesman Septimus Kaikai, 'we are looking at firms ... one company will be here or two companies, within mining, within marketing ... and will help us to decide which security should be put in place'.[50] In addition, the government is considering the re-introduction of strict movement controls in the diamond mining areas, controls introduced by the British colonial government in the 1930s, and which operated during the Stevens era. The decision by the Kabbah government to return to the privatisation of security for the diamond industry had been largely due to the advice of the British and American governments. Private military companies in both countries are therefore strategically placed to win security contracts from the Kabbah regime. The outsourcing of security functions to private military companies is hardly the solution for long-term peace and stability in war-torn Sierra Leone.

However, the debate on the privatisation of security in Africa will not disappear in the foreseeable future. Some analysts argue that private military companies have strategic military capabilities which could help stabilise a crisis, for example, EO's military involvement in Sierra Leone and Angola were instrumental in bringing the rebel factions to the negotiating table.[51] Based on their capability to effect a strategic military balance, some military and political analysts argue that PMCs should be employed to provide security for collapsed states. It is also asserted that due to the failure of UN peacekeeping operations, PMCs could be legally contracted to bring peace and security in war-torn societies. They therefore argue for the outsourcing of UN peacekeeping responsibility to PMCs. An Open Letter written by Sandline on 5 June 2000 to the UN called on:

> The UN to consider supplementing the efforts of the troops by contracting private military companies to provide the cadre of experienced officers and non-commissioned officers who can plan, lead and enhance skills of these forces in the field.[52]

It is argued that their capability to exercise military coercion to resolve conflict helps to create a fragile but conducive environment for ceasefires and the introduction of peacekeeping forces. Hence, private military companies could complement the military and security responsibilities of international peacekeeping forces operating in conflict zones. The capability for rapid deployment in conflict situations has shown that private military companies have a clear advantage over ad hoc multinational forces such as ECOMOG, NATO and the UN. It is further argued that they are cost-effective when compared with the cost of international peacekeeping and the maintenance of government forces. Also, they are willing to sustain loss of life as 'soldiers of fortune', or 'guns for hire', something most states fear because of the political repercussions.[53] Private military companies also provide a foreign policy proxy and plausible deniability for western governments who do not want their involvement in a particular conflicts to be acknowledged. In the case of Sierra Leone, EO demonstrated the capability to temporarily bolster the weak democracy in the country.

However, some analysts contest the so-called merits of the privatisation of security. It is argued that the link between strategic minerals and low-intensity conflicts means that financially poor and weak states with mineral resources will virtually mortgage their mineral resources to private military companies. Their involvement would possibly lead to the prolongation of the war since they profit out of instability and wars.[54] The profit motivation, i.e. exploiting war for profit, led to some 'shady' deals. For example, former EO soldiers have been hired by the RUF-Taylor faction to train fighters and provide strategic military advise. The operations of private military companies are most of the time bereft of transparency. They are accountable only to their shareholders and board of directors. This therefore jeopardises the interests of their clients, i.e. beleaguered governments. Private military companies, through their association with war economies, have led to the privatisation of violence, and contributed to arms proliferation, drug trafficking and money laundering. Also, their glossy corporate image belies their involvement in gross human rights violations. The Global Coalition for Africa (GCA) states:

> That PMCs have emerged to provide security is a stunning indication of the weakness of some Africa states and may have ramifications in many countries. PMCs whether operating in the military or civil spheres are not a long-term solution to African problems. Indeed, relying on them may aggravate already difficult situations by further eroding the capacity of public institutions to ensure order. This could undermine the legitimacy of the state.[55]

Diamonds and Human Security in Post-war Sierra Leone

The human security costs of conflict diamonds are enormous in Sierra Leone. This is unlike Botswana, Namibia and South Africa, where the diamond wealth has been used to generate economic development, infrastructural and social progress. In Sierra Leone, it has contributed to war and underdevelopment. According to the British Foreign Office Minister Peter Hain, 'Diamonds must be used to help rebuild Sierra Leone's schools and hospitals, not destroy them'.[56] It therefore becomes obvious that long-term peace and security, sustainable development and democratic participation are linked to efficient management and redistribution of resources from the diamond industry. Diamonds and other strategic resources should be used to finance post-war reconstruction and development. Major investment by government and external donors in improving human and economic security, creating viable and sustainable democratic and accountable governing institutions, are central to winning positive peace in post-war Sierra Leone. It also involves the establishment of an equitable framework to ensure that the wealth from the natural resources of the country are used to create jobs, infrastructural development and access to social services such as education, health care and transportation. These pro-active human security measures would go a long way to remove the incentives for relapse into further war and the economic exploitation of violence.

The campaign against conflict diamonds led by *Global Witness* and other NGOs are positive international efforts to ensure that natural resources are utilised to enhance human security in war-torn societies. The *Global Witness* 'Fatal Transactions' campaign has called on the public and other interested organisations to request the 'diamond trade to implement effective controls to ensure that diamonds do not fund rebel armies in Africa'.[57] This campaign has been taken up by politicians in western governments. The U.S. Congressman Tony Hall, introduced the CARAT Act legislation that required the diamond industry to provide written certification for the origin of diamonds. The proposed law desires to create consumer awareness to 'avoid purchase from countries in which war or human right abuses are funded through the sale of diamonds ... and to protect democratic countries that depend on diamond revenue from any collateral damage of a consumer backlash'.[58] The Belgian government, for its part, in March 2000 introduced new controls on diamond imports into Antwerp. A Foreign Ministry statement acknowledged that:

> Since Antwerp is the World Centre for the import and export of

diamonds, our country has been involved in this issue. Everything possible must be done to make sure the UN sanctions are applied and that, in general, the suffering of the people in countries torn apart by civil war, such as Angola and Sierra Leone, is alleviated.[59]

However, the campaign against conflict diamonds will be unsuccessful as long as there is no simultaneous campaign against arms proliferation and lax international gun control. Arms proliferation in Africa poses the greatest threat to human security, not only in terms of loss of lives and injuries, but their potential for massive disruption and the implications for internal displacement, refugee flows, economic and agricultural dislocation. Though conflict diamonds provide the resources for fuelling wars in Africa such as in Sierra Leone, Angola and DRC, the guns actually do the killings and destruction. Excessive focus on conflict diamonds is an oblique recognition of the failure of the international community to control illegal arms flows into Africa that are used to fight Africa's bloody wars. Martin Rapaport opines that:

> After all, it is much easier to control the movement of tanks, ammunition and fuel than small easily transportable diamonds. Why are arms merchants allowed to ply their trade in Africa? Why are oil companies allowed to do business and fund wars?[60]

Another aspect of this recent international focus on conflict diamonds is that it is potentially unhelpful in understanding the causes of African wars. It is obvious that resources from conflict diamonds fuel and prolong African wars, but to claim that diamonds are the primary cause of wars in countries such as Sierra Leone, DRC and Angola, is rather simplistic. Why is it the case that, though diamonds were discovered in Sierra Leone since the 1930s, the country did not degenerate into civil war in the pre-1990s era due to diamond 'greed'? The simplistic interpretation of conflicts such as Sierra Leone demonstrates, yet again, the failure of the international community to analytically engage the fundamental causes of African conflicts. It becomes obvious that a focus on 'conflict diamonds' provides a simplistic, do-able, entry point in terms of responding to complex emergencies in Africa. What this focus on conflict diamonds does is to shift the debate from pigeon-holing African conflicts as mere 'ethnic' and 'tribal' wars. But is this international focus on conflict diamonds not a pretext by western governments to protect the legitimate diamond trade and arms industry, both of which are multi-billion dollar business enterprises with serious implications for their national economies? Instead of analytically engaging the problems facing Africa, such a simplistic entry point, i.e. conflict diamonds, potentially holds back the constructive debate on Africa. Blair's blueprint for 21st Century Africa, 'Africa Partnership Initiative' states that, 'We need a new partnership for Africa, in which Africans lead but the rest of the world is committed where all the problems are dealt with, not separately but together in a coherent and unified plan'.[61] Britain has been in the vanguard promoting the campaign against conflict diamonds and calling for the regulation of the diamond industry through the implementation of an international certification scheme. However, it is obvious that no matter how effective the diamond certificate scheme, which is yet to be proven, as long as the fundamental causes of the war remain unaddressed, there would always be the potential for relapse into war and political instability.

The international campaign against conflict diamonds has also become another 'donor-driven' analysis of African conflicts. The Finance Minister, James Jonah, in a speech to the German Foundation for International Development in October 2000, reduced the war in Sierra Leone to being 'simply about diamonds'.[62] It is obvious that the Finance Minister is merely dancing to the tune of the donor-driven analysis of the war in Sierra Leone, i.e. saying what the donors want to hear. This is hardly surprising given the role played by key western governments in leading the campaign against conflict diamonds, and the heavy dependence of war-torn Sierra Leone on donor funding.

Conclusion

The exploitation of conflict diamonds clearly demonstrates the link between civil wars, strategic minerals, arms smuggling, drugs trafficking and money laundry. The international diamond industry, under the umbrella of economic globalisation, has contributed to fuelling wars in Africa. The diamond related criminal activity extends beyond the ECOWAS region to include world financial and trading centres such as Switzerland, Antwerp, Tel Aviv, Bombay and London, in an informal transcontinental network that involves not only diamonds, but arms, drugs and money in search of laundering. The privatisation of security in Sierra Leone has further complicated the human security situation in the war-torn country. Therefore, sustainable peace and development lies in simultaneously addressing the 'twin-partners' of conflict diamonds and arms trafficking in Sierra Leone.

Notes and References

[1] For further discussion see Alfred B. Zack-Williams, *Tributors, Supporters and Merchant Capital: Mining and Underdevelopment in Sierra Leone* Avebury Press, 1995; 'Diamond Mining the Rural Economy and War', paper presented at the International Conference on State, Conflict and Intervention in Sierra Leone, Centre for African Studies, St. Anthony's College, University of Oxford, 13-14 May 2000.

[2] A. Zack-Williams, op. cit., 1995.

[3] Ibid.

[4] M. Harbottle, *The Knaves of Diamonds* London: Seeley Service Company, 1976, cited in Zack-Williams, May 2000.

[5] Ian Smillie et al., *The Heart of the Matter* January 2000, p. 5.

[6] A. Zack-Williams, 'Diamond Mining and Underdevelopment in Sierra Leone' *Africa Development* Vol. XV, No. 2, 1990, p. 24.

[7] Zack Williams, op. cit. May 2000, p. 10.

[8] Ibid.

[9] Zack-Williams, op. cit., 1995, p. 122.

[10] Ian Smillie et al., op. cit., 2000, p. 6.

[11] Zack-Williams, op. cit, 1995, p. 122. See also: H. L. van Dev Laan, *Sierra Leone Diamonds: An Economic Study Covering the Years 1952 - 61* Oxford: Oxford University Press, 1965.

[12] See Ian Smillie et al., op. cit., 2000; Zack-Williams, op. cit., 1995.

[13] William Reno, *Warlord Politics and African States* Boulder, Colorado: Lynne Rienner, 1998, p. 116.

[14] Paul Richards, op. cit. 1996.

[15] William Reno, op. cit., 1998, p. 120.

[16] C. Magbaile Fyle, 'Conflict and Population Dispersal: The Refugee Crisis in the Mano River Tri-State Area' Dakar: CODESRIA, 1995, p. 5.

[17] Arthur Abraham, 'War and Transition to Peace: A Study of State Conspiracy in Perpetrating Armed Conflict' *African Development* Vol. 22, No. 3-4, 1997.

[18] *Report on the Crisis in Sierra Leone*, Major General Vijay Kumar Jetley, May 2000, available at http://www.sierra-leone.org/.

[19] William Reno, op.cit. 1998. Reno describes the 'Kalashnikov lifestyle' as the culture of war and a means of accumulation, 'Shadow States and the Political Economy of Civil Wars' in Berdal and Malone (eds) *Greed and Grievance* 2000, p. 54.

[20] Jimmy Kandeh, 'Ransoming the State: Elite Origins of Subaltern Terror in Sierra Leone', 1999, p. 349.

[21] Ibid. pp. 362-364.

[22] De Beers defines conflict diamonds as 'diamonds which originated from areas in Africa controlled by forces fighting the legitimate and internationally recognised governement of the relevant country' The London-based NGO, Global Witness, which has led the campaign against conflict diamonds contests the restrictive definition advanced by De Beers. It defines conflict diamonds as those diamonds 'that originate from areas under the control of forces that are in opposition to elected and internationally recognised governments, or are in anyway connected to those groups ...' The Global Witness definition embraces not only rebel factions, but also government forces and government-held territories trading in illegal diamonds. Global Witness, *Conflict Diamonds: Possibilities for the Identification, Certification and Control of Diamond* London: Global Witness Ltd, 2000, p. 1.

[23] Robert Fowler was the Canadian Ambassador to the UN. The report was commissioned by the UN in its attempt to resolve the Angolan civil war after the failure of the democratization process in 1993.
[24] Robert Neild, 'Expose the Unsavory Business Behind Cruel Wars', *International Herald Tribune* 17 February 2000.
[25] 'What Price Diamonds?' *West Africa* 26 June - 2 July 2000, p. 2.
[26] cited in *West Africa* 2000.
[27] Mark Duffield, 'Globalization, Transborder Trade, and War Economies', in Berdal and Malone (eds) *Greed and Grievance*, 2000.
[28] Ibid. p. 84.
[29] Ian Smillie et al, op. cit.
[30] 'De Beers', 'All that glitters is not gold', *Financial Times*, 11 June 2000, p. 17.
[31] Ian Smillie et al, op. cit., p. 4.
[32] Ibid., p. 5.
[33] 'Between a rock and a hard place' *Financial Times* 12 July 2000, p. 8.
[34] 'De Beers and Africa's crisis' *Financial Times* 12 July 2000.
[35] William Reno, op. cit., 1998.
[36] 'The Bay Guys of West Africa' *West Africa* 14-20 August, 2000, p. 9.
[37] Ibid.
[38] Robert Fowler, op. cit.
[39] 'Liberia Chief fuels diamond war' *Sunday Telegraph* 28 May 2000.
[40] James Rupert and Douglas Farah, 'The man in the middle: Liberia President Taylor, may hold the key to peace in Sierra Leone' *The Washington Post* 30 May 2000.
[41] Mark Duffield describes transborder trade as trade that is wider than conventional ideas of parallel or informal economic activity. This transnational trading operations which implies a large-scale tradeborder trade involves both legal and illegal goods. Mark Duffield, op. cit., p. 76.
[42] Ibid., p. 69.
[43] Ian Smillie et al, p. 6.
[44] Ibid.
[45] For detailed discussion of the link between strategic minerals and the privatisation of security see; David J. Francis 'Mercenary Intervention in Sierra Leone: Providing national security or international exploitation?' *Third World Quarterly* Vol. 20, No. 2, 1999, pp. 319-338; Abdel-Fatou Musa and J. 'Kayode Fayemi (ed.), *Mercenaries: An African Security Dilemma* Pluto Press, 2000.
[46] Ian Smillie et al, op. cit., p. 8.
[47] David Francis, op. cit., 1999, p. 331.
[48] The Legg Report 1998.
[49] Ian Smillie et al, p. 9.
[50] Professor Septimus Kaikai, interview on BBC Newsnight Programme 22:30 GMT, 2 June 2000.
[51] David Shearer, *Private Armies and Military Intervention* Adelphi Paper 316, Oxford University Press, Oxford, 1998.
[52] Stepen Mbogo, 'Mercenaries? NO, PMC' *West Africa* 18 - 24 September 2000, pp. 18-19.
[53] Henry Sanchez, 'Why do States Hire Private Military companies?' available at http://newarkwww.rutgers.edu/global/sanchez.html.
[54] David Francis 'Mercenary intervention in Sierra Leone' 1999.
[55] *West Africa*, Ibid.

[56] Clarence Roy-Maculey, 'Sierra Leone Diamond Trade Targeted' *Associated Press* 16 January 2000.
[57] Martin Rapaport, 'Blood Money' March 2000, available at http://ww.diamonds.net/news/new.asp?nf=0.
[58] Ibid.
[59] Wednesday, 8 March 2000, available at http://www.unfoundation.org/unwire/unwire.cfm#1.
[60] Martin Rapaport, March 2000.
[61] Speech by Prime Minister Tony Blair at the UN Millennium, New York, 7 September 2000.
[62] James Jonah, 'Economic Dimensions of the Conflict in Sierra Leone', op. cit.

7 Political Implications of Sierra Leone's ECOWAS Regionalism

Introduction

This chapter critically examines the political implications of Sierra Leone's ECOWAS regionalism. Since the creation of the economic community, the impact of membership upon individual states has been an issue for evaluation by governments, elites, academic researchers and the general public, though in a rather haphazard manner. The renewed momentum of regionalism within the Community in the 1990s has seen expansion into the security domain and a revised Treaty. All these have contributed to bring the debate about the costs and benefits of regionalism on member states to the forefront. There is a growing demand from the public, particularly in the immediate post-ECOMOG period, to know more about ECOWAS matters. The generally vague economic ideas about ECOWAS shared by the people are being compounded by the new security, military, and foreign policy dimensions of the Community. The desire to know about the advantages, disadvantages and wider implications, has been crystallised into an evaluation of Sierra Leone's ECOWAS regionalism.

Any attempt to evaluate the politics of Sierra Leone's ECOWAS regionalism is an ambitious endeavour, even if it were to be restricted only to a superficial approach based on some general assumptions. It is difficult to quantify or estimate the positive and negative effects from a political perspective. A number of problems also emerge because of the variation in policy areas, and the selection of goals and criteria. Most academics, politicians and interest groups are in agreement that membership of ECOWAS is advantageous for all sixteen states, although they are aware of the fact that these gains may not be evenly distributed among or within the member states. Even in times of serious political crisis within the Community, the majority of the member states are reluctant to consider leaving the economic grouping. The case of the withdrawal of Mauritania from ECOWAS in 1999 is an exception. There seems to be a positive correlation between elite values and regionalism in West Africa. It is generally the case that elites are in the vanguard promoting regionalism because they tend to be the principal beneficiaries, although generally society as a whole does benefit from the regionalisation processes. Therefore the political and ruling elites sometimes endeavour to take stock of the costs and benefits of membership of regionalism. The implementation of ECOWAS' economic objectives and ECOMOG's security policies demonstrates that the actions that deliver beneficial consequences in one context can deliver undesirable ones in another. Generally speaking, member states in an economic community always seek to maximise the greatest benefits from regional co-operation, but in times of crisis over costs of regionalism, their response is to retreat into some kind of economic and political nationalism.

An assessment of Sierra Leone in ECOWAS is an exercise which economists would term cost-benefit analysis. This evaluation is from a politics perspective and as such will include effects that cannot be easily estimated in financial terms, benefits that are tangible and quantifiable, as well as effects that are not valued generally as positive or negative. The analysis of the benefits and losses, positive or negative effects of Sierra Leone's ECOWAS regionalism is compounded by the dynamic, multi-sectoral and complex regionalistion process.

The preamble to the ECOWAS Treaty explicitly accepts the need for a fair and equitable distribution of the benefits of economic co-operation among member states. Such benefits are normally perceived in practical and immediate terms. History has shown that most of the benefits of integration are long-term and intangible. The question of gains and losses accruing from integration has always been a contentious issue. It has been a common problem plaguing economic regionalism schemes in developing regions. The regionalisation process in CACM, EAC, LAIA, and CARIFTA led to unequal benefits with relatively adverse effects on some member states' growth rate.[1] Expectations of immediate and spectacular benefits have been the driving force for the politics of regionalism. Failure to achieve this often led to disappointment, frequent breakdown and disintegration of the regionalism projects. The perception of positive and negative effects of regionalism also vary from country to country and within a country due to socio-economic and political forces or shifts, or as a result of spectacular events in which the people pay the price in 'blood and money'. Therefore what one country regards as a benefit or a cost may well not be so to another country. This depends on the country's political, security and economic characteristics and circumstances. The objectives pursued by countries in an integration scheme may also differ, which invariably affects the notion of benefits and losses. For instance, if a member country's objective is purely economic development whilst another wants to achieve the traditional ends of politics, then the benefits and costs will vary from country to country. In other words, each country will regard something as a benefit or a cost according to the objectives it is pursuing.

The lack of any comprehensive study of the costs and benefits of regionalism leads to a very subjective and general discussion about the impact. Decisions therefore tend to be based more on vague perceptions than on sound economic and political facts. The politics of regionalism among weak and fragile economies forces them to concentrate on short-term gains and losses rather than long-term opportunities arising from integration. It is evident that the integration process cannot be expected to benefit all participatory countries equally and may have detrimental effects for some of them.

In a developing region like West Africa, the politics of regionalism become part of the problem. The majority of West African leaders tend to evaluate the gains accruing from regionalism in predominantly national terms. For example, the Nigerian government constantly wants to know how much it has gained from ECOWAS regionalism. What often happens is that once the development goals are not forthcoming under conditions of immediacy specified by leadership, the legitimacy of the integration process is seriously brought into question and the result is either stagnation or disintegration of the integration effort.[2]

Politico-Diplomatic Relevance of ECOWAS Regionalism

Sierra Leone is a member of a variety of intergovernmental and multilateral organisations through which it strives to achieve its foreign policy and national development objectives. ECOWAS has increasingly become the principal forum for the pursuit of the traditional ends of politics for the country. The prevailing view is that, since the economic benefits of integration are not immediately forthcoming, the politics of regionalism and co-operation provide the opportunities for tangible and intangible benefits. Hence, the politico-diplomatic relevance of regionalism to a small state like Sierra Leone is gradually taking centre stage. The general perception is that tangible political gains of regionalism will counter-balance economic disappointment. ECOWAS therefore provides the platform for the realisation of the country's external relations such as foreign and security policy, and external trade policy. The achievement of these external political, security and economic policies are geared towards national development.

Sierra Leone joined the economic community mainly for pragmatic reasons, not out of a realistic conversion to the ideal of a united Africa or political union in West Africa. The rationale was to provide a forum where the country would pursue more effectively its economic and foreign policy objectives. There was no marked opposition at the national level to Sierra Leone's ECOWAS regionalism. The fear of exclusion was more poignant than any foreseeable costs of membership. In the parliamentary debate on ECOWAS in 1975, some representatives expressed reservations about the possible loss of sovereignty that would be involved, but consideration of politico-diplomatic gains was more persuasive. However, the parliamentary debate on ECOWAS was merely a democratic formality because Siaka Stevens as president was the principal foreign policy decision maker.

One such area is the holding of the chairmanship of ECOWAS. Sierra Leone has twice held the chair of ECOWAS, during the presidency of both Siaka Stevens and Joseph Momoh. The chairmanship of ECOWAS is a coveted office since the holder acts as both 'political manager' and external spokesperson of ECOWAS. This role has provided unprecedented intangible benefits for the country. The political influence that goes with the position immediately converted Sierra Leone into a prominent regional actor. The international profile of the country was boosted and the international status and prestige of the president was enhanced. Sierra Leone was immediately placed firmly on the international map of political relevance. The international publicity that goes with the summits and ministerial conferences hosted reflects positively on the image of the country. The publicity generated by the holding of the ECOWAS chair, moreover, is far less expensive than mounting a public relations campaign in the international media to publicise the country in terms of attracting investment and tourist opportunities. Summits and ministerial conferences attract huge international media coverage. Thus under the banner of ECOWAS the country receives free positive international media coverage, which every country needs from time to time. These summits also have economic benefits as local staff are being employed to serve as conference attendants, interpreters and drivers. The hotels also come into business and money, mainly in foreign currencies such as dollars and pounds sterling. Both Stevens and Momoh used their position to promote external economic relations and co-operation with industrialised and newly industrialised states.

The May 1981 ECOWAS summit, coming after the hosting of the OAU conference, further developed the international image of the country and its president. The holding of the OAU and ECOWAS chair in 1980 and 1981 respectively provided enormous publicity for the country. Freetown could, after all, more easily afford to host another international summit, thanks to the infrastructural facilities bequeathed by the OAU conference. But the ECOWAS summit, coming on top of the OAU conference, also left in its wake huge financial costs amounting to millions of dollars. Stevens, in a political realist justification of the financial costs of hosting ECOWAS, argued that 'there are things you cannot measure in money', alluding to the intangible benefits of such projects. The following three ECOWAS protocols were signed in Freetown: i. Protocol relating to the definition of the concept of originating products of the member states of ECOWAS; ii. Protocol relating to the institutions of the Community; iii. Protocol relating to Mutual Assistance in Defence.

This international public relations exercise in ECOWAS is often an attempt to show how important the respective member states are and in particular, governments that lack domestic legitimacy will cash in on this opportunity to present a credible international image for domestic consumption. The 1981 Protocol on Mutual Assistance in Defence signed in Freetown was more for domestic political considerations than for external security. At that time, Siaka Stevens was facing increasing domestic opposition and as such needed a platform to stem the tide of his unpopularity. Domestically, the military aspects of this protocol were hardly emphasised. The military establishment which was important to maintain Stevens in power saw the ECOWAS defence initiative as a positive development and thus gave its total support to ECOWAS as an indirect way of protecting the country.

The politico-diplomatic relevance of the Chair of ECOWAS is all the more apparent in the jostling for chairmanship among Community leaders who sometimes regard themselves as 'president' of West Africa. Through the mediation of Siaka Stevens as chairman of ECOWAS, Sierra Leone's international image was further enhanced by a positive contribution to the resolution of the Senegalese and Mauritania dispute. In comparative terms, the politico-diplomatic relevance of the presidency of the EU is instructive to the analysis of the West African scenario.

Another area of politico-diplomatic relevance is the position of the Executive Secretary of ECOWAS. The chief executive of the Community, like that of the presidency of the European Commission, carries a lot of political weight. It is a post coveted by member states. Member states regard administrative and professional positions in ECOWAS as benefits of economic regionalism to be shared. Sierra Leone became the second holder of the executive secretaryship of the Community from 1985 to 1992.

Alhaji Mumodu Munu was first appointed, but due to his poor performance, Sierra Leone was requested by the Authority of the Community to nominate another representative to the post. The choice of Dr. Abass Bundu, with a previous international civil service experience, was an attempt to limit the damage done by the poor performance during Munu's tenure. The sacking of Munu reflected negatively on the international image of the country. Munu's situation however, has since had a parallel in the removal of the Guinean Executive Secretary, Dr. Edouard Benjamin in August 1997. The performance of Bundu, especially during the expansion of the Community into the defence and security domain, helped to restore the international image of the country and Sierra Leonean staff at Community institutions. A good or bad performance of an international civil servant reflects on the country. It has implications on the educational and administrative systems and competence of the country, and there is a general reluctance to recruit from poor performing countries.

The criteria for the allocation of posts is based on geographical, equitable distribution and technical competence. However, since the appointments are political in nature, it does not necessarily mean that the best brains will be attracted. As far as the government of President Momoh was concerned, it was happy to let Munu complete his term of office without consideration to what meaningful contribution (or lack of it) he would make to the Community. The ECOWAS Authority had to intervene because it was not benefiting from the leadership capability of Munu. The Munu case led to a strategic evaluation of the system of appointment and brought new criteria for the selection of the Executive Secretary. New emphasis was then placed on political and technical considerations, rather than mere geographical and equitable distribution. The post also became open to competition in the country that has the responsibility to nominate. The final selection then became the responsibility of the Authority. The Revised Treaty explicitly provides for this in Article 18. 2.3.[3] Sierra Leone thus indirectly effected a positive development within the Community in terms of the selection of its chief executive, as a result of the poor performance of Momodu Munu. A corollary to this is that Sierra Leone civil servants and technical experts working at the Secretariat and Community's specialised institutions acquire detailed knowledge of the Community, which complements the knowledge of their own country's administration. The national government ministers whose portfolios fall within the area of Community competence also gain from similar insight.

The politics of regionalism within ECOWAS has helped the member states to forge a common regional political and security co-operation from time to time. This common regional foreign and security co-operation has become a permanent feature of ECOWAS as provided for in the Revised Treaty, Chapter X, Articles 56 and 58.4.[4] It enables member states like Sierra Leone to hide behind a collective position on controversial international issues. Sierra Leone's political ideology, during the Cold War era though generally non-aligned, was in reality a mixed bag of capitalist and socialist orientation. The 1986 American raid on Libya was a good example of ECOWAS as an alibi. Sierra Leone had cordial diplomatic relations with both the United States and Libya, though the balance was in favour of America. The regional position adopted by ECOWAS was a total condemnation of the American action against Libya. Without this regional political cover, Sierra Leone would have preferred to remain silent, neither supporting, nor condemning the aggression. The solidarity of collective action and a common foreign policy approach afforded Sierra Leone a degree of anonymity, where a unilateral policy would have exposed the country to greater potential costs. This has often proved useful as a cover for national foreign policy decision makers and thus avoiding the diplomatic embarrassment of a single position. On certain controversial international issues, the government could deflect any criticism of its national policy by referring to the 'alibi' of an agreed ECOWAS policy or position. Another classic example is the Arab-Israel War in 1979 and the common Community approach which led to the cutting of ties with Israel, though Sierra Leone had strong Israeli diplomatic links.

ECOWAS therefore provides a platform for Sierra Leone to conduct its foreign and security policies, and also articulate its views and grievances. The close interaction with Francophone states has generated new understanding of individual countries, which has invariably led to the solution of regional problems. President Momoh's view was that 'the values of community and hospitality to brother and sister Africans have been the bedrock of our national behaviour and firmly nurtured in our national psyche'.[5] Through this, there has evolved a spirit of collective diplomacy at ECOWAS level. Such regional political co-operation provides the government with detailed knowledge of the partner's point of view on international politics and development, thus widening individual perspectives and facilitating decision making. It is especially the geographically small and the politico-economically weak states such as Sierra Leone that profit from this regional political and security co-operation, as in the ECOWAS effort to restore constitutional rule in the country after the May 1997 military coup. It therefore strengthens the country's voice in the chorus of the sixteen members.

The mere existence of the Community serves as a venue to launch politico-diplomatic offensives. The NPRC military junta under the young and inexperienced leadership of Captain Strasser was quick to capitalise on the politico-diplomatic advantage provided by ECOWAS. The overthrow of the APC government did not go down well with the international community, hence the barrage of criticisms and condemnations. The new military junta, though not lacking in some domestic support, needed a platform to launch a diplomatic initiative that would earn it some semblance of international recognition and legitimacy. ECOWAS provided the perfect opportunity for the military junta. The attendance of the new military leader at the 1992 ECOWAS summit gave the military government instant recognition, which invariably meant recognition and international legitimacy by the world community. In contrast, the new military leader of Liberia, Master-Sergeant Samuel Doe' was unwelcome at the 1980 ECOWAS summit. This damaged the international image of Liberia's military leader. In the words of the Liberian Foreign Minister, Gabriel Bacus Mathews, 'some of the heads of state in Lomé were afraid that anything that legitimises Liberia's Master-Sergeant Doe may give encouragement to a Master-Sergeant Doe within their own countries'.[6] It could be argued that because of the politico-diplomatic advantages provided by ECOWAS, military leaders have been more predisposed to support ECOWAS regionalism. Similarly, the international campaign led by ECOWAS against the illegal AFRC junta which overthrew the civilian government of President Kabbah, denied it any international recognition and de facto legitimacy.

The regional defence and security arrangements, like the non-aggression pact, mutual defence protocol and ECOMOG, have added a new dimension to national security. Within the framework of security regionalism, there also exist bilateral military agreements and defence pacts with Nigeria and Guinea. The regional security body has become a vital complement to national security and defence arrangements. The former Commander of the Armed Forces Major-General Tarawalli, stated categorically that 'there is no meaningful substitute for a collective regional defence arrangement'.[7]

However, this regional political and security co-operation is also bound to bring some diminution of the country's autonomy in foreign affairs. There is therefore a price to pay for regional political and security co-operation. It entails a departure from historical tradition, a certain bending of national principles, and a departure from the 'purity' of national foreign policies,[8] i.e. if there is any such thing as 'pure' foreign policy exposued by Sierra Leone. Often, the reaction of ECOWAS members to controversial international issues gives proof of the divisive geo-politics and their limited room for manoeuvre when they are forced to go beyond their policy of declaratory diplomacy, for example, ECOMOG's intervention in Liberia and Sierra Leone. From a general perspective of foreign policy, once regarded as the exclusive preserve of the nation-state, it is becoming increasingly difficult for each ECOWAS partner to follow exclusively their own foreign policy inclinations without adopting from time to time the line dictated by the Community in the name of regional solidarity.[9] Therefore, Sierra Leone's obligation to ECOWAS inevitably tied the foreign policy of the country to the economic community. Though it is undeniable that the country gains through increased capacity to influence regional policy outputs, there is nevertheless a loss in decision making autonomy as in the case of providing a military base to facilitate ECOMOG's operation in Liberia. Arguably, the national balance sheet of this regional political co-operation contains more credits than debits. For example, the ECOWAS-ECOMOG intervention to restore democratic rule in Sierra Leone was made possible because of the regional political and security co-operation. This is further discussed later in this chapter.

There are regions in the world where Sierra Leone has little diplomatic, political and economic contact or influence. Access has been made possible by membership of the ECOWAS. The ECOWAS-ACP-EU Industrial Forum has provided investment opportunities for Sierra Leone's economic operators. ECOWAS serves as a politico-diplomatic forum for member states in their economic relations with international trade organisations such as GATT and WTO. Negotiating agreements under the auspices of ECOWAS provides an enhanced bargaining power and political leverage as a result of their combined strength in facing other groups or powerful states. ECOWAS spoke as one in the Uruguay Round of 1986 and in an alliance with other developing regions, was able to secure preferential treatment in their external trade. A spin-off of this regional economic diplomacy is that it increases understanding between ECOWAS partners and brings about mutual confidence that goes beyond trade issues. The diplomatic solidarity often used by all regional groupings is most effectively portrayed at multilateral conferences.[10]

It is important to note that the political benefits of Sierra Leone's ECOWAS membership is usually perceived in intangible terms. The politics of regionalism in West Africa, based on consensus, preserved the basis of external sovereignty, while a small state such as Sierra Leone enjoys obvious advantages in terms of enhanced politico-diplomatic status. The extent to which these benefits are translated into influence with other governments varies according to particular circumstances. It would of course be difficult to reject the general assumption that a collective voice on behalf of 200 million people will have a more potent force than the individual policy advanced by a government of 4.9 million people. It also has the advantage of persuading important third parties to act in a way favourable to Sierra Leone, which in normal circumstances they might not.

ECOWAS and the Defence of Democracy in Sierra Leone

The most controversial and politically debated aspect of Sierra Leone's ECOWAS regionalism is the democratic intervention of the regional community under the aegis of ECOMOG to restore the democratic government of President Tejan Kabbah. The intervention has become one of the most important developments in the history of the regional economic community. This unique ECOWAS intervention to restore constitutional order in war-torn Sierra Leone has important implications for African inter-state relations and the traditional norms of international society, namely non-intervention and state sovereignty. The ECOWAS democratic intervention can also be located in a wider debate about the international dimensions of democratisation. This section therefore evaluates the domestic, regional and international implications of ECOWAS' novel defence of democracy in West Africa.[11]

The overthrow of the 15 month old civilian government of President Kabbah on 25 May 1997 by the AFRC, led by Major Johnny Paul Koroma, effectively suspended democratic governance in Sierra Leone. The junta banned all political activities, dissolved parliament and suspended the constitution. The retrenchment of democracy in Sierra Leone further threatened the fragile peace in war-torn Liberia and also the wider security of the region. It meant that ECOWAS and ECOMOG had failed in their peace and conflict settlement efforts in Liberia and West Africa in general. The military coup was an affront not only to the ECOWAS declaration of political principle of 1991, but also the 1997 Harare Declaration which committed the OAU member states to intervene to protect recognised governments.

To understand why it became possible for there to be external multilateral intervention on behalf of democracy in Sierra Leone, one has to look at the nature of domestic politics, and the failure of the post-colonial state, both politically and economically. The genesis of the May coup led by Major Koroma could be traced to the loss of political power and exclusion of the military from the economic and political processes since the election of the civilian government in March 1996. The military establishment had been politicised by successive governments in order to keep them out of politics and to ensure regime survival. The Republic of

Sierra Leone Military Forces (RSLMF) had become enmeshed in the patrimonial politics and predatory accumulation. Loyalty to the political leaders therefore took priority over the institutions they represent. The corruption, indiscipline and the 'sobel' phenomenon within the national army made the civilian government more dependent on the Kamajors – a civil defence force. With the election of the new SLPP government, the Kamajors were transformed from an obscure civil defence organisation into a mass movement largely of Mende ethnic origin. The Kamajors now eclipsed the military and political dominance of the national army, and also threatened their privileged position in the lucrative war economy, especially in the diamond fields. This was thoroughly resented by the army. However, the Kamajors simply played the role the constitutional army had historically abandoned.[12] The quasi-national status of the Kamajors further alienated the army from the new regime, and 'the policy of reducing the size and privileges of the army set the theatre for civilian-military confrontation'.[13] The Kamajor perception of the army was one of an ineffective, corrupt, unpatriotic lot bent on undermining 'the first Southern dominated Government in thirty years' and a 'threat to the country's new democracy'.[14] With the withdrawal of Executive Outcomes and the delayed arrival of the UN peacekeeping force, coupled with poor domestic policies implemented by the new government, and after series of attempted coups, the junior ranks of the army, who felt marginalised by the clientelistic mode of accumulation, succeeded in overthrowing the civilian government.

The ECOWAS attempt to do an Aristide[15] in Sierra Leone is a product of a combination of both domestic and international factors which forced the regional community and key actors to act on behalf of democracy.

The ousted president Kabbah appealed to the Nigerian Head of State, General Sani Abacha, in his capacity as ECOWAS chairman, to intervene and restore constitutional order. Realpolitik explains why General Abacha seized this opportunity to champion the ECOWAS cause for the restoration of democratic governance in Sierra Leone. Some political analysts and media commentators argued that Abacha, himself a military dictator and the epitome of anti-democratic forces, was the least qualified to undertake such a venture. The Nigerian military under General Babangida had, in the June 1993 elections, subverted the democratic wishes of the Nigerian electorate; therefore the democratic motives of the military in Sierra Leone were also suspect. However, to the General, domestic and international political considerations alike warranted such a robust stance. The resolution of the Liberian conflict and the return to democratic rule in that country was a major boost for the domestic and international credibility of the Nigerian leader. Another military venture to restore democratic rule in Sierra Leone might go a long way to silence his domestic and international critics who had been instrumental in the suspension of Nigeria from the Commonwealth in 1995 following the execution of several human rights activists, most prominently Ken Saro Wiwa.

The ECOWAS international pro-democracy condemnation of the military junta in Freetown was instrumental in bringing about the international isolation of the junta by the international community. A diplomatic offensive was launched by ECOWAS and OAU, calling on the international community not to recognise the illegal regime. According to the OAU Secretary General Salim A. Salim:

> The United Nations and the International Community firmly uphold the principle that the will of the people shall be the basis of authority of governments and that governments democratically elected shall not be overthrown by force....It is lamentable that some soldiers who have no mandate to rule at all should decide to challenge the legitimate position of the people. It is a setback for Africa's transition to democracy...This development will not be welcome in Africa.[16]

The OAU, at its 33rd Summit in Harare, decided to support the ECOWAS initiative to restore constitutional order in Sierra Leone since the crisis was perceived as a threat to continental peace and security.

In an attempt to reverse the coup in Freetown, ECOMOG, under the authority of the ECOWAS chairman, launched a failed military intervention through bombing raids on the capital city. The Nigerian gunboat diplomacy was domestically and internationally criticised. This forced ECOWAS to rethink its strategy of resolving the Sierra Leone crisis. It recognised that military intervention or coercive diplomacy was insufficient to resolve the crisis, and had to formulate an exit strategy in order to avoid becoming embroiled in the conflict as had happened in Liberia. ECOWAS therefore took the political and diplomatic initiative to negotiate the restoration of constitutional rule in Sierra Leone. A series of ECOWAS consultative meetings at ministerial and presidential levels led to the formulation of the Conakry Peace Accord under the auspices of the Guinean President Lansana Conte. The Accord formulated an ECOWAS Peace Plan for Sierra Leone which broadly committed all parties to the re-instatement of the legitimate government of President Kabbah; return of peace and security; and a resolution of the issue of refugees and displaced people. In order to achieve these objectives, three measures were advanced in the Peace Plan: i. imposition of sanctions; ii. enforcement of an embargo;

and iii. possible use of force. The ECOWAS Peace Plan had important implications for African inter-state relations. Though military coups have been a constant feature of West African politics, the Sierra Leone crisis is important because it was the first time a regional community has taken a collective and unanimous stance in defending democratic rule. What is more, the agreement to use force to reverse a military coup is unprecedented in West Africa. The ECOWAS example, coupled with the terms of the 1997 Harare declaration were later to serve as justification for the Zimbabwean-led SADC intervention in DRC in 1998.

To ensure the implementation of the Peace Plan, an ECOWAS Contact Group, known as the Committee of Five was established to monitor the situation in Sierra Leone. In an attempt to negotiate a political settlement of the crisis, ECOWAS pursued twin track objectives of political negotiation and use of force, and further approved the use of sanctions against the military junta because of its intransigence to agree to the restoration of constitutional rule. The territorial scope of ECOMOG was expanded to include not only Liberia, but also Sierra Leone, known as ECOMOG II. The Committee of Five also secured the mandate of the UN Security Council for its sanctions and embargo decisions. The Security Council Resolution 1132 of October 1997 gave legal backing to the ECOWAS peace efforts in Sierra Leone and rendered mandatory and universal any sanctions adopted by ECOWAS against the military regime. The resolution provided for the following: travel restrictions on members of the junta and their families; an arms embargo; and no supply of petroleum and petroleum products, except for humanitarian assistance and operations of the military observer group and commodity transactions. The Council empowered ECOMOG under Nigerian Command to impose and enforce a land, sea and air blockade on the junta. It is ironic that Nigeria, a non-democratic, military dictatorship should be empowered by the UN Security Council to reverse a military coup and restore democracy. However, the Security Council itself is hardly a democratically representative body.[17] The UN Security Council authorisation of ECOWAS to use force is not new. Other examples of multilateral military intervention authorised by the Security Council include: military coalition in the Korean conflict in 1950, the Allied coalition in response to Iraq's invasion of Kuwait in 1990 and the multinational enforcement actions in Somalia, Rwanda, Haiti and Bosnia and Herzegovina. The stated objective in all these examples was to use all necessary means, including force, to deal with armed conflict or threat to peace.

Resolution 1132 mandated ECOMOG to apply the measures stipulated in the Conakry Accord which called for political settlement, imposition of sanctions and enforcement of an embargo, and the use of force if necessary. Subsequent ECOWAS political negotiations led to agreement with the military junta to return the country to constitutional rule and the cessation of armed hostilities, return of refugees and displaced persons, and immunities and of exception from prosecution for all those involved in the events of 25 May 1997.

The post-Conakry period saw a variety of obstacles put in the way of the peace plan. By January 1998 it became apparent that peaceful negotiations and sanctions had failed to resolve the crisis. ECOWAS therefore resorted to the use of force in order to oust the illegal regime. On 9 February 1998, a Nigerian-led ECOMOG force launched a pro-democracy invasion of the capital, code named 'Operation Sand Storm'. By the end of February, the military was overthrown and an ECOWAS Task-Force comprising Col. Max Khobe and the Vice-President Albert Demby constituted the ad hoc administrative body to supervise the affairs of state before the return of the ousted president. As a confidence building measure, a cross-section of West African leaders and the international community accompanied President Kabbah on 10 March 1998. Present at the re-installation ceremony were General Sani Abacha, Guinean President Lansant Conte; Nigerian President Ibrahim Bare Mainassara; the OAU and ECOWAS Secretaries General; the UN Special Representative and ECOWAS Foreign Ministers. Ed O'Loughlin writing in *The Independent* opined that 'When forces acting in the name of democracy overthrow a dictatorship, the international community is supposed to applaud. But when a Nigerian-led peace-keeping force chased Major Johnny Koroma's military junta from Freetown, the world responded with only a polite murmur . . . foreign diplomats in the region say their governments feel unable to congratulate Nigeria too publicly'.[18] This, of course, was understandable, given Nigeria's anti-democratic and human rights violation record which resulted in its international isolation.

Divisive Geo-politics in the Defence of Democracy

Nigeria's dominant role in the defence of democracy in Sierra Leone has generated considerable debate. Some critics contend that Nigeria's posturing was simply part of a 'Pax Nigeriana' designed to dominate the region. This criticism however underestimates the realities of the Sierra Leone crisis and its impact on regional peace and security. The post-Cold War international neglect of Africa means that the UN and Western powers cannot and will not any longer police African problems. Africa's security must therefore be its own responsibility. In the case of West Africa, whether desired or not, Nigeria has the capacity and potential to provide leadership for regional security. Nevertheless some observers see UN support for a Nigerian-led ECOMOG as 'a blue leaf and legitimacy for Nigeria's gun boat diplomacy' in West Africa.[19]

The use of force prior to UN Security Council authorisation is another contested issue. It has been argued that Nigeria's aerial bombardment of Freetown on the 2, 12 and 13 June 1998 was illegal, since the ECOWAS Authority had not met to give its formal approval, and was without Security Council authorisation. Did this therefore constitute a violation of the sovereignty and territorial integrity of Sierra Leone? The AFRC junta was quick to label it a naked act of Nigerian aggression and a violation of the state's political sovereignty. Arguably this could not be the case. Actually, there was no legitimate government in Sierra Leone. The military regime was recognised neither domestically nor internationally and as such lacked any semblance of internal and external claim to sovereignty. The ousted president was still internationally recognised as the legitimate head of state as was evident in his attendance at the June OAU summit, the August ECOWAS summit and the Commonwealth Heads of State and Government summit in Edinburgh in 1997. The military junta could not claim territorial integrity as they had no control over the territory of Sierra Leone. The Civil Defence Force - the Kamajors, together with the RUF, effectively controlled the eastern and southern parts of the country. Even the Nigerian military intervention was at the request of the ousted civilian president. That request was within the ambit of the bilateral defence agreement between the two countries under the Status of Forces Agreement (SOFA). Some critics argue that the defence agreement between former Presidents Babangida and Momoh was only a goodwill gesture, and did not amount to any formal agreement to ensure the re-instatement of any government overthrown. Arguably, however, the Nigerian intervention was not in breach of sovereignty, given the collapsed nature of the state.

Perhaps it is on humanitarian grounds that the use of force can be most easily justified. In the aftermath of 25 May coup Sierra Leone degenerated into chaos and anarchy, with serious repercussions in terms of loss of lives and destruction of property. Complex emergency situations such as Somalia and Rwanda, have increasingly seen the jettisoning of traditional notions of non-intervention. Forcible humanitarian intervention seems to be gradually gaining credence in the post-Cold War period. Although it could be said that Nigeria was only acting on the request of the *de jure* president, the initial occupation of the international airport and imposition of a land, sea and air blockade on the country by the Nigerian-led ECOMOG had no legal basis. To some extent, therefore, it amounted to a violation of the UN Charter as provided for in Chapter VIII. However, the complex emergency situation in Sierra Leone made the Nigerian-led ECOMOG intervention part of a much larger debate on what can be acceptable breaches of international law.

The ECOWAS intervention has set a new security agenda in world politics, that is, restorer/defender of a democratic system and constitutional order in the region.[20] This in itself is a major departure from the coup-prone public image of West Africa. Arguably, ECOWAS intervention has politically helped to lay the foundation for the proscription of *coups d'etat* in West Africa. It takes Africa beyond the situation in Burundi in 1996 when the military overthrew the democratically elected government. There was a chorus of half-hearted condemnation of that coup and the region's economic grouping imposed sanctions. But the Burundian situation was largely perceived as an internal affair, and in the absence of a regional hegemon and UN support, the military junta was able to stay in power and to this day still constitutes the *de facto* government of the country. Even so, it is premature to conclude that ECOWAS' democratic intervention will deter further coups in West Africa. The recent military coups in Guinea-Bissau, Niger and Côte d'Ivoire in 1999 have not led to any form of intervention from ECOWAS.

In the defence of democracy in Sierra Leone, three issues have become prominent, i.e. the tensions and divisiveness inherent in a regional collective political and security co-operation, the vested interests of the major actors; and the domestic and international implications of the ECOWAS democratic intervention. By all indications, the Sierra Leone coup and the ECOWAS democratic intervention have repercussions far beyond the borders of Sierra Leone. The ECOWAS defence of democracy in Sierra Leone revealed tensions and divisions in West African politics, often simply described as the Anglophone, Francophone and Lusophone divide. There was constant disagreement about the use of force to reverse the military coup in Sierra Leone. ECOWAS member states such as Ghana, Togo, Liberia and Burkina Faso expressed strong reservations about the use of force in defence of democracy. They cited the high human casualties and destruction of property that would accompany such an act, even though it became increasingly apparent that some show of force or use of force was necessary to make the coup leaders see the futility of their actions. The reservation expressed by some of the regional leaders is not surprising because some of them have either been warlords or coup makers and are hardly committed to genuine democracy in their respective states. Their opposition to the use of force was a front to hide their resentment of Nigeria's exercise of hegemony, and a mask for their opposition to such a precedent that might be used against them in future. They were also faced with the dilemma of choosing between acquiescence in the familiar tradition of coups and implementing a new regional political and security initiative with all its accompanying military adventurism.

Democratic intervention: New Political Order or Co-operative Exploitation?

The democratic intervention by ECOWAS set a new political and security precedent in post-colonial Africa. Democratic intervention is an activity undertaken by a state, a group of states or a regional or international organisation which intervenes forcibly in the internal affairs of another state with the objective of establishing law and order and restoring democratic governance or create a conducive environment for holding democratic elections. It is inextricably linked with collective forcible humanitarian intervention, that is, intervention motivated by humanitarian considerations. It is important to note that there can also be non-forceful democratic interventions, such as the UN's involvement in Namibia's founding elections. So far, most examples of democratic intervention have been occasioned by the fragmentation of political authority and the collapse of the state apparatus as a result of civil war or military intervention in civilian politics.[21] In these situations, where governmental authority has ceased to exist, democratic intervention offers an insurance policy for post-conflict societies. The role of ECOWAS in Sierra Leone can be placed within this framework. It is correct to say that such interventions breach the traditional norms of international society.[22] But, somewhat like the democratic intervention of the UN in Cambodia, Mozambique and Angola, and ECOWAS in Liberia, they also amount to issuing a certificate of legitimacy to reconfigured states, where the state has been on the verge of collapse or has collapsed in all but name. Hence the interventions actually endorse the familiar state basis of international society.

Furthermore, Walzer argues that the use of force in complex humanitarian emergencies should be employed as part of a long-term project of conflict-resolution and political, economic and social reconstruction.[23] Joaquin Tacsan argues that 'intervention for the protection of democracy is an established principle in the western hemisphere, but it does not seem to be a fully recognised entitlement in the universal context'.[24] The Organisation of American States (OAS) has provided hemispheric leadership for the promotion of democracy and human rights in the Americas for example, seeking the restoration of democratic order in Peru, Guatemala and Haiti. In fact, the OAS has given creative interpretation of the doctrines of sovereignty and non-intervention in respect of regional collective action in 'matters concerning the survival of a democratic government'.[25]

The ECOWAS democratic intervention in Sierra Leone can thus be seen as part of the normative development in international law and politics, especially as the intervention has not been limited to the formal restoration of democracy but has also been involved in such peacebuilding efforts as the re-organisation and retraining of the army and police forces, and disarmament and demobilisation of combatants. There are therefore some striking similarities to the American-led OAS initiative in Haiti. The OAS recognised deposed President Aristide as the legitimate president and sanctioned economic, financial and arms embargos on Haiti. This provided the basis for UN-OAS co-operation, thereby legitimising OAS intervention. Similarly, the UN-ECOWAS partnership legitimised intervention in Sierra Leone. When the Cedras military junta in Haiti rejected the Protocol of Washington of 23 February 1992 calling for peaceful resolution of the crisis, the OAS was driven to invoke the provisions of Chapter VIII of the UN Charter which authorised enforcement actions. The justification was that Haiti posed a threat to regional peace and security. Similarly, when Koroma's AFRC regime in Sierra Leone reneged on its promise to settle the crisis peacefully, ECOWAS secured Security Council authorisation for the enforcement of its own peace plan, in Resolution 1132.

However, a post-mortem examination would also reveal some less savoury aspects as well. The mercenary company Sandline International, which assisted ECOMOG in ousting the military junta was motivated by the desire to exploit mineral resources - a link between low-intensity conflicts and commercial rivalry over strategic minerals which has been examined in detail elsewhere.[26] DiamondWorks, a multinational company with which Sandline had business dealings, secured major mining concessions in the diamond-rich southern province. Nigeria took the lead in the restoration of constitutional rule in Sierra Leone possibly because it hoped to install a puppet government and in turn tie the political autonomy and national security of the country to Nigeria. The Nigerian Brigadier General Max Khobe has in fact been appointed Chief of Defence Staff by the restored president. Britain too as a result of commercial and political interests in this former colony co-operated with both the Nigerian military regime and Sandline in reinstating the ousted civilian government. *Africa Confidential* claims that America's intention was to limit the international credibility of the Nigerian military regime. That may or may not be true; but in effect the US's considerable financial and logistical support to ECOMOG propelled Nigeria into a leading role.

The foreign policy interest of Nigeria, Britain and the US in the restoration of democracy in Sierra Leone leads us towards a wider debate about the merits and/or propriety of humanitarian intervention. Realist and pluralist international society theorists argue that such democratic intervention masquerading as forcible humanitarian intervention, is nothing more than a front for the pursuit of national interests, and the pretext of humanitarian consideration is often abused by powerful states. But there are counter-arguments (associated with solidarist international society theorists) that maintain the promotion of human rights should be ranked alongside international peace and security as provided for in Articles 1 (3), 55 and 56 of the UN Charter. They further posit that common humanity necessitates correlative moral duties which legitimise collective humanitarian intervention, even on behalf of democracy.[27] Democratic intervention as part of the wider process of reconstructing collapsed states therefore has the potential to establish the foundation for universal respect for human rights and fundamental freedoms, equity and the rule of law. This will strengthen states, making them a stable pillars of the international system rather than undermining the international system in its present form.

ECOWAS-UN Co-operative Security in Sierra Leone

The 'strategic over-stretch' or over-burden of the UN in the 1990s and the inability of ECOWAS to respond effectively to violent intra-state conflicts has led to the emergence of a new form of co-operative security and task sharing between the world body and the West African regional community. Co-operative security is broadly conceptualised as regional and international responses and approaches to containing deadly civil wars within states as a viable mechanism for limiting the contagion effects of the war. It is a sort of 'fire brigade' response to civil wars, and to a large extent, legitimises the traditional state-centric approach to security.[28]

The co-operative security formula was first experimented within the African context during the Liberian civil war. According to the UN Secretary General Kofi Annan:

> If the Liberian conflict has a silver lining it was the very close working relations which we built up between ECOWAS and the United Nations. We developed a new form of co-operation which I am sure will serve as an important model of co-operation for the resolution of other conflicts, whether in Africa or elsewhere.[29]

The ECOWAS-UN co-operation in Sierra Leone is predicated on the assumption that co-operation with regional intergovernmental collective security organisations in the management and resolution of conflicts will reduce the burden of maintaining international peace and security through task sharing.[30] ECOWAS-UN co-operative security and task sharing is a practical realisation of systematic co-operation between the UN and a regional organisation as envisaged in Chapter VIII of the UN Charter. ECOWAS-UN co-operative security and task sharing has been manifested in the following areas: facilitating and negotiating the civil war peace settlement; peacekeeping; and peacebuilding and reconstruction.

Facilitating and Negotiating Civil War Peace Settlement

The UN, in collaboration with other governments, regional intergovernmental organisations and NGOs, has been instrumental in facilitating and negotiating settlement of the civil war in Sierra Leone. The UN mobilised its diplomatic, political and economic resources to find a negotiated settlement of the conflict in view of the effects of the civil war on regional peace and security, and gross violations of human rights perpetuated by all parties to the conflict. Following the outbreak of the civil war in Sierra Leone, the UN worked closely with ECOWAS and other intergovernmental organisations to help bring peace to the country. The UN supported the re-introduction of democratic governance in war-torn Sierra Leone and encouraged the ECOWAS peace negotiation processes. The co-operation between ECOWAS, UN, OAU, Commonwealth and other NGOs led to the signing of the Abidjan Peace Accord in 1996 between the RUF and the government of Sierra Leone under the auspices of the president of Côte d'Ivoire Henri Konan Bedie, in his capacity as ECOWAS chairman. The Abidjan Peace accord was suspended when the Kabbah regime in May 1997 was overthrown. Against the background of the heavy investment of the UN in facilitating peace making and efforts to reach a negotiated settlement of the civil war, the military intervention by the AFRC was to derail all these efforts. The UN therefore supported the diplomatic and political initiative of ECOWAS to internationally isolate the military junta, and refused to recognise the regime as constituting the government of Sierra Leone.

UN Security Council Resolution 1132 on the Sierra Leone crisis gave legal backing to the ECOWAS initiative. The resolution imposed comprehensive mandatory sanctions and an embargo on the military regime. The UN enjoined all states and regional organisations to strictly adhere to the sanctions on Sierra Leone. A special committee on Sierra

Leone was established by the Security Council to oversee the implementation of sanctions. The Committee included Sweden, Costa Rica and Kenya, countries presumably selected for their neutrality on the Sierra Leone crisis. To facilitate liaison and effective co-ordination, the UN Secretary General appointed a Special Envoy, Francis Okello, to work with the ECOWAS Committee on Sierra Leone.

The UN also played an influential role in supporting ECOWAS' political and diplomatic efforts to restore constitutional rule. ECOWAS Ambassadors at the UN also played a crucial role in lobbying the Security Council to support ECOWAS' peace and democratic efforts in Sierra Leone. In the deliberations leading to the adoption of resolution 1132, the Permanent Representative of the Republic of Korea to the UN stated that:

> ...the action we take today will set yet another example of the success of co-ordinated approach between the Security Council and regional organisations in addressing conflict situations in Africa. What is at stake is the great cause of democracy and we therefore believe that the international community should continue to stand as one in prevailing upon the junta that there is no compromise on this principle.[31]

The May 25 coup in Sierra Leone therefore became a litmus test to measure the commitment and sincerity of the UN, ECOWAS and liberal democracies to global democratic governance and the rule of law.

The diplomatic and political support of the UN contributed to the signing of the Conakry Peace agreement between the illegal military junta and ECOWAS on behalf of the exiled government of President Kabbah. The Conakry accord was overtaken by the overthrow of the military junta by the Nigerian-led ECOMOG force. Perhaps the most important contribution of ECOWAS-UN task sharing is in the negotiation of the Lomé Peace Accord of 7 July 1999.[32]

The Lomé Peace Accord is the most important peace settlement which formally ended the armed conflict between the government and the warring factions, though armed hostilities still continued. This reinforces the point that merely signing a peace document will not immediately end a civil war or guarantee sustainable peace. The Lomé agreement was a political settlement which provided a framework for power sharing and a blanket amnesty. A broad-based government of national unity through cabinet appointment legitimised the RUF Leader Foday Sankoh as a major political player. Sankoh was offered the chairmanship of the board of the Commission for the Management of Strategic Resources with the status of Vice-President, in effect, giving him control of the diamond resources. The RUF was transformed into a political party with four cabinet positions and four deputy ministers. The Lomé Accord further granted the RUF leader absolute and free pardon, as well as a blanket amnesty for all war crimes and gross violations of human rights by all combatants since the start of the conflict in 1991.

The UN, ECOWAS and Sierra Leone's western backers have been criticised for sponsoring an unjust civil war peace settlement. The power sharing deal has been criticised as a political forge potentially detrimental to genuine post-war justice and reconciliation. It has also been criticised as a mechanism for rewarding political violence.[33] The blanket amnesty provision provoked serious controversy both domestically and internationally because of the implications of leaving war crimes unpunished under international law and humanitarian conventions relating to the conduct of war. The UN, despite playing a vital role in negotiating the Lomé Accord, issued a disclaimer that it would not recognise any amnesty granted to rebels and soldiers. Generally, the blanket amnesty provision bartered crimes against humanity for fragile peace and security; in effect, it sacrificed justice for stability. Francis argues that:

> After years of de-legitimizing the RUF and branding Sankoh a war criminal, London and Washington pressured the Kabbah regime to do business with him as a 'legitimate' political actor. The Lomé agreement is a product of a hastily negotiated peace settlement, preoccupied with short-term objectives and glossing over issues of justice . . . .[34]

In an attempt to deflect international criticism, Britain, America and the UN, whilst supporting the Lomé agreement as the only alternative for war-torn Sierra Leone, also endeavoured not to exclude the possibility of prosecutions for crimes against humanity. In fact, as far as the British minister for Africa Peter Hain was concerned, 'it was a myth that Britain and the US foisted the Lomé peace agreement on the people of Sierra Leone; on the contrary, it was negotiated by President Kabbah ... and supported by the various African organisations involved.'[35] It is obvious that, had this Faustian deal being successful, the British, Americans and UN, who helped broker the peace agreement, would have been the first to claim credit for their efforts in bringing about a peace settlement in Sierra Leone.

UN Peacekeeping in Sierra Leone: From Humiliation to Strategic Rethinking

The UN Security Council resolution 1132 legalised ECOMOG's

peacekeeping and enforcement operations in Sierra Leone, and made it possible for the deployment of a United Nations Observer Mission in Sierra Leone (UNOMSIL). The mandate of UNOMSIL was to provide security for UN staff and humanitarian relief agencies, and assist in the post-war peacebuilding in such areas as disarmament, demobilisation and reintegration of ex-combatants. The Lomé peace accord provided for the phased withdrawal of the Nigerian-led ECOMOG and the deployment of an expanded peacekeeping force and new mandate under UNAMSIL. Resolution 1270 established UNAMSIL to takeover the functions of UNOMSIL, and created the UN's largest peacekeeping force in the world, totaling 11,000. The peacekeeping force included contingents from Kenya, Zambia, India, Nigeria, Ghana, Guinea, Bangladesh, Jordan, Russia and some ECOMOG contingents.

After the withdrawal of ECOMOG, the UN peacekeeping mission was humiliated by the RUF, the rebel faction that the UN sponsored in the controversial Lomé peace deal. In a dispute over the disarmament and demobilisation of RUF combatants, the RUF responded by taking hostage more than 500 UN peacekeepers and killed 4 soldiers in May 2000. The largely ill-equipped, un-coordinated and poorly armed UN peacekeepers were powerless and lacked the robust mandate needed to respond to RUF aggression and for their breaking the terms of the Lomé Accord. The near collapse of UN peacekeeping in Sierra Leone was internationally criticised. The UN was criticised for the failure of its troops to use force to defend itself, and for sending poorly-armed peacekeeping troops into a conflict zone. The humiliation of the UN peacekeepers in Sierra Leone evoked memories of spectacular failures of recent UN peacekeeping operations in Rwanda, Somalia, and Bosnia-Herzegovina. The UN peacekeeping mission in Sierra Leone was salvaged from a humiliating failure by the intervention of well-equipped, heavily armed British paratroopers and special forces. The military intervention by Britain prevented the capture of the city by the RUF, and stabilised the UN peacekeeping forces.

The humiliation and near failure of UN peacekeeping in Sierra Leone is to some extent the result of the politics of peacekeeping. From Bosnia to Somalia and Rwanda, it has been recognised that sending peacekeepers into conflict zones without a robust mandate and effective fighting force would only create the recipe for failure and disaster. In the case of Sierra Leone, most of the major powers were reluctant to contribute troops to the UN peacekeeping force. America still suffers from the 'hangover' of the Somalia syndrome, and though a staunch supporter of the Sierra Leone peace settlement, would not commit the involvement of US troops in Sierra Leone. Even the commitment of the new UNAMSIL contingent to enforcing the peace has been questionable. This resulted in the all too easy disarming of UN peacekeepers and the holding of hundreds as hostages by the RUF.

The personality conflict, institutional and regional rivalries have compromised the effectiveness of UN peacekeeping in Sierra Leone. The ECOMOG high command, supported by the Nigerian government, and the Indian-led UNAMSIL commander have had a fractious working relationship. A scathing report on the crisis in Sierra Leone written by the UNAMSIL Commander, Gen. Jetley stated:

> The accord called for deployment of a peacekeeping force comprising ECOMOG and UNOMSIL to oversee the peace process. This was interpreted by the Nigerians [who formed the major chunk of ECOMOG] that ECOMOG would form a major part of the UN peacekeeping Force and that this Force would be headed by the ECOMOG Force Commander Maj. Gen. Kpamber. However when Gen. Kpamber went to UNHQ New York, he was very disappointed to learn that he was not going to be the Force Commander of UNAMSIL...The Nigerians therefore felt that they were not getting a fair deal in the peace process in Sierra Leone despite the sacrifices they had made to pave the way for the peace process . . .It is my opinion that the ECOMOG Force Commander along with the SRSG and DCF have worked hard to sabotage the peace process and show Indians in general and me in particular in a poor light ... keeping the Nigerian interests was paramount even if it meant scuttling the peace process and this also implied that UNAMSIL was expendable.[36]

Metaphorically, therefore, whilst these two 'elephants' were fighting, the grass (people of Sierra Leone and the peace process) suffered considerably. Furthermore, the failure of the peacekeeping mission was not only due to the criminal complicity of some elements of Nigerian-led ECOMOG with the RUF in the exploitation of the diamond resources, but also logistical difficulties made UNAMSIL peacekeeping an impossible task to accomplish. The UNAMSIL forces were adversely affected by lack of effective communications equipment, limited fuel, water, food rations, inadequate camp infrastructure, and the inadequate military capability of units such as the Guineans, Kenyans and Zambians. Therefore, General Jetley's conclusion is that:

> UN peacekeeping operations are a combination of diplomacy and tact. Generally in African countries the Peace Accord signed is shaky and fragile. In a mineral rich country like Sierra Leone, politics has a very major role to play in finding solutions to civil wars. In my case, the Mission Directive given to me and which I tried to follow implicitly,

directly conflicted with the interests of not only the warring factions but also of the major players in the diamond racket like Liberia and Nigeria.[37]

There has been ample evidence to substantiate the allegations of General Jetley against some key Nigerian-ECOMOG Officers and its implication for the ineffectiveness and failure of UN peacekeeping. For instance, the close working relationship between the ECOMOG Force Commander and the RUF in the immediate Post-Lomé period led some Sierra Leoneans to describe Gen. Kpamber as 'Sankoh's ADC'. Also, some senior Western diplomats based in Nigeria confirmed the allegations of diamond smuggling and drug running by the Nigerian military in both Liberia and Sierra Leone.[38] However, it is difficult to substantiate the claims of these western diplomats given the covert nature of any such complicity between the Nigerian army and the RUF. It would also be erroneous to generalise such a claim for the Nigerian forces in Sierra Leone. The UN and US have also been criticised for their failure to support Gen. Jetley in the crisis over his allegations that senior Nigerian ECOMOG officers were making the peacekeeping objectives difficult to accomplish. Their failure to support Gen. Jetley was a realist political ploy not to antagonise the Nigerian leadership, given the country's dominant role in ECOMOG. The only exit strategy was for the UN, with the support of Britain and America, to acquiesce to the demands of Nigeria who called for the replacement of Gen. Jetley. ECOWAS had earlier called for the replacement of the Indian-led UNAMSIL commander with a Nigerian Commander who is familiar with the dynamics of the civil war in Sierra Leone and African realism. Gen. Jetley had since being replaced by Lt. General Daniel Opande, the Deputy Chief of General Staff of the Kenyan armed forces. The replacement of Jetley led to the withdrawal of the Indian contingent from UNAMSIL. The above analysis shows that the politics of regionalism invariably affects peacekeeping operations.

The ECOWAS community, based on the ECOMOG peacekeeping and enforcement experience in Liberia and Sierra Leone, has been instrumental in pressurising the UN to change its peacekeeping mandate from the traditional neutral inter-positionary force, to peace enforcement as the only means to stabilise war-torn countries. The humiliation and near collapse of UN peacekeeping in Sierra Leone has led to a fundamental strategic rethinking of UN peacekeeping in the world. After the May peacekeeping crisis, the UNAMSIL contingent was increased to 13,000, with most of the additional troops coming from Nigerian-led ECOMOG. The expansion of UNAMSIL made it the largest UN peacekeeping force in the world. In August 2000 a further expansion of UNAMSIL to 20,500 troops was recommended by Kofi Annan. In recognition of the limitations of its traditional peacekeeping, UNAMSIL's mandate has been expanded to incorporate implicit peace enforcement activities. Annan recommended that UNAMSIL be provided with 'special equipment that is not usually associated with traditional peacekeeping duties'.[39] This 'special equipment' includes: night vision; laser range finding and designation equipment; surveillance and target acquisition equipment; and global positioning systems equipment and radar.

The ECOWAS-UN task sharing in the resolution of the civil war in Sierra Leone has fundamentally affected the nature and scope of UN peacekeeping. UNAMSIL has become the largest and most challenging UN peacekeeping deployment in the world. The US representative to the United Nations, Richard Holbrooke, opines that 'It could be a mistake to see the tragedy of Sierra Leone as a metaphor for all of Africa or for the failure of all United Nations peacekeeping'.[40] The humiliation of UN peacekeeping in Sierra Leone warranted the setting up of the Lakhdar Brahimi Commission to review UN Peace and Security operations. The Brahimi Report recommended changes to the traditional concept of peacekeeping. Though it endorsed the traditional principles of consent of parties and impartiality of UN operations, the report recommended the need for a robust, well-armed and well-equipped peacekeeping force, with realistic mandates, and the imperative to distinguish between the victim and the aggressor. The report further recommended that 'Rules of engagement should be sufficiently robust and not force UN contingents to cede the initiative to attackers'.[41] In addition, the report recommended the creation of a kind of rapid reaction force, a multinational, brigade-size force with capacity for speedy deployment to complement the UN Standby Arrangement System through which member states commit a unit for peacekeeping operations at short notice.[42] At the UN Millennium Summit in September 2000, a special session of the Security Council approved strengthening the capacity and mandate of UN peacekeeping, especially in Africa. Jean Kamara argues that:

> Sierra Leone has become a special test case for the UN in its role as the keeper of world peace. But what the UN does in Sierra Leone may just be the beginning of a change that is coming to UN peacekeeping activities ... Sierra Leone will therefore serve to test the willingness of UN member states to make peacekeeping work.[43]

The international solidarity to salvage the UN peacekeeping operation in Sierra Leone is a manifestation of how the backing of major powers such as America and Britain is instrumental to the success of any peacekeeping operation.

In response to international criticism of the UN for sponsoring an unjust peace and for the near failure of peacekeeping in Sierra Leone, in order to burnish its battered image the UN came up with two important recommendations on the Sierra Leone crisis:

> i. The imposition of a UN ban on the sale of Sierra Leone diamonds until the recognised government develops a system of certification for official diamond production and sales. This was subsequently introduced.
> ii. Recommend the formation of an international war crimes tribunal to try those guilty of gross violations of human rights and atrocities committed during the civil war.

The special war crimes tribunal would be largely modelled on the international criminal courts for Rwanda and former Yugoslavia. The mandate for the war crimes court covers 'those most responsible' for the conflict in Sierra Leone, i.e. those responsible for mass killings, extra-judicial executions, widespread mutilations, sexual violence against girls and women, the abduction of thousands of children and adults, forced labour and recruitment into armed groups, looting and burning of urban dwelling and villages.[44] The special court would have jurisdiction to prosecute those accused of crimes against humanity, war crimes and other seroius breaches of international humanitarian law in connection with the 9-year conflict.[45]

A major limitation of the court is that its temporary jurisdiction would extend to acts committed since 30 November 1996, the date for the signing of the first peace accord (Abidjan). The crucial question is what happens to the perpetrators and victims of war crimes and breaches of international law between March 1991 and October 1996? It could be argued that this limited jurisdiction is hardly the means to address the important issue of justice and lasting peace in post-war Sierra Leone. Another contentious issue is the proposed prosecution of minors. The prosecution of children has been acknowledged by the UN Secretary General as a 'difficult moral dilemma'. However, Kofi Annan made the case that:

> more than in any other conflict where children have been used as combatants, in Sierra Leone, child combatants were initially abducted, forcibly recruited, sexually abused, reduced to slavery of all kinds and

trained, often under the influence of drugs, to kill, maim and burn. Though feared by many for their brutality, most if not all of these children have been subjected to a process of psychological and physical abuse and duress which has transformed them from victims into perpetrators.[46]

The prosecution of children, according to the recommendation, must be based on safeguards which include: a special juvenile chamber, due process protection, psychological counselling and rehabilitation, instead of imprisonment. The formation of an influential war crimes tribunal is a precedent in the West African sub-region and would potentially deter the excesses of insurgents, soldiers and warlords.

International Co-operation for Disarmament, Demobilisation and Re-integration

ECOWAS-UN co-operative security and task sharing has succeeded in mobilising international support for disarmament, demobilisation and re-integration (DDR) of ex-combatants. DDR has been a central element of all the civil war peace settlements in Sierra Leone. The Lomé Peace Accord provides for a DDR commission. The rationale is that disarming and dismantling warring factions, reducing the proliferation of arms in society and socially re-integrating ex-combatants are crucial to maintaining and sustaining security and stability for peacebuilding and reconstruction. Removing the instruments of violence through disarmament and demobilisation would limit the threat to the fragile peace process and allow the democratisation and development processes to recommence.

UNAMSIL is mandated with the responsibility to disarm and demobilise warring factions. UNAMSIL is given this responsibility because it is regarded by the warring factions as a neutral, impartial body that would generate confidence building in the DDR process. With the co-operation of ECOMOG, UNAMSIL organised the demobilisation camps, and supervised the disarmament of ex-combatants in collaboration with the Lomé mandated DDR Commission. The warring factions have come to view ECOMOG as a party to the conflict and its pro-government leanings have made it difficult for ex-combatants to disarm to ECOMOG forces or even allowed to be demobilised by them. UNAMSIL involvement was therefore crucial in providing credibility, confidence and a security guarantee for the disarmament and demobilisation of ex-combatants.

ECOWAS-UN task sharing has led to the involvement of major powers including key western governments and other NGOs in the peacebuilding and reconstruction process in Sierra Leone. Britain's political, diplomatic, military and financial support has been crucial in reaching a negotiated settlement of the civil war and facilitating the peacebuilding and reconstruction process. Britain, a key member of the UN Security Council, has used the platform to promote the case of war-torn Sierra Leone. Britain has also used its privileged and influential position in the IMF and World Bank to facilitate and mobilise international financial and economic support for post-war reconstruction. Britain has established and co-ordinated the International Contact Group on Sierra Leone.[47] Britain has also been influential in the reform of Sierra Leone's ineffective and politicised security sector. A senior British police officer, Keith Biddle is the Acting Inspector General of the Sierra Police Force. British forces are also training and restructuring the rag-tag national army. The head of the British forces in Sierra Leone, who works closely with both the UNAMSIL Commander and the Commander of the Sierra Leone Forces, is the *de facto* head and co-ordinator of the national armed forces. The British support for Sierra Leone may not necessarily be entirely altruistic. A variety of neo-colonial, strategic, political, diplomatic and economic motivations largely account for the British support for war-ravaged Sierra Leone. The British Prime Minister Tony Blair argued that Britain has 'historic responsibilities to Sierra Leone and British military intervention to bolster the fledging democracy and prevent humanitarian catastrophe in war-torn Sierra Leone fits in with the new Labour 'ethical foreign policy'.[48]

The British Ministry of Defence (MOD), with the tacit support of the Blair government, launched 'Operation Palliser' as a 'protective evacuation' of British nationals from Sierra Leone in May 2000. This paved the way for a full-scale military involvement and eventually led to the rescue of British hostages held by the rag-tag rebel faction, the so-called West Side Boys in September 2000. 'Operation Palliser' became the opportunity to test the MOD's capability for rapid deployment of British forces in conflict zones. According to the Defence Secretary Geoffrey Hoon 'The deployment of British Forces for a limited period on these tasks is a model of the rapid deployment concept that was at the heart of the Strategic Defence Review'.[49]

It becomes obvious that the internal politics of the MOD and the opportunity to test the rapid deployment capacity of the British defence establishment were also important considerations for British military involvement in Sierra Leone. One cannot but wonder at the rationale for deploying approximately 1,300 British troops, from the army, navy and air forces just for the protective evacuation of roughly 500 British nationals, the majority of whom were in Freetown. It is therefore not surprising that Sierra Leone has become a divisive party political issue in domestic British politics. The opposition Conservative party talks of 'mission creep' i.e. the possibility of being embroiled in a messy domestic conflict with no possible exit strategy. Sierra Leone has considerably contributed to the recent policy change of the new Labour government when it abandoned the phrase 'ethical foreign policy'.

The Nigerian government has also contributed to the post-war peacebuilding and reconstruction process through the training of the Sierra Leone Junior Officer corps at the Nigerian War College. According to diplomatic sources, the British government's criticism of other governments for being 'abandoned' in its efforts to bring peace and stability in war-torn Sierra Leone prompted the response of the American government. Though the US has contributed to the negotiation of the civil war peace settlements and post-war peacebuilding, it has not shown sustained commitment to the resolution of the civil war in Sierra Leone. After the collapse of the Lomé peace agreement in May, the Clinton administration refused a UN request to contribute to the peacekeeping force for Sierra Leone. Rachel Stohl observed that according to a report in *The New York Times* the US government 'tried to charge expensive rates for the use of Pentagon aircraft to ferry soldiers of other nations to Sierra Leone'.[50] In August 2000, President Clinton approved US$ 20 million of aid to enhance the military capability of the Nigerian and UN troops in the peacekeeping operations in Sierra Leone. In addition, the Clinton administration deployed US Special Forces to train the Nigerian-led peacekeeping forces in Sierra Leone. According to the US Under-Secretary of State Thomas Pickering, the objective was to:

> train and equip West African battalions that will then be dispatched to Sierra Leone to bolster beleaguered government troops and United Nations peacekeepers....Our goal is to return the freely elected government to full control of the territory of Sierra Leone and to get the guerrillas demobilised.[51]

However, some analysts are critical of the US military contribution to peacebuilding and reconstruction in war-torn societies. Rachel Stohl argues that exporting US military knowledge and expertise is not a substitute for peacebuilding and peacekeeping efforts. The US, as the world's largest arms exporter, and given its world market dominance considerably undermines its credibility to end armed conflicts in Africa.[52] Furthermore, the Clinton administration has been criticised for failing to do more in Sierra Leone before the January 1999 massacre; a massacre which shocked the world community through the CNN and BC direct impact effect. Prior to this, the OAU and ECOWAS had been abandoned to fend for themselves in terms of resolving the crisis in Sierra Leone. For instance, whilst ECOWAS was given a paltry $15 million dollars by the Clinton administration for its peace support operations in Sierra Leone, NATO was given billions of dollars for the bombing of Serbia in 1998 and for post-war reconstruction.[53]

ECOWAS Rescues the UN

What has emerged out of this strategic and systematic partnership between ECOWAS and UN is the potential capacity of the West African regional organisation to rescue the world body in the achievement of its primary objective of maintaining international peace and security. ECOMOG, which has been criticised on the grounds of 'how not to conduct peacekeeping operations outside the traditional UN framework', is now leading the debate on the new kind of partnership for security and development between regional organisations and UN. ECOWAS is therefore showing the way for other regional groupings such as the EU on how to conduct peacekeeping through UN co-operative security and task sharing. The ECOWAS-UN partnership is important because the UN peacekeeping roles in the Gulf region, Kosovo and Somalia demonstrates the growing inability of the world body to adequately respond to diverse conflicts faced by the international community.[54]

The ECOWAS-UN partnership helps deflect some of the political, and financial pressures on the world body in assuming direct responsibility for every conflict situation in the world. What is important about the ECOWAS-UN partnership is that it is a co-operative relationship beneficial to both. In fact, ECOWAS and ECOMOG conflict management and resolution in West Africa not only reduces the financial burden on the UN for a potentially costly and protracted civil war, but also helps the world body to fulfil its primary mission of maintaining international peace and security. The UN's moral, political and diplomatic authority and access to international financial resources lends international legitimacy to ECOWAS conflict management and resolution efforts in West Africa and in the process helps to revamp the largely ineffective economic community. Also, the legitimacy, structure and mandate of the UN provides the most impartial and preferred means for extra-regional involvement in local conflicts.[55] Clement Adibe therefore argues that the fact that 'the UN-ECOWAS partnership took place at all, given the circumstances of widespread fears of domination and mistrust, is indicative of progress in African diplomacy, in particular and inter-institutional co-operation in general'.[56]

However, it is argued that UN support and legitimacy for ECOMOG's peace enforcement actions in Sierra Leone have sometimes compromised UN impartiality. ECOMOG's *modus operandi* in Sierra Leone has not conformed with international law and humanitarian norms relating to the conduct of war. The documentary *Out of Africa* by Sorious Samura showed how ECOMOG troops have been involved in gross violations of human rights and summary executions of suspected rebels. Also, the lack of a peacekeeping doctrine and the non-accountable posture of ECOMOG's military operations have been criticised. Political analysts and media commentators argue that UN support of the Nigerian-led ECOMOG complex contingence operations is a blue leaf and legitimacy 'for Nigeria's gunboat diplomacy and dominance of West Africa.[57] The difficulty is that the UN cannot ensure the neutrality of ECOWAS and ECOMOG. In addition, though Chapter VIII of the Charter gives the UN primacy over regional organisations in the maintenance of international peace and security, the dominant role of the sub-regional hegemon, Nigeria, and the preponderance of its military forces ensured that the UN sometimes played 'second fiddle'. For example, Nigerian-led ECOWAS demanded and secured the change of the UNAMSIL commander and the large inclusion of Nigerian troops in UNAMSIL. However, this UN 'second fiddle' role is not only peculiar to West Africa. The intervention of NATO in the Kosovo crisis meant that the UN was forced to play 'second fiddle' to NATO.

ECOWAS and the Erosion of National Sovereignty

The question of constraints on national sovereignty has always plagued economic regionalisms. The move towards closer political and economic union, for example the adoption of a single currency in the EU, has brought to the fore the debate about the limitations, if not undermining effects, of integration on national sovereignty. The issue of sovereignty is even more contested in integration schemes in developing countries. It was clear from the outset that membership of ECOWAS would involve a substantial loss of national sovereignty in the light of the extended economic and social objectives of the Community Treaty, a fact not lost on member states in 1975. The preamble of the Treaty accepts the fact that the integration of member states into a viable regional community may demand the partial and gradual pooling of national sovereignty within the context of a collective political will. However, the politics of regionalism made the leaders of West Africa underestimate the constraints that go with this process. Even in the European Union, the status quo seems to remain the same for some time because Europe's nation states find it increasingly difficult to yield their sovereignty. In West Africa, national sovereignty is jealously guarded by community members.

The concept of sovereignty in international relations discourse has been used by political analysts, media commentators, jurists, government officials and politicians without identifying the sense in which they are using the term. Michael Fowler and Julie Bunck point out that the 'concept of sovereignty has been used not only in different senses by different people, or in different senses at different times by the same people, or in different senses by the same person in rapid succession'.[58] Like the elusive term 'national interest', the concept becomes a term of convenience at the service of government officials, political analysts, media commentators and politicians. Sovereignty denotes the capacity of the state to exert domestic political and external authority. Sovereignty is both a juridical status and a political concept. Some analysts contend that sovereignty is a legal fiction for the very fact that states take directives from some international institutions or regional economic groupings.[59]

The constraints on national sovereignty of Sierra Leone's ECOWAS regionalism have been most apparent in the following areas: economic and trade liberalisation policies; the free movement protocol; common regional political and security policies; and the supranationality provision. The implementation of regional trade, political and security decisions and measures often conflict with the national economic interest of the state. Sierra Leone, like other community partners, depends to a great extent on revenue from import and export duties and its primary industries need some degree of protection from external competition. Yet in the interest of ECOWAS regionalism, the country has had to commit itself to eliminate customs duties and establish a common external tariff. The huge loss of revenue to the government is a serious constraint on the fiscal sovereignty of the state. The former President of The Gambia, Dauda Jawara, commenting on the historic ECOWAS Treaty, noted that 'the co-operation the Community would require might impose hardship on certain countries, not necessarily the least developed'.[60]

For ECOWAS to work effectively and for member states to accrue meaningful benefits, they have to cede some degree of sovereignty to the Community, some 'pooling of sovereignty'. Governments have to grasp the fact that the signing of the ECOWAS treaty is bound to bring some unanticipated consequences. It is doubtful whether Sierra Leone, like other Community countries, fully appreciated the implications that membership of ECOWAS would necessitate a loss of sovereignty over economic and commercial policies in a way unprecedented among the newly independent African states. All the member states in 1975, whether capitalist or socialist, agreed to free movement of persons, goods and capital in the service of economic development. It inevitably made it difficult to exercise total economic autonomy. General Olusegun Obasanjo of Nigeria in his remark at the opening of the 1977 ECOWAS Heads of state summit opined that 'There is no easy way of achieving ECOWAS' objectives, . . . As we urged here, ECOWAS necessitates a loss of sovereignty over economic and commercial policy of a kind unprecedented in Africa'.[61] The paradox of levelling of national barriers to the free flow of the factors of production required a substantial transfer of sovereignty to Community institutions. Thus, the integration body becomes a powerful and intrusive influence on national politics.

Successful economic regionalism requires not only a harmonisation of trade policies but also of fiscal and monetary policies. This form of policy integration may well conflict with other national policy objectives. Generally, the pursuit of economic and development goals might in some circumstances be impossible without external co-operation and a degree of pooling of sovereignty. Chris Brown, using the example of the pooling of sovereignty in the Universal Postal Union, states that:

> The bundle of power that a state posses as a sovereign body is thereby simultaneously diminished and enhanced - the state now has the capacity to set up an effective postal system, but it buys this capacity by giving up part of its capacity to regulate this system, because there are now rules it must accept if it wishes to remain part of the wider body, that is, if it wishes to preserve its capacity to exercise its sovereign powers and run an effective postal service.[62]

Brown's conclusion is that for a state to be truly sovereign it may have to surrender part of its national sovereignty. ECOWAS therefore provides the platform for a significant derogation of sovereignty. However, developing nations such as Sierra Leone, are increasingly unwilling to surrender their juridical status as sovereign, but yet attempt to effectively exercise their political sovereignty, thereby creating an extensive network of governance dilemmas. This could be regarded as the paradox of sovereignty. Sovereignty itself is a colonial legacy, something which the African states cling to with almost 'primitive loyalty', but at the same time they want to make a total break with colonialism and all its vestiges, except for a few Francophone West Africans. The dynamics of the global market economy shows that the requirements of multinational co-operation driven by the ever increasing volume of transnational flows have led to a growing appreciation among states of the obsolescence of traditional notions of sovereignty. Righter considers the 'demythification of sovereignty' as having started in the poor countries as illustrated in the India and Zimbabwe proposal to develop 'general principles and guidelines' for intervention to create 'corridors of peace or tranquillity' during the Security Council meeting in January 1992.[63]

The harmonisation of economic policies is interpreted by some national policy makers as a loss of something they have spent many years waiting for, i.e. political independence. Though Sierra Leone has in some cases adopted indigenisation policies to protect the economic interests of its citizens, it has not ruled out joint endeavours in the form of economic regionalism. It has been argued that even if economic regionalism 'holds out the promise of improving the viability and performance of each territorial economy, the problem exists of reconciling itself to economic (real or apparent) sacrifice of part or all of its sovereignty'.[64] The dynamics of economic and political co-operation within ECOWAS has shown that it will always be difficult for the political leadership in West Africa to surrender a substantial measure of its sovereignty when its feels insecure and see the basis of its claim to national leadership eroded by regional policies. In recognition of this problem, the ECOWAS Executive Secretary in his 1982 report noted that:

> There are important and crucial variables such as national interest and ceding of some aspects of national sovereignty which are not normally given the weight they deserve in the analysis but which are crucial for the success of any integration among developing countries. As the work of the Community is based on consensus, our activities are sometimes bogged down because member states are unwilling to part with some aspect of national interest for the greater benefit of the Community.[65]

However, recent trends within the Community seem to indicate that member states have gradually taken cognisance of the fact that there is no such thing as absolute national sovereignty, and that if they want to exploit the benefits of regionalism, then they must pool their sovereignties. The popularity and controversy generated by the free movement aspect of the regionalisation process highlights the threats to national sovereignty as perceived by the state. On the other hand, it is arguable that this type of regionalism indirectly weakens the ability of the government to control its territory. The emphasis on open regionalism and its free market principles inevitably calls into question governments right to regulate the economy.

Another area of constraint on national sovereignty is regional political and security co-operation. As has already been shown, Sierra Leone's participation in the common ECOWAS political and security process, i.e. ECOMOG, entails a substantial erosion of national sovereignty. When Sierra Leone signed the ECOWAS economic charter it did not anticipate that subsequent political and security co-operation would lead to a virtual surrender of its territory to the regional security body. The December 1999 ECOWAS Protocol relating to the Mechanism for Conflict Prevention, Management, Resolution, Peace-Keeping and Security contains further restrictions that would erode the sovereignty of the state. However, the politics of regionalism as an aspect of economic development, and its interdependent forces invariably create negative consequences not originally anticipated. The increasing relevance of market-led interdependence, coupled with the need for regional peace and stability leads to an erosion of legal autonomy of member states. Sierra Leone is gradually shifting from being a national decision maker to 'co-decision maker' at ECOWAS level. It is this governance dilemma that makes the doctrine of 'naive sovereignty' counterproductive. As Shirley Williams puts it: 'Governments do not sacrifice their powers absolutely. That is why sovereignty has been pooled rather than transferred'.[66] In a variety of ways the ECOWAS defence protocols and the regional political and security approach do have constraining effects on the state, in spite of its putative benefits. It has therefore been argued that clinging to sovereignty in the process of economic development under modern conditions has the adverse effect of relegating development and growth to the sidelines. Peter Gray is of the view that 'countries which are not willing to denounce the desire for nationhood or which have lost any opportunity to achieve the minimum standard of economic efficiency required, may be condemned to a perpetuity of underdevelopment'.[67]

An area that has generated a lot of debate is the impact of the Free Movement Protocol on the sovereignty of the state. At the signing of the ECOWAS Treaty in 1975, President Stevens was more cautious about the free movement proposal and even urged member states to delay decision on this matter until an 'ECOWAS consciousness' within the countries had been created. As far as Stevens was concerned, there was no point in adopting a decision that would be difficult to implement. Stevens' ECOWAS consciousness argument was only a front for securing the national interest of the state. Stevens, like the majority of Sierra Leoneans, was mindful of the considerable economic, political and social impact an unrestricted free movement of persons would have on the economy. The diamondiferous areas of the country were already overcrowded because of a huge influx of foreign nationals, mostly West Africans. The ECOWAS protocol on free movement envisaged a common people - citizens of the Community. In spite of its popularity, it remains even today a politically sensitive matter. The free movement, right of residence and establishment entails elimination of national discriminatory laws relating to employment and working conditions. It has led to intense competition from West African nationals for scarce jobs. Some of these migrant workers are ready to work for wages far below the national average, thereby exacerbating the unemployment problem. Their presence creates the need for more social overheads in terms of schools, health and social services facilities. The diamond areas are the worst affected regions of the country. In 1979, government refused entry to 200 Ghanaians on the grounds that they intended to settle and become fishermen and bakers in the coastal towns. The influx of West African nationals has often led to closure of the Sierra Leone borders, and to the actual expulsion of illegal immigrants from the country in 1982, even though this went against the spirit of the ECOWAS Treaty. However, the protocol did not provide for a free for all movement of persons. It specifically stipulates that in the interest of national security appropriate measures could be taken by member states. Some of these immigrants, with diverse religious and political persuasions have constituted a threat to the security of the state. The Fullahs from Guinea and the Via from Liberia have often been prominent in domestic political crises in the country. During general elections, they have been mobilised as thugs by unscrupulous politicians. It has been pointed out that the invading rebel force in 1991 took advantage of the free movement protocol and the porous border to attack Sierra Leone. However, this is a general ECOWAS problem and each member state has adopted different policies on how to address the problem.

The supranationality provision of the treaty is another area for potential derogation of sovereignty. The revised ECOWAS Treaty provides for supranationality, in that legislation passed by the Authority of the Community and the Council of Ministers becomes binding on member states after 90 days. In international law, decisions made by international organisations on the basis of ratified treaties have precedence over national laws. In the same way, EU legislations have precedence over national laws of member states whenever they run into conflict. This therefore implies that ratifying the ECOWAS Treaty, results in a general obligation for member states to comply with Community legislation. The traditional decision-making principle of consensus has now been replaced by a supranationality within ECOWAS regionalism. The increasing volume and scope of ECOWAS legislations clearly represents an erosion of national sovereignty, particularly when the supranationality provision comes into force. Sierra Leone's ECOWAS regionalism involves extensive and intensive co-operation across a range of policy issues not found in its relations with other international organisations. By joining ECOWAS, the state opted for the pooling of sovereignty which inevitably might erode formal legal sovereignty. However, the general assumption is that all forms of international co-operation involve some diminution of sovereignty. The very nature of the international system in which Sierra Leone operates, characterised by increasing interdependence, erodes sovereignty. Thus, what Sierra Leone is doing is not necessarily a damaging erosion of sovereignty but sharing or pooling of sovereignty within the context of ECOWAS regionalism.

Conclusion

A political balance sheet of Sierra Leone's ECOWAS regionalism will show that some meaningful gains and negative effects have been bestowed on the country. At the political-diplomatic level, the country has benefited tremendously from the political and diplomatic relevance of the ECOWAS chairmanship and that of the Executive Secretaryship. It has enhanced the international profile of the country and the domestic and international status of the leaders. It has also helped firmly to place Sierra Leone on the international map of political relevance. The chairmanship has been used to negotiate investment opportunities for the country and help mediate in regional conflicts. The international publicity generated by conferences and summits has been advantageous to the country at relatively low financial cost. A negative effect is that these conferences are a huge financial burden on the state which it can ill afford. The ECOWAS platform provides the opportunity for military leaders to secure international recognition and 'legitimacy'. The common regional foreign and security co-operation has the advantage of giving the country a degree of anonymity on controversial international issues. This co-operation and the protocols on regional security, conflict prevention and peacekeeping however leads to an erosion of autonomy in foreign affairs. On the other hand, the collective bargaining power provided by ECOWAS strengthens the position of Sierra Leone in its negotiations with international trade organisations.

It is arguable whether the decision to provide a base for ECOMOG operations in Liberia had anything to do with the outbreak of the civil war. The general perception is that the immediate cause of the war in Sierra Leone was blamed on ECOMOG. Part of the problem was the failure of strategic policy to address the threats to national security and territorial integrity posed by the Liberian civil war. However, the decision to provide the base amounted to 'sacrificing' of the political autonomy and territorial integrity of the state in the interest of regional security and defence operation. This in itself entailed a substantial derogation of national sovereignty. The West African security regionalism as manifested by ECOMOG also involves huge financial costs for the country. The 'ECOMOG phenomenon' did provide, however, an opportunity for the country to refresh the body politic after 24 year of APC misrule. The ECOMOG phenomenon describes the radical political and revolutionary ideologies propagated amongst the ECOMOG contingents deployed in Liberia. The majority of ECOMOG soldiers questioned the decadent political culture and authoritarian regimes in their respective countries. These young military officers, imbued with radical ideas, returned to their countries with the desire to reform the decaying polity. This ECOMOG phenomenon was first manifested in Sierra Leone in 1992. It was later replicated in The Gambia in 1994 when young military officers who had served in ECOMOG overthrew the 30 year rule of Sir Dauda Jawara.

The defence of democracy by ECOWAS is perhaps the most important gain for Sierra Leone. ECOWAS in the process has set a new security agenda that has important implications for the dynamics of African international relations and a rethinking of the security problematique in Third World politics. The total dependence of Sierra Leone on ECOWAS for its political survival is a virtual erosion of political autonomy. The politics of regionalism and the expansion of ECOWAS into the security domain has led to a new co-operative partnership with the UN and the management of Sierra Leone's civil war.

ECOWAS membership has led to a substantial diminution of national sovereignty in such areas as regional foreign and security co-operation; economic and fiscal autonomy; free movement and supranationality provisions. However, the logic and politics of economic regionalism, and the increasing interdependence of the global economy makes inevitable a pooling of sovereignty.

Notes and References

[1] I. Gambari- *Political and Comparative Dimensions of Regional Integration: The Case of ECOWAS*, 1991.
[2] Asante, 1986, p.104.
[3] ECOWAS Publication - *Economic Community of West African States (ECOWAS): Revised Treaty* Abuja, Nigeria, 1993.

[4] Ibid., pp. 35-6.
[5] *Contact: The Magazine of ECOWAS*, October 1992, No. 4, p. 17.
[6] West Africa, 9 June 1980, p.1044.
[7] Interview, 26 October 1997.
[8] This analysis draws from the Welters and Coffrey (eds.) *The Netherlands and EC Membership Evaluated* London: Pinter, 1990.
[9] Ibid.
[10] Ibid., see also, Wright (ed.) *African Foreign Policies* 1999.
[11] This section draws extensively from David Francis, 'The Economic Community of West African States, the Defence of Democracy in Sierra Leone and Future Prospects' *Democratization* 6, 4, 1999, pp.139-165.
[12] Max Sesay 'Sierra Leone's Intractable War' *Africa World Review* November 1997-March 1998, p. 7-8.
[13] Zack-Williams- 'Coping with Complex Emergencies: Aetiology of COPE in Sierra Leone 1991-98', 1998, p. 2.
[14] Ibid., p. 18.
[15] The US-led OAS-UN force intervened in Haiti in 1994 to restore the deposed government of President Aristide.
[16] Sierra Leone website; 29 November 1997, available at http://www.sierraleone.org/Slnews.html.
[17] UN, *1948-1998: 50 Years of United Nations Peacekeeping Operations*, New York, United Publication, October 1999, p. 2.
[18] *Independent*, 2 March 1998.
[19] Thomas Weiss (ed.), *Beyond UN Subcontracting: Task Sharing with Regional Security Arrangements and Service Providing NGOs* London: Macmillan, 1998, p. xiii.
[20] For further discussion of the new security agenda see David J. Francis, 'ECOMOG: A New Security Agenda in World Politics', in Simon Bakut and Sagarika Dutt (eds.), *Africa Towards the Millennium: A Mature Approach to Development* London: Palgrave, 2000, pp. 177-202.
[21] For further discussion of this view see I. William Zartman (ed.), *Collapsed States: The Disintegration and Restoration of Legitimate Authority* Boulder, Lynne Rienner, 1995; Paul Richards, *Fighting for the Rain Forest* 1996.
[22] See Article 2 (7) of the UN Charter. The 1980s and 1990s have seen a progressive erosion of this principle in defence of universal values. There is an impressive literature on the breaching of traditional interpretations of international law, particularly with reference to sovereignty. See amongst others: James Mayall (ed.), *The New Interventionism 1991-1994: United Nations Experience in Cambodia, former Yugoslavia and Somalia* Cambridge: Cambridge University Press, 1996; M. Lewis, *Making History in Somalia: Humanitarian Intervention in a Stateless Society* Discussion Paper 7, Centre for the Study of Global Governance, London School of Economics, 1993; Janet Heininger, *Peacekeeping in Transition: The United Nations in Cambodia* New York: Twentieth Century Press, 1994.
[23] Michael Walzer, 'The Politics of Rescue', *Dissent* (Winter) 1995, pp. 35-6.
[24] J. Tacsan, 'Searching for OAS/UN Task-Sharing Opportunities in Central Africa and Haiti', in Thomas Weiss, op. cit., 1998, p. 102.
[25] Ibid.
[26] Francis, 'Mercenary Intervention in Sierra Leone', op. cit.
[27] Nicholas Wheeler, 'Humanitarian Intervention and World Politics' in John Baylis and Steve Smith (eds.), *Globalization of World Politics* 1997, pp. 394-5.

[28] See also: Gareth Evans, 'Co-operative security and intra-state conflict' *Foreign Policy* 96, 1994.
[29] United Nations Special Representative Address, June 1997.
[30] For a detailed discussion of UN task sharing see: Thomas Weiss (ed.) *Beyond UN Subcontracting: Task Sharing with Regional Security Arrangements and Service-Providing NGOs* London: Macmillan 1998.
[31] Statement by Ambassador Park Soo Gil, Permanent Representative of the Republic of Korea on the situation in Sierra Leone at the Security Council, 8 October 1997, New York: UN Plaza.
[32] For more details on role of UN in facilitating Lomé, and criticisms of UN for supporting power-sharing and blanket Amnesty, See: David Francis, 'Torturous Path to Peace' *Security Dialogue*, Vol. 31, No. 3, 2000.
[33] Ibid.
[34] Ibid.
[35] Foreign Affairs Select Committee (FAC) *Minutes of Evidence for Monday 22 May 2000 Sierra Leone: Mr Peter Hain MP and Mr J. Bevar*, London: The Stationery Office, 20 July 2000, response to question 23.
[36] Maj. Gen. Vijay Kumar Jetley, *Report on the Crisis in Sierra Leone* May 2000, Freetown.
[37] Ibid.
[38] 'Nigeria Military Rejects Accusation Over Sierra Leone', AFP Report, Saturday, 9 September 2000, 9:58 GMT, Lagos.
[39] Jean Kamara, 'Annan talks up peacekeeping' *West Africa* 4-10 September 2000, p. 15.
[40] Richard Halbrooke, 'Africa Needs a Decisive United Nations' *International Herald Tribune* 24 August 2000.
[41] Lakhdar Barhimi is former Algerian Foreign Minister.
[42] Jean Kamara, p. 16.
[43] *West Africa* pp. 15-16.
[44] *UN Secretary General's Report on War Crimes Tribunal for Sierra Leone* Sierra Leone Web, 5 October 2000, available at www.sierra-leone.org/.
[45] Ibid.
[46] Ibid.
[47] The International Contact Group includes Belgium, Canada, China, Egypt, France, Germany, Italy, Japan, The Netherlands, New Zealand, Nigeria, Norway, Sweden, United Kingdom, United States, Commonwealth, UN and World Bank/IMF.
[48] Tony Blair, 'Britain's role in Sierra Leone' BBC Broadcast on 19 May 2000.
[49] Geoffrey Hoon, statement on Sierra Leone to the House of Commons, 15 May 2000. For a discussion of the strategic defence concept see, Colin McInnes, 'Labour's Strategic Defence Review' *International Affairs* 74.4, 1998, pp. 823-845.
[50] Rachel Stohl 'Doubts about US training missions' *West Africa* 28 August - 3 September 2000, p. 23.
[51] Ibid.
[52] Ibid.
[53] Jesse Jackson, 'A Tale of Two Countries: Sierra Leone and Kosovo: Why Isn't America Paying More Attention to the War in Africa?' *Newsweek* 7 June 1999, p. 4.
[54] David Francis, 'ECOMOG: A New Security Agenda in World Politics' in Bakut and Dutt, 2000.
[55] M. Alagappa, p. 270.
[56] Clement Adibe, in Thomas Weiss (ed.) *Beyond UN Subcontracting* 1998, p. 81.
[57] Thomas Weiss; op. cit., 1998, p. xiii.

[58] M. Fowler & J. Bunck, 'What Constitutes the Sovereign State?' *Review of International Studies* Vol. 22, p. 398.
[59] Chris Brown, 1997, pp. 125-6.
[60] *West Africa* 16 June 1975, p. 689.
[61] Ibid, 1 August 1977, p. 1570.
[62] Brown, 1997, p. 126.
[63] Righter, *Utopia Lost* cited in *Review of International Studies* Vol. 22, 1996, p.103.
[64] Asante, 1986, p. 147.
[65] Ibid.
[66] Keohane and Hoffman, 1991, p. 158.
[67] Peter Gray, 'Globalisation versus Nationhood: Is Economic Integration a Useful Compromise?' *Development and International Co-operation* Vol. IX, (16), 1993, p. 48.

8 Economic Implications of Sierra Leone's ECOWAS Regionalism

Introduction

This chapter examines the economic gains and losses, or missed opportunities, of Sierra Leone's ECOWAS regionalism. Economic motivations have been the overriding consideration for the country's participation in the economic community. Sierra Leone, like other ECOWAS partners, enjoined itself to promote the harmonious economic development of the region through collective self-reliant economic regionalism and co-operation, the primary objective being to create welfare and improve the living standards of the people.

Assessing the economic gains and losses of regionalism is often difficult because international trade and economic regionalism potentially benefit some and harm others. That is, economic regionalism has the potential for uneven development because some more developed states are in a strategic position to benefit from regionalism than less developed states. It therefore results in problems in evaluating the positive and negative economic effects of regionalism. The costs of 'non-integration', i.e. where integration objectives are not implemented, and protectionist policies are maintained, also becomes part of the problem. It is this failure to generate tangible economic benefits that in some cases leads to an erosion of sustained political support for regionalism projects at national level. The limited economic benefits (or lack of it) have also made the politics of regionalism prominent by focusing more on political pursuits. This chapter seeks to evaluate the impact of ECOWAS economic policies and development strategies on national economic growth and the development of the country.

Sierra Leone and the Traditional Benefits of Economic Regionalism

The primary purpose of economic regionalism is to accelerate growth and development in member countries through the elimination of tariff and non-tariff barriers to trade across national borders. Thus, the freeing of trade or factor movements is not an end in itself but a means to accelerate economic growth and development. The orthodox trade theories such as trade creation and trade diversion lead us to expect that Sierra Leone's ECOWAS regionalism would alter the pattern of goods produced and traded in Sierra Leone. The theory predicts that the country would specialise in those activities most favoured by its relative abundance of labour, natural resources and land. Consequently, the removal of tariff barriers with other Community countries would provide a window of economic opportunities for growth and development. But these putative welfare effects have been found wanting when applied to developing regions like West Africa.

However, the traditional economic benefits of regionalism served as a powerful source of attraction for regionalism in West Africa. Theoretically, the traditional economic benefits of regionalism are to be derived from the following areas: economies of scale; industrialisation; investment opportunities; comparative advantage and specialisation. However, many of the benefits and costs of regionalism are only potential. The realisation of benefits to a very large extent depends on the measures the member countries take. Economic regionalism projects, in fact, open up new opportunities and possibilities, but whether their benefits and costs are realised will depend to a large extent on the political will and sustained commitment of the member states. Some of these ideas about traditional benefits will now be applied to Sierra Leone in ECOWAS.

Economies of Scale

It is assumed that the regionalisation process will broaden the national markets to which enterprises within the integrated area have access without the hindrance of quota restrictions, licensing or customs duties.[1] The argument is that larger markets are superior to smaller markets, and that a considerable share of the benefits of larger markets is to be expected from the effects of competition, cheaper goods and open avenues for investment opportunities. A large market is thought to encourage new industries and efficient cost of production.

The large market for Sierra Leone, with unrestricted access to 200 million potential consumers in West Africa, is definitely an economic advantage. However, the country has not been able to exploit the benefits of economies of scale because of its weak economic and manufacturing base, which is largely agro-based. The cash crop and mineral export-oriented nature of the economy makes Western markets more attractive than the ECOWAS market. Its underdeveloped industrial base, like most regional economies, offers little or no competition. Since independence, the protected nature of the domestic market was based on the strategy of import-substitution industrialisation, which relied on high protective tariffs or production subsidies. This strategy has however changed in the wake of economic liberalisation in the country in the 1990s. What is evident is the fact that Sierra Leone has clearly not yet exploited the opportunities provided by the large market. That aside, the regional Customs Union itself has not been fully operationalised as there still remain some quantitative and qualitative restrictions to trade between Community partners.[2]

Anti-regional marketeers in the country have often argued that ECOWAS regionalism would expose infant industries to a wave of intense competition from more prosperous economies such as Nigeria and Cote d'Ivoire, which they would be unable to resist. For instance, the competition from the Nigerian imported 'Gulder' and 'Star' beer posed a serious threat to the local brewery industry. The large market however provided welfare benefits derived from greater choice that consumers enjoyed due to the availability of a variety of foreign manufactured goods. Cheap consumer goods such as kitchen utensils, chemical products, pharmaceuticals, textile materials, toiletries, stationery and vehicle spare parts, mainly from Nigeria, Côte d'Ivoire, The Gambia and Liberia, are available in markets throughout the country. With the elimination of tariff barriers some amount of trade creation has occurred in the sense of an increase in imports of Community manufactured goods to Sierra Leone. The dynamic effect of trade liberalisation also exerts its influence on prices as manifested in the availability of cheap Community goods, though not necessarily of the highest quality. The lower prices of consumer goods and the broader choice of products are positive effects of ECOWAS regionalism. The presence of ECOMOG in Sierra Leone has added new commercial and economic opportunities and possibilities to ECOWAS regionalism. Nigerians dominate this ECOMOG generated intra-regional trade and commerce, a large proportion of this trade is transacted through the informal market. The ECOWAS market is increasingly becoming an important market for the country, particularly in the post-civil war period.

Another dimension of the economies of scale is that of the 'polarisation' or 'backlash' effects of economic regionalism. The more developed community partners are in a better position to exploit economies of scale thereby making them 'growth poles' around which, smaller economies tend to focus their regional trade.[3] The polarisation effect is manifested in, for example, large imports by smaller economies from relatively developed community partners, but with no corresponding significant exports. Sierra Leone's intra-ECOWAS trade with Nigeria and Côte d'Ivoire is a classic example.

Industrialisation

Industrialisation has been a major attraction for ECOWAS regionalism. In line with the modernisation theory of development, economic growth through industrialisation became a primary objective for developing countries. Most national development strategies adopted were based on import-substitution industrialisation or export-oriented industrialisation. Some countries such as Sierra Leone tried a mixed economy, i.e., combining both models of industrialisation. Sierra Leone, like other Community members, expected to develop its industrial sector and generate economic growth through regional co-operation. Article 26 of the Revised ECOWAS Treaty provides for the promotion of industrial development in member states, joint industrial development projects and multinational enterprises.

The existence of a large Community market has not stimulated industrialisation in Sierra Leone. The previously protectionist and inward-looking bias of the regionalism objective partly explains Sierra Leone's inability to generate net benefits from industrialisation. In addition, industrialisation is a capital-intensive project, and Sierra Leone has not been able to generate enough resources or attract adequate external funding to promote viable industrialisation. The industries that were expected to be established in member states have not materialised because the fragile economies within the Community have not been able to generate the resources needed for community industrialisation. Even the few primary industries established in Sierra Leone have been adversely affected by the nature of domestic politics.

Sectoral industrial planning proposed by ECOWAS to ensure complementarity in production rather than unnecessary regional competition has not produced the expected dividends. What could be regarded as sectoral industrial projects operating within the Community were not established within the ECOWAS framework. In fact, there is no project that could be exclusively regarded as an ECOWAS enterprise. The smoked fish industry in Sierra Leone and the cement factory in Togo are both recognised as industries with the potential of becoming Community enterprises within the ECOWAS framework.

Investment

The importance of a harmonised industrial and investment policy in an integrated area can not be overemphasised. Each Community partner expected a fair share of potential industrial investments through ECOWAS regionalism. ECOWAS therefore has encouraged private and public multilateral investment in the Community. At the July 1996 ECOWAS summit, the 25 per cent domestic equity participation for investment in the Community was scrapped as a means to open up the region to foreign direct investment and to integrate the Community within the global economy. This is in line with the neo-liberal economic policies adopted by member states of the Community. It is a response to the new regionalism. Such free market policies would provide the enabling economic environment in order to attract the inflow of foreign direct investment (FDI), technology, and cross-border investments, all of which are deemed necessary for national and regional development. However, an important point needs to be made that foreign investment is not necessarily the solution to industrialisation and development in Africa. Caroline Thomas criticised the neo-liberal 'propaganda' that FDI is a good thing for developing regions. Foreign investment, in the guise of importing capital for development invariably ends up exporting capital from Africa. Even the welfare benefits of the 'trickle down' effects from trade and investment have not reached the majority of the people who remain marginalised and impoverished.[4] What is more, the disintegration of the Soviet Union and instability in Africa saw a huge flight of capital from the continent mainly to Eastern Europe and Asia.

It is in this regard that the ECOWAS removal of the 25 per cent equity participation in Community investment could be seen as an avenue for the influx of unregulated multinational corporations in West Africa. It could also be argued that though the intention is to encourage capital investment in the region, MNCs will inevitably end up exporting capital out of the Community because their profits are sent back to their parent bodies located in the Western metropoles. S. K. B. Asante argues that, by making use of the transnational linkages established between foreign capital and local political and economic elite, MNCs weaken the effectiveness of mechanisms designed to correct the inequitable distribution of regionalism costs and benefits.[5]

Notwithstanding this, however, the evolving regional investment policy has created a variety of investment opportunities for smaller economies such as Sierra Leone. Under the auspices of the ECOWAS-ACP-EU Sectoral Industrial Forum, there is a growing partnership between West Africa and European economic operators on the one hand and, on the other, an increase in South-South co-operation through bilateralism and multilateralism. The Forum creates the channel for private foreign investment to help develop the West African market. A European Union-West Africa Industrial Forum was organised in 1995 to promote development of agro-industry. As a result of the EU-West Africa Forum co-operation, the following industrial business projects from Sierra Leone were submitted for private foreign or joint investments: cut flower production; fishing company expansion and acquisition of fishing facilities; smoked fish plant; rehabilitation of fishing company; dessicated coconut plant project; ginger production; and animal feed mill. Through the investment opportunities provided by ECOWAS, these Sierra Leone industrial business ventures have the possibility of attracting foreign investments and joint ventures with European economic operators. An additional spin-off benefit is the employment opportunities that go with such investment enterprises.

The dominant intra-ECOWAS investment in Sierra Leone is in the form of Nigerian investment in the country. The Nigerian petroleum re-marketer, Unipetrol company has 11.45 million Naira (US $145.000) (1997) investment in Sierra Leone Oil Refinery Corporation, i.e. 20 per cent equity holding in the refinery. The relative Nigerian economic presence is not surprising, given the significant political and military role played by Nigeria in the civil war peace settlement and conflict management in the country. Political realists would therefore argue that economic and political influence had been the driving force for Nigeria's involvement in Sierra Leone under the umbrella of ECOWAS, rather than any notion of Pan-West Africanism and common humanity.

In Sierra Leone, the sizeable Lebanese community who monopolise economic activities, have often taken advantage of ECOWAS trade liberalisation provisions to exploit further the region's economies of scale. Previous indigenisation policies have been ineffective and have in fact been against the spirit of the ECOWAS goal of expanded intra-regional trade.

Specialisation

Specialisation is another area which would be expected to produce benefits for Sierra Leone. ECOWAS regionalism is expected to generate specialisation in the following ways: manufacturing and agriculture, specialisation based on comparative advantage; and intra-industrial specialisation. The West African sub-region can boast of large and valuable quantities of mineral and agricultural resources, for example, diamonds, oil, cocoa, coffee, but allowed itself to be reduced to the role of producing and exporting all its valuable primary products and importing finished products at very high prices. The region has been regarded as a case of producing what it cannot eat, and eating what it cannot produce.[6] The complementarity of resources in the region has not been transformed into meaningful comparative advantage. For instance, cocoa, which is produced in large export quantities by Ghana, Côte d'Ivoire and Sierra Leone, could serve as a basis of Community industrial specialisation.

In Sierra Leone, only one industry can be claimed to be the result of regional specialisation, that is the manufacture of glass bottles.[7] The country is therefore a regional market for the supply of glass bottles within the Community. However, the civil war has adversely affected this industry. What has become evident is the fact that the country has not utilised its resource endowment for regional specialisation. This could be attributed to the scarcity of capital and skilled labour, and the general politics of underdevelopment. The country's dependence on external economies, high transportation costs due to underdeveloped infrastructural facilities, and difficult regional communications systems are all unattractive for investors.

Arguably, the traditional benefits of economic regionalism have been difficult to realise in Sierra Leone for a variety of complex reasons. Orthodox trade theories and Custom Union theory on which these benefits of integration are based have limited applicability to developing countries. They are based on the premise that the conditions for regionalism already exist and that market forces will subsequently produce benefits. This is however not the case in West Africa. Sierra Leone's underdeveloped economy and absorptive capacity do not create a conducive environment for exploiting the benefits of economic regionalism. Asante makes the point that the extent of the benefits which a regionalism scheme can bring depends largely on the economic development already achieved by the partner countries, on the size of their subsistence sector and on their natural resources, their labour supply and capital for investment.[8]

Sierra Leone and ECOWAS Trade Liberalisation Programme

The liberalisation of trade and free movement are at the heart of the regionalisation process in West Africa. Trade liberalisation encapsulates the mains goals of ECOWAS, i.e. increased intra-regional trade and economic development. It is an essential part of ECOWAS internal market policy wherein all barriers to trade and factor movement are eliminated.[9] Article 35 of the Revised Treaty provides for the liberalisation of trade as a priority within the Community.

In general, trade liberalisation constitutes a significant aspect of economic regionalisms. It is argued that a country participating in such a scheme benefits from the elimination of barriers to its exports on the part of the partner countries. This removal of restrictions would ensure the significant development of international trade. It is particularly important for the West African economies, whose exports of manufactured goods often suffer discrimination in the developed region's markets, such as EU, in spite of the Lomé Conventions. ECOWAS aims to achieve the combined elements of greater intra-regional trade, but with some element of protectionism against countries outside the grouping. It is assumed that the adoption of a common tariff on imports from third countries and the harmonisation of other measures affecting imports and exports will eliminate distortions in competitiveness among the partner countries. It is also assumed that a common customs tariff and the harmonisation of tariff nomenclature will greatly minimise the problem of unrecorded trade which is so endemic in the region.[10] It is argued that the divergence in the regional tariff structure and the inevitable price differentials are the main motivations for smuggling.

The removal of quantitative and qualitative restrictions to trade and free movement is crucial for the success of the trade liberalisation programme. Sierra Leone is one of the countries that has removed all non-tariff barriers of a monetary nature. It means that in principle payment of airport tax, hotel bills and flight tickets can be made in any West African local currency. However, there still exist unofficial barriers within the Community among economic operators. The reality is that, hotels and airline operators, in both Anglophone and Francophone West Africa, refuse to accept payments in other Community currencies outside the CFA zone or national currency.[11]

Trade Liberalisation, Promotion of Handicraft Industry and the Extinction of Endangered Species

Through the liberalisation programme, Sierra Leone's traditional handicraft industry has benefited from the free movement of unprocessed goods and traditional handicrafts without qualitative restrictions and exemption from import duties. Craft products including country cloth, rope, sail canvas, boats, wood carvings, baskets and leather goods and some other products have benefited from the programme. These products and tariff preferences have brought economic benefits financially and employment-wise for the rural population. The economic gains generated from this trade have become an alternative for some sections of the rural community not engaged in agriculture, the main economic occupation.

The liberalisation scheme dealing with traditional handicrafts exempted such items as raw hides and animal skins, articles of animal guts, and worked ivory from import tax duties within the Community. The traditional handicraft industry depends on the 'raw materials' of flora and fauna to survive.[12] In spite of its economic gains, it has had some accompanying negative effects. The trade liberalisation scheme in promoting such industry indirectly affected environmental and wildlife protection. The trade in tanned reptile skins (crocodiles, iguanas, snakes), horn and teeth (pigmy hippopotamus, antelopes, lions), and worked ivory (elephants), has had a devastating effect on the wildlife in Sierra Leone. It has led to the near extinction of endangered species, like the pigmy hippo, and a depletion of the elephant population. The trade in ivory contravenes the international ban on the ivory trade, thereby making the ECOWAS trade liberalisation programme dealing with traditional handicrafts a contravention of international regulation. However, two relevant points should be made here. Sierra Leone's situation is not different from other ECOWAS members. In particular, there is lack of comprehensive wildlife protection policy in most member states. The people, in trying to eke out a living need the animal meat for their protein supply. It is also important to note that with or without the trade liberalisation provisions, member states were already using animal materials for the traditional handicraft industries. The ECOWAS scheme therefore only formalised what was already in existence.

The Politics of Trade Liberalisation and the Loss of Fiscal Revenue

There is considerable interest among exporters and economic operators for an ECOWAS-wide trade liberalisation. Recorded intra-ECOWAS trade in 1994 was estimated to be about 10 per cent of the total trade of the Community.[13] A variety of obstacles still remain in utilising the trade liberalisation provisions in Sierra Leone, as in other member states. Some of the problems include: inefficiency and rent-seeking behaviour of some government officials, including security agents responsible for clearing imports and exports; inadequately trained officials at border posts and too many unofficial check points along Community international highways, which encourages rent-seeking activities by customs and immigration officials; high transportation costs as a result of inordinate delays and poor infrastructural facilities.[14] The apparent political support given by Sierra Leone, like other Community partners, to the trade liberalisation programme since it became operational in 1990, has not been met by the same degree of commitment to implement the scheme. A combination of factors accounts for this. Sierra Leone generates most of its revenue from customs duties. The possible large loss of government revenue accounts for this lukewarm commitment. This is not surprising as most ECOWAS countries depend on international trade taxes for over a third of their government revenue. There is a lack of confidence in the ECOWAS Compensation Fund's ability to reimburse likely losses of customs revenue.[15]

Before the establishment of the Community, each ECOWAS country applied its own customs tariffs to goods imported from third countries. The establishment of a common customs tariff therefore meant a major loss of fiscal revenue for the government. Within the context of national development and economic planning, the tariff is a taxation instrument available to national authorities to be deployed in the raising of revenues or the allocation of national economic resources.[16] In this context, the tariff carries with it some degree of flexibility in raising fiscal revenue and allocation. It is this degree of flexibility that tariff harmonisation removes from the national governments and its removal imposes an element of constraint on their freedom of action, since the common tariff is established by agreement of the partners.[17] The ability of governments to allocate or raise fiscal revenue also goes to the heart of national sovereignty in the sense that taxes are the prerogative of parliament and raising revenue lies at the core of a legislature's power in any democracy.[18] Table 3 illustrates the significance of customs revenue to different Community members.

Table 3: Taxes on International Trade Transactions – ECOWAS Countries

International Trade Taxes as a Percentage of Total Government Revenue Annual Average per cent

Country	1985-89-MRE	1990-MRE
Benin	n.a.	33.2
Burkina Faso	32.1	n.a.
Cape Verde	n.a.	n.a.
Côte d'Ivoire	33.0	32.1
Gambia	66.4	42.5
Ghana	39.8	33.1
Guinea	n.a.	32.4
Guinea Bissau	33.9	n.a
Liberia	29.6	n.a
Mali	23.2	39.3
Mauritania	34.6	30.9
Niger	33.1	39.3
Nigeria	11.6	n.a
Senegal	31.3	35.6
Sierra Leone	40.0	37.3
Togo	32.1	38.2

MRE: Most Recent Estimate
Source: World Bank *African Development Indicators* 1996.

As shown in the table Sierra Leone's official customs revenue as a percentage of total government revenue is the second highest within the Community for the period 1985-89. The highest was The Gambia, with a percentage of 66.4. Nigeria's customs revenue for the same period was a mere 11.6 per cent of revenue. This is not surprising because of its huge returns from oil.

Apart from the problems associated with constraints on customs revenue, mistrust among governments arising from political differences, severe economic setbacks, are part of the problems in implementing the liberalisation scheme. Other problems include: stringent and complex rules of origin for Community goods which discourage cross-border investments; introduction of new non-tariff barriers by some member countries, including Sierra Leone, despite agreement that these be progressively dismantled; inadequate development of the financial sector and difficulty in obtaining trade credit; inordinate delays in processing transactions channelled through the Clearing House in Sierra Leone; and the overlapping mandates of regional grouping comprising sub-sets of ECOWAS countries like MRU and UMEOA.[19]

Trade liberalisation however, is a necessary, but not sufficient condition for increasing intra-ECOWAS trade. It is instructive to note that though the trade liberalisation programme has not generally made a significant contribution to intra-trade of member states, it still holds a lot of economic potential and opportunities for Community partners to exploit when it eventually becomes fully operational. The same could be said of the EEC Common Market in the pre-1987 period. The Common Market did not make a very significant impact on the intra-trade of member states until the Single European Act of 1987, which internalised the common market.

It is in this regard therefore that, in evaluating the impact of Community trade policies on member states, one should take into account the loss of opportunities and the increase in costs arising from national deficiencies.[20] Sierra Leone, with a relatively underdeveloped economy and weak industrial base, is less likely to be able to exploit aggressively the opportunities offered by the liberalisation scheme. It was only in 1993 that Sierra Leone made an application for the inclusion of some of its products in the liberalisation scheme for export within the Community. The exporting impact on the country has been negligible. Part of this could be attributed to the civil war in the country and its effect on economic activities. The implication is that two additional costs of regionalism are borne by the country. The existence of a common external tariff encourages the importation of manufactured goods from within the Community, rather than from abroad. The industrially well advanced members like Nigeria and Côte d'Ivoire (see Table 5 for Sierra Leone's trading partners), are able to exploit the protective cover of the trade liberalisation scheme to export into the country. Thus, Sierra Leone finds itself a net importer. The commercial balance of the country is therefore increasingly in deficit.[21] Domestic industries must therefore compete locally with products imported from member states.

Some aspects which are vital to the realisation of the trade liberalisation objectives will now be addressed. They include: intra-regional trade; free movement; compensation scheme; customs regime; and monetary co-operation.

Sierra Leone and Intra-Regional Trade

Intra-regional trade has been regarded as an important indicator of the level of success of the regionalism scheme and the contribution to the economic growth of member states. The ECOWAS region, like SADC and SACU, has an unusually high degree of openness compared to other African regional arrangements. Between 1980 and 1994, on average, merchandise exports and imports as a proportion of GDP were more than 50 per cent for the ECOWAS region. Yet, trade within the region, i.e. exports and imports, is still a very small proportion of GDP. It is claimed that unrecorded trade within the region is equivalent or more in value to official trade among member countries. Even if this is taken into account, intra-regional trade is still a relatively small proportion of the Community's GDP or its total trade. Intra-regional exports and imports doubled in 1994 from their levels in 1980. Exports increased from US $1.2 billion to US $2.1 billion, and imports from US $1.2 billion to US $2.4 billion.[22] During this period, intra-regional exports and imports as a percentage of the ECOWAS GDP also increased from 1 per cent to 3.2 per cent and 1 per cent to 3.6 per cent respectively. Even after more than two decade of the ECOWAS Treaty, intra-regional trade is only a small proportion of the Community GDP.[23]

Sierra Leone's total contribution to the intra-ECOWAS export as a percentage of GDP was a mere 0.2 per cent in 1985, while intra-Community imports as a percentage of GDP rose from 2.5 per cent in 1985 to 5.9 per cent in 1993 but fell slightly to 5.6 per cent in 1994.[24] This shows that the country is a recipient economy, with a very weak industrial base for exports. The table below shows that intra-Community exports from Sierra Leone have been consistently low. In comparative terms, some other relatively less-endowed Community members, such as Burkina Faso, Togo, Niger, and The Gambia, have fared better in terms of intra-ECOWAS exports. The table shows how negligible Sierra Leone's intra-regional trade is in comparison with other ECOWAS countries.

Table 4: Intra-ECOWAS Trade

	Intra-ECOWAS Trade									
	Imports / US $ million					Exports/US $ million				
Country	1989	1990	1991	1992	1993	1989	1990	1991	1992	1993
Benin	47	67	18	23	21	15	37	8	10	9
Burkina Faso	87	142	163	124	127	20	26	19	19	28
Côte d'Ivoire	414	568	528	548	550	444	604	641	667	720
Gambia	7	10	9	9	9	6	11	10	13	16
Ghana	95	72	86	92	97	235	221	216	232	264
Guinea	14	8	10	14	17	5	5	6	9	14
Guinea Bissau	12	10	11	12	14	2	2	2	4	6
Liberia	11	1	1	6	7	3	1	2	4	10
Mali	106	183	212	337	356	94	241	100	137	152
Niger	98	102	38	92	92	29	38	69	73	69
Nigeria	14	19	29	49	44	459	780	514	713	592
Senegal	123	170	158	166	172	92	89	78	115	122
Sierra Leone	15	12	17	19	23	1	1	2	3	5
Togo	44	86	48	59	31	29	37	38	48	19

Source: *ECOWAS Handbook of International Trade* (1995, p.9).

The underdeveloped industrial base of Sierra Leone and the complementarity of resource endowment in the region, coupled with the politics of decline and the debilitating effects of the civil war in the country have considerably limited intra-Community trade. The direction of Sierra Leone's intra-ECOWAS trade vividly illustrates the problem.

Table 5: Direction of Sierra Leone's Intra-ECOWAS Trade

	Direction of Sierra Leone's Intra-ECOWAS Trade					
	Imports/'000 Leones			Exports/'000 Leones		
Country	1992	1993	1994	1992	1993	1994
Côte d'Ivoire	877	1619	2476	361	..	48
Gambia	..	395	556	528	65	83
Ghana	30	6	316	..	15	157
Guinea	758	93	319	959	945	154
Guinea-Bissau	..	1	..	..	3	6
Liberia	315	27	66	244	219	355
Nigeria	1433	2377	1204	1	..	..
Senegal	266	259	434	6	2	..

Source: *Annual Statistics Digest*, Central Statistics Office, Freetown.

The products that account for the majority of Sierra Leone's intra-regional trade include: fish, live cattle (re-export to other coastal countries from the Sahelian countries), kola nuts, palm oil and timber. Local manufactures consist mainly of textiles, beverages and confectionery, soaps and detergents, plastic products and glass bottles. The above tables illustrate the limited intra-regional trade and the extra-regional nature of Sierra Leone's economy.

The country's economy is largely Western market oriented, with UK, Belgium, Netherlands, and Luxembourg, taking most of the country's exports. Since 1990, the USA and Germany have also figured among the major trading partners. Nigeria, UK, and Germany have regularly supplied over 50 per cent of imports, although there are signs of increased imports coming from the USA and Côte d'Ivoire, replacing Nigeria's role. The principal exports for Sierra Leone in 1996 included: diamonds - US $18.7 million; rutile - US $2.1 million; cocoa - US $1.8 million; fish and shrimps - US$1.8 million. The principal imports for 1994/95 comprised: foodstuffs - US $53.9 million; fuel and energy - US $23.6 million; machinery and transport equipment - US $19.9 million; chemicals - US $16.5 million. The main destinations of exports for 1995 were: USA - 20 %; Belgium-Luxembourg - 20 %; Spain - 13 %; UK - 6 %. The main origins of imports for the same period were: Côte d'Ivoire - 17 %; UK - 17 %; India - 9 %; Belgium/Luxembourg - 8%.[25] The heavy dependence on extra-regional trade also explains the rather weak intra-Community economic orientation of the country. Sierra Leone's extra-Community trade orientation is a familiar picture of the West Africa sub-region, partly due to the incorporation of these economies into the world market through colonial rule.

The Sierra Leone export situation reflects the general economic climate within the Community. In 1992, the share of manufactured exports of ECOWAS in its total export to the world was a mere 4.8 per cent. When fuel exports mainly from Nigeria, which constitute about 43 per cent of the region's total exports, are excluded, the share of manufacturing rises to just about 8.3 per cent.[26] ECOWAS countries have not succeeded in industrialising the region. Of all Africa's sub-regions, West Africa is the least industrialised, accounting for about 8 per cent of Africa's manufacturing value added in 1994, compared with nearly 20 per cent for Eastern and Southern Africa, and about 15 per cent for North Africa.[27]

Sierra Leone, like other ECOWAS countries, has suffered acutely from the global economic recession and national economic difficulties manifested in falling per capita incomes, high inflation rates, falling terms of trade, wide fluctuations in growth rates of export earnings, overvalued exchange rates, underdeveloped production infrastructure, and the heavy burden of external public debt. Under these unfavourable economic conditions, it becomes difficult for the country to achieve the goal of intra-ECOWAS trade. The very nature of the existing non-tariff barriers in Sierra Leone, especially with the free movement of goods and the customs regime, also accounts for its low share of intra-regional trade.[28]

Free Movement and its Pressures on the Economy

Free movement and intra-regional trade are fundamental to the regionalisation process in West Africa. The trade liberalisation programme can only work efficiently and accrue benefits to member states if there is unrestricted movement of the factors of production within the Community. Free movement is the most popular aspect of West African regionalism, and at the same time, the most controversial. The rationale is that it constitutes the fundamental basis for strengthening ECOWAS and also influencing the harmonious development of all economic, social and cultural activities within the region. The principle underlying the idea of Community citizenship is that irrespective of nationality, all member state nationals should have the same rights and freedom. Article 2 of the Supplementary Protocol on the Second Phase of the Protocol on Free Movement dealing with right of residence provides for the rights of Community citizens and duties of member countries. It provides that jobs can only be denied to Community citizens on the grounds of public order, public security, and public health.[29] Migrant workers are therefore entitled to the same rights as nationals of the country where they secure employment. The Protocol on Free Movement explicitly provides that it is the responsibility of the member states to take corrective measures to regulate the negative effects of free movement within the Community.

The mobility of production factors within the Community has given rise to certain benefits and costs for the country. The unstable economic and political situation has led to the exodus of labour force, management skills and capital to other member countries. This inevitably affects the long-term development prospects of the country. Sierra Leone nationals had extensively utilised the window of opportunity provided by the Free Movement Protocol, especially during the civil war period. Though there are no available statistics, informal sources point to the fact that thousands of Sierra Leoneans are gainfully employed in almost all West African countries. Similarly, the movement of labour into Sierra Leone in the pre-war period has posed problems for the already over-stretched economy. This labour migration was especially acute in urban cities and diamond regions.

Article 8 of the free movement protocol is the most widely abused by member states. It provides that for reasons of internal security, member states can impose measures restricting the implementation of the protocol and if necessary, close borders. This has been widely interpreted by some heads of state, to the extent that petty quarrels and political misunderstandings have led to the use of this provision, as, for example, in the Sierra Leone-Liberia border closure in 1983, the Ghana-Togo dispute in 1992 and the recent border skirmishes between Liberia, Guinea and Sierra Leone, and Côte d'Ivoire and Burkina Faso.

Border area workers, seasonal workers and itinerant workers have all frequented the Sierra Leone job market, taking advantage of the free movement provisions. Most West African nationals resident in the country, especially in the diamond regions, do not bother to get resident permits as required by ECOWAS. Some migrate into the country even without the stipulated ECOWAS travel certificate. It was this situation that forced the government to declare Kono district a Diamond Protected Area, accessible only to foreign nationals with valid permits. This has been violated by most West African citizens, who settle and engage in the diamond business with few constraints. Lack of government supervision, corrupt and rent-seeking activities of immigration officials and politicians, and weak implementation of immigration regulations are largely responsible for this problem.

The free movement of goods and persons, improvement of border procedures and elimination of unofficial road blocks are vital to the realisation of the trade liberalisation objective. Though all ECOWAS member states have abolished visa requirements for Community citizens, numerous road blocks exist and Community citizens fall victims to harassment by officials and extortion in practically all the member states. The writer, during field trips to West Africa, experienced the practical difficulties along the Trans-West African Highway, from Lagos (Nigeria) through Cotonou (Benin) to Lomé (Togo) to Ghana, and from The Gambia, through Senegal to Mali. Harassment and extortion is the norm along this route. The researcher, even with all the correct documents, was subjected to inordinate delays and questioning by the security agents. Numerous unofficial checkpoints litter the routes between Sierra Leone, Guinea and Liberia, with the accompanying harassment and extortion. However, the problems relating to the free movement of persons and goods differ from country to country.

The recommendations put forward by the ECOWAS Minimum Agenda for Action in 1993 on free movement calls for a combined control team and reduction of road blocks to a single checkpoint between the borders. These recommendations only scratch the surface of the problem. The root lies in the fragile economic position of the member states and the impoverished nature of the citizens of the Community. Immigration and Customs officials, including the police and other security agents, are poorly paid.[30] Extortion, which is now informally recognised, has become the only viable way for these officials to eke out an existence. Smuggling or unofficial trade is also big business, with huge connection to the vested economic interests of the political elite and their cronies. Immigration officials are often bribed with thousands of Nairas, Cedis or Leones by traders, which they cannot resist in the face of their economic realities. Some government functionaries and politicians actively promote smuggling because of the financial benefits accruing to them. Economic operators, traders, and travellers, who do not want to be bothered by the ECOWAS free movement and travel certificate provisions, are willing to bribe in order to save time and harassment. Addressing the problem of free movement in West Africa, unlike the EU, is a complex matter that requires not only regional institutional prescriptions, but also tackling the fundamental domestic problems of the member states.

Mano River Regionalisation: The Monkey Trade and Smuggling

An integral part of Sierra Leone's intra-Community trade and free movement is that of smuggling and the monkey trade phenomenon. It has been suggested that the total value of unofficial trade exceeds that of the value of recorded trade in the country. The corrupt nature of the border controls, national price differentiations and the porous nature of the borders have led to an endemic culture of smuggling in the country. The Monkey trade and smuggling was further enhanced by the creation of the Mano River Union (MRU) in 1973. The MRU is a sub-regional intergovernmental co-operation grouping that brought together Sierra Leone, Liberia and Guinea. The Union was a political project fashioned as a result of the ideological and personal ties between presidents Stevens of Sierra Leone and Tolbert of Liberia. The construction of the Mano River Bridge enhanced the movement of peoples and other production factors between Liberia and Sierra Leone, and further gave a new economic and commercial dimension to the Koindu border market town in eastern Sierra Leone.

The unofficial export of Sierra Leone's diamonds and gold to Liberia, and cocoa and coffee to other neighbouring countries operates on a large scale. Liberia and Guinea are making profitable business from the smuggling activities of their nationals and other West Africans who operate behind the cover of the ECOWAS free movement protocol. Here, we see some kind of trade creation amongst ECOWAS countries though obviously not the kind expected to result from the formation of an integrated economy. The high rate of smuggling to Liberia in the pre-1985 period, primarily due to the American dollar used in that country, created a huge distortion in Sierra Leone's economy. The attractiveness of the US dollar made the Liberian market a more attractive business proposition. Not only mineral and agricultural products were smuggled out of the country but also essential items such as fuel, which could fetch a better price in Liberia.

The endemic smuggling in the region has been aided and abetted by the ECOWAS free movement provisions. Traders circumvent export regulations in Sierra Leone and smuggle out products to be sold for the convertible CFA Franc and US dollar. The traders then buy goods, the importation of which is prohibited, or something which is difficult to get. This is not a feature peculiar to Sierra Leone. A significant portion of Togo and Benin imports of commodities such as beverages, textiles, spirits and cigarettes end up in Nigeria through the informal market. Niger, a land-locked economy is heavily dependant on unofficial imports from Nigeria.

Trans-border regionalisation through the Mano river axis enhanced the operations of the monkey trade especially in Liberia. The monkey trade is a trade in smoked monkey, a delicacy in Liberia, that is exported unofficially. It is a thriving market between the two countries, especially the eastern region of Sierra Leone. Traders commission the hunting of monkeys in the forests of Sierra Leone. The processed monkeys are then exported to Liberia through the informal market. The traders in turn used the then Liberian US dollars in pre-1985 era, to purchase luxury items, household goods and designer clothing from the free ports of Liberia, which were then imported into the country through the same unofficial channels. It was a very lucrative business for both countries and brought numerous economic benefits but at the same time some costs for the country. The economic crises and the deterioration in the standard of living in both countries made the trans-border informal economy an alternative opportunity for survival by rural and urban communities.

Another facet of this trans-border trade was the Koindu emporium. The town became a commercial meeting point in the pre-war years that brought together traders and economic operators from Guinea, Liberia and Sierra Leone. It is difficult to estimate the economic benefits generated by this trading town because of the lack of trade statistics. It is however reasonable to assume that it brought significant gains to the people and the country, though the loss of revenue to the government cannot be underestimated. Thus, the monkey trade and the Koindu commercial hub were at the heart of the Mano River Union intra-trade in the pre-civil war period.

The economic costs of free movement in West Africa have been immense for Sierra Leone. Some economists argue that Liberia stands to lose a lot if the illegal trade were to stop. The following example of the politics of regionalism illustrates this point. In 1983, a diplomatic row broke out between the two countries, as a result of a newspaper allegation against the wife of the Liberian military leader Master Sergeant Samuel Doe. The Liberian head of state unilaterally closed the border. The unanticipated consequence was the sudden abundance of local commodities in the Sierra Leone market, which made President Stevens quite reluctant to resolve the dispute that would eventually have led to the re-opening of the border. The business community in both countries pressurised their respective governments to re-open the border. Deardorff and Stolper argue that smuggling in African circumstances is a blessing in disguise for the economies, the people and even the government. They are of the view that smuggling in Africa can sometimes be considered to be a healthy reaction to bad situations caused by bad policies.[31] In effect, the informal economy provides economic and material benefits for the majority of the people in times of unfavourable economic conditions. However, the crucial objection is that this kind of evaluation ignores the fact that smuggling is detrimental to long-term development. It also takes no account of the tax revenues which are lost to the government. The argument could be advanced for a need to develop a common regional approach to control smuggling. Though a common approach would be the rational thing to do, the interests of member states that benefit from smuggling activities or informal trade are bound to undermine any such regional approach. Niger and other land-locked ECOWAS countries make no secret of their economic dependence on smuggling or what they prefer to describe as trans-border informal trade. In addition, the porous nature of the borders and endemic corruption in West Africa makes the realisation of a common regional approach to smuggling almost unattainable.

The ASYCUDA Project and Sierra Leone's Customs Regime

The Automated System for Customs Data (ASYCUDA), is the computerisation of Community customs data and management systems. Customs activity for most Community members constitutes a major source of revenue for the government. The previously rudimentary and manual system of customs management has often hampered the collection and processing of customs revenue and procedures. In recognition of this, ECOWAS in the early 1980s sought the assistance of UNCTAD in the design of an articulated system of computer-based procedures governing dutiable and duty-free goods that enter and leave the Community.[32] The objective was to computerise the customs regime/systems in ECOWAS member states. It was geared towards the co-ordination and centralisation of customs information at local, national and regional level. The general framework of co-operation is with government departments and other agencies like the National Statistics Office, Inland Revenue, Police, Immigration, and Health. It also includes customs activity with international trade co-operation organisations and financial institutions like the Customs Co-operation Council (CCC), IMF/World Bank, and UNDP.[33]

This automated data processing encourages the modernisation of customs and external trade procedures. Against the background of the complex structure of customs activity and its relevance for revenue generation in the fragile economies of the sub-region, the role of ASYCUDA as a customs administrative and management information tool and as an inexpensive method for automation, is crucial to revenue generation. It is also a mechanism to address not only the notorious problem of corruption, but also the issue of debt management in the region.[34]

Duties and taxes collected by the customs on foreign trade form about 33 per cent of government revenue of most developing countries. It is the customs documents which provide trade data and statistics necessary for economic planning and trade negotiations. The mechanism for the collection of customs revenues is an essential part of a governments' financial strategy. Its proper functioning is a *sine qua non* for the development of sound fiscal policy, the management of foreign trade and ultimately the development of the country. Therefore, customs services and the speed with which they clear consignments for imports and export play a key role in the country's development.[35] Fraud and malpractice which is endemic within the customs regime in the Community have often led to the lack of up-to-date trade data, and gross inefficiency.

The outcome of the ECOWAS-UNCTAD Customs support negotiations led to the setting up of the ASYCUDA Management Information System. In order to implement this programme, the Community Computer Centre was established in 1985, to work towards the full realisation of the ASYCUDA project in Community countries. This framework is to serve as a national and regional tool for management of information delivery within ECOWAS.[36]

As of January 1996, 12 member states had implemented the National ASYCUDA systems within ECOWAS. The francophone states were at an advanced stage of implementation. The implementation of Sierra Leone's National ASYCUDA project started in January 1995. The total cost of the implementation of phase 1 of the project was put at US $55,082.78.[37] The expenditure covers preparatory installation, equipment acquisition, evaluation missions and training. The original funding of the project was started by the Overseas Development Assistance (ODA). The statistical project, EUROTRACE, is funded by EU. Political and civil unrest in the country, coupled with the corrupt attitude of customs officials, have contributed to the slow implementation of the project.

The ASYCUDA system therefore has the potential to revolutionise the customs regimes within the Community. The revolution of the customs systems and procedures in Sierra Leone is important because it puts an end to the manual, disorganised, and mediocre customs information systems and procedures.[38] Sierra Leone is therefore utilising the tangible benefits of economic regionalism and co-operation to develop and replace its outdated customs regime. Through ECOWAS regionalism, the sum of US $55.000 was spent on behalf of the government of Sierra Leone to reform its customs regime. In the face of the declining economic situation and the dislocating caused by the civil war, the funding of the ASYCUDA project is a great financial and infrastructural help to the country. When the project is fully operational it should lead to an increase in revenue collection through easy collection procedures, eliminate corrupt practices within the customs regime and provide for transparency within the system. The system reinforces customs controls and monitors the perception of customs duties.[39] In Mauritania for example, the US $1 million invested in the system over the period 1984-1988 led to a US $4 million increase in government revenue.[40]

The problem with the implementation of the ASYCUDA project in the anglophone countries, particularly Sierra Leone and Nigeria, is the rent-seeking and patronage system that are almost institutionalised within the customs systems of these countries. In Sierra Leone, the customs department is a 'state within a state'. The customs department is a manifestation of William Reno's 'shadow state', wherein the customs institutions have been privatised and informalised to serve the patrimonial interests of the office holders and their political patrons.

However, the implementation of the ASYCUDA project in the country, coupled with the necessary political will and constructive reform policies, the customs regime will be revolutionised with all its attendant benefits. Mohamed Mansaray argues that the customs computerisation and rationalisation will speed up the clearance of goods and reduce delays in deliveries to overseas customers. As a result, the associated overhead costs which adversely affect the cost of imports and the price of exports are greatly diminished.[41] The Mauritania example is worthy of mention here, in that it has reduced the transit time of goods through customs from one week to one day since the introduction of the system. Furthermore, the computerised database on trade can be used for statistical economic analyses and in the formulation of realistic economic development plans. ASYCUDA thus has the advantage of generating reliable foreign trade data within a few days of the end of the reporting month. This will enhance the effective control in customs clearance procedures and provide more precise customs accounting.[42] The government will then be in a better position to take economic decisions and enter trade liberalisation and compensation schemes with confidence. Mansaray further argues that the computerisation of the clearance procedure at customs department will bring about a functional re-organisation of work such as systematic working methods and optimal allocation of tasks, something which the Customs department in Sierra Leone urgently needs. It will not only lead to the rationalisation and simplification of customs documents, but also enhance internal electronic exchange of information between bodies including the central bank, and the Trade, Finance and Economic Planning Ministries. The centralisation of data will create a liaison between the trading community and port and airport operators, importers and exporters, forwarding agents, airlines and shipping companies, clearing agents and banks, all of whom interact with the customs system.[43] Sierra Leone is therefore able to utilise the immense benefits from the reform of its moribund customs system through the opportunities provided by ECOWAS regionalism.

Considering the limited technological skills available in the region, training is a major feature of the ASYCUDA project. Training was organised for customs experts and statisticians from ECOWAS member states in October 1996. The meeting considered the Single Customs Document (SCD), which replaced the numerous customs documents in the member states. The harmonisation of customs regulations and procedures is important in promoting intra-regional trade. Two delegates from Sierra Leone were among the 36 participants from the Community countries. From April 1991 to September 1997, a total of 27 ASYCUDA and Customs related seminars and workshops were organised by the Community Computer Centre. Only 7 technical and managerial staff from Sierra Leone attended these courses, out of a total of 246 participants over the period.[44] There has been criticism that the appropriate personnel, i.e. the operators, are not often sent to attend these courses. Most times, officials who have nothing to do with the ASYCUDA project are sent. Part of the reason for the poor attendance is that, customs officers are often reluctant to leave their posts because of the personal loss of revenue from corrupt sources. The government also finds it increasingly difficult to finance the training requirements of Sierra Leonean participants.

The harmonisation and computerisation of Sierra Leone's customs systems and procedures has the potential to be a major positive development, against the background of millions of dollars lost in government revenue through the mediocre system and corrupt practices of the existing customs regime. The revolutionisation of the customs regime has significant advantages for the country. The ASYCUDA project is one area where the country has been able to utilise the opportunities provided by economic regionalism and co-operation for the development of the country.

West African Clearing House and its Impact on Sierra Leone

The West African Clearing House (WACH) is the first experiment in multilateral monetary co-operation in West Africa. The harmonisation of the different monetary zones and payment systems in the region will promote intra-Community trade. In March 1996, WACH was transformed into the West African Monetary Agency (WAMA), with the signing of the Articles of Agreement by the Central Banks in West Africa. This elevated WAMA to a full-fledged specialised institution of ECOWAS that will manage the monetary process in the Community. The Central Banks of the region established the Clearing House as a means to eliminate some of the problems that affect intra-regional trade. Because of the plurality of monetary zones in West Africa, each with a different exchange rate, all transactions are expressed in West African Unit of Account, which is equivalent to 1.4 (1997) Special Drawing Right (SDR) of the IMF. WAMA therefore, underpins the need for currency convertibility and a single currency for the sub-region.

WAMA has a role to play in overcoming payments obstacles to trade and regionalism, especially in a region where normal trade finance linkages are absent.[45] The Monetary Agency reduces to some extent the need for foreign exchange for intra-region trade transactions. However, due to the low level of intra-regional trade, the role of WAMA remains modest. Over the period 1976 to 1984, transactions channelled through WAMA rose steadily from about SDR 50 million to about SDR 225 million. It declined sharply to SDR 14 million in 1990. Since then, the level of transactions recovered reaching SDR 90 million in 1994.[46] The reasons for this unimpressive performance include the existence of large outstanding debts by some member states which led to the suspension of certain members from participating in the operations of WAMA, and the foreign exchange difficulties experienced by many countries within the context of the regional economic crisis. The wide exchange rate differentials between the administered rates of government and the parallel market rates encouraged traders to use the parallel market. Also, the relatively weak banking system in the region, with few outlets in the member countries, hampered transactions through WAMA.[47]

WAMA has created the opportunity for Sierra Leone's business community and economic operators to pay for imports from the ECOWAS region in the local currency. The settlement of payments for goods and services in the national currency limits the use of foreign exchange reserve and transfer costs for the government and economic operators. The total of transactions channelled through the Clearing House mechanism by Sierra Leone from 1976 - 77 to 1988 - 89 amounted to 2,028.9.UA, i.e. approximately US $28,404.6 million. From 1986/87 to 1988/89, transactions dropped to this lowest, 115 UA- -1986/87; 395 UA- -1989/88; 309 UA- -1988/89.[48] Sierra Leone's position reflects the general trend at Community level. The 1988/89 fiscal year recorded the lowest level of Community transactions in the sum of 28.2 UA million.

The ratio of Sierra Leone's trade transactions channelled through the Clearing House arrangements as a percentage of intra-regional trade remains low due to government restrictions imposed on payments, such as the Economic Emergency Regulation imposed in 1987, the IMF stabilisation conditionalities, as well as the complicated exchange rate disequlibrium. The homogeneity of Community products, inadequate transport and communications facilities are part of the reason for low transactions through the Clearing House.[49] Some exporters in Sierra Leone avoid the Clearing House arrangements because they prefer payment in foreign currencies such as US dollars and pound sterling.

The benefits derived from the Clearing House are not limited to an increase in the use of national currencies in intra-Community trade transactions, but also the enhancement of a corresponding relationship with other Community central banks and monetary authorities. But even the opportunity to pay for imports in local currency is becoming increasingly difficult due to the ever deteriorating economic circumstances and socio-political dislocations caused by the war. The economic advantages conferred on Sierra Leone by the Clearing House are many, but also entail some disadvantages. The short-comings include risks and uncertainties surrounding the exchange rate of currencies of member states which may affect the central bank and monetary authorities; the risk of devaluation and default in the payment of exchange losses or inconvertibility.[50]

A corollary to this is the ECOWAS initiative of policy harmonisation in the areas of exchange rates, rate of inflation, ratio of budget deficit/GDP and central bank credit to government. In pursuit of the ECOWAS commitment to the creation of a favourable regional business environment in 1997, the Community adopted a decision to co-ordinate and harmonise the macro-economic policies of member states. The target indicators for eventual economic and monetary union are set as follows: reduction of exchange rate variability to 10 per cent by 1998; attainment of a single digit inflation rate; reducing the ratio of budget deficit/GDP to 5 per cent; reduction to a ceiling of 10 per cent of central bank credit to government.[51] A regional monitoring and supervision mechanism is being put in place to assess the performance of national economies towards the achievement of these target indicators. The achievement of this macro-economic policy convergence largely depends on the political willingness and economic viability of the member states. Theoretically, the harmonisation of macro-economic policies is a positive development that will help the medium and long-term stability of member states economies, something that still remains desperately elusive. The economic development potential of the regional initiative for smaller states like Sierra Leone are numerous. However, one wonders how realistically attainable are these convergence criteria, against the background of poor economic performance and political instability of West African states.

ECOWAS Trade Fair and Private Sector Participation

The promotion of intra-regional trade through trade fairs and exhibitions is an integral part of not only achieving the ECOWAS economic regionalism objectives, but also to encourage the involvement of the private sector and the informal economy. The first ECOWAS Trade Fair was organised in Dakar, Senegal in June 1995, to mark the 20th anniversary of the Community. Sierra Leone participated in both the ECOWAS Trade Fairs in 1995 and 1999.

The Sierra Leone Export Development and Investment Corporation (SLEDIC) formed in 1993 as a forum for indigenous entrepreneurs, is entrusted with the responsibility for organising Sierra Leone's participation in the ECOWAS Trade Fair. This in itself is an important development because the private sector, as an organised interest group, is brought into the regionalisation process. It provides a valuable channel for private sector participation in Sierra Leone's ECOWAS regionalism. The objective of the country in participating in the trade fairs is to give international publicity to national products. Generally, participation in the trade fairs has been seen as a means to explore external markets for the country's export products. It is also perceived as an opportunity to learn about what other export competitors were doing in order to adjust national export strategies in the face of the challenges of a global market economy. Attracting private investors and motivating small scale producers to the need for export oriented production and marketing are some of the reasons for participation.[52]

In preparation for the ECOWAS Trade Fair, SLEDIC organised a mini-trade fair in order to select products and companies that would represent the country. The following companies represented Sierra Leone at the Trade Fair: i. Whitex Industry (plastic containers, soap and detergents); ii. Floko Arts and Works (textiles i.e., local garments) and home decorations); iii. SAYENU Industries (garments, dress-making materials); iv. Batik Design (handicrafts and home decorations); v. CORINA Designs (home and office decorations, tailoring and designing); vi. YAMINA Industries (shoes, bags, textiles and batik); vii. Eastern Farmers Multi-Purpose Co-operative Union (cocoa, coffee, kola nut, agricultural tools, carvings).[53]

The benefits derived from participation by the private sector are many and varied. Besides the international exposure of Sierra Leonean products, the ECOWAS Fairs provided the first opportunity for the private sector to organise the participation of the country in a regional international trade fair. Participation in itself was a learning process for the private sector. It provided a valuable organisational and marketing experience. The Sierra Leone participants had the opportunity to interact with other exhibitors and as such were able to assess the quality of their products. This first hand experience of new designs, production techniques, product variety and the utilisation of local materials, pricing and price negotiations, and the level of production technologies, all proved a valuable learning process for the participants. The Sierra Leonean exhibitors were able to assess the market demand for their products according to the volume of sales. Some products like batik designs, projected the cultural heritage of Sierra Leone as evidenced by the kind of questions the foreign visitors asked. They were also able to learn that production for the export market is quite different from that for the local market. Some participating companies were able to negotiate new sales contracts, while others established business links with intra-African trade groups such as the African Network for Support to Women Entrepreneurs (ANSWE).[54] The representative of Floko Arts and Works Company stated that 'I had the opportunity of interacting and establishing contacts with Senegalese and American representatives. We should be communicating with each other and sharing new ideas on technology in textile designing.' The Whitex Company's assessment is that:

The Trade Fair itself was a good start for ECOWAS and being the first, it provided every country and participant the opportunity to see what others are doing and could do in terms of trading with each other and exchanging ideas within the region. The Fair also provided manufacturers, producers and marketeers a mirror to look at themselves and to evaluate their products before venturing into the competitive world of export.[55]

Participation in the Trade Fair brought some valuable lessons in showing that market competitiveness only favours those producers with top quality commodities. The marketing and commercial experience learnt during the Dakar Trade Fair considerably helped SLEDIC to organise Sierra Leone's participation in the Accra Trade Fair. It is therefore not surprising that the country won the 'Asanti Stool' as prize for best exhibit, and had 70 per cent of exhibits sold. However, the majority of the exhibitors were small scale producers who do not have the capacity to pay for their own bills without serious financial consequences to their small business.[56] The trade fairs have been held at a time when the government was faced with increasing financial and political difficulties, due to the civil war. Therefore, neither government nor SLEDIC could make much financial input. Donor support from EU, UNDP and ECOWAS ensured Sierra Leone's participation in the fairs. It is important to note that the fair provided an opportunity for the private and informal sector in Sierra Leone to participate in the ECOWAS regionalisation process. It also made it possible to promote the economic potential of the country and encourage commercial exchanges with economic operators in Community countries and the rest of the world.

Sierra Leone and ECOWAS Regional Agricultural Development Strategy

The majority of economies in West Africa are agro-based. Agriculture constitutes a large share of the GNP, and accounts for more than half of the foreign exchange earnings, and also employment opportunities. The centrality of agriculture in the generation of national wealth and employment of labour in West Africa cannot be over emphasised. In recognition of the relevance of agricultural development to food security and nation building, the ECOWAS Community formulated a Regional Agricultural Development Strategy in 1982 as a framework for the development of common agricultural development. Article 25 of the

Revised Treaty provides for the adoption of a common agricultural policy in such areas as research, training, production, preservation, processing and marketing of the products of agriculture, forestry, livestock, and fisheries.[57] The ECOWAS agricultural development strategy covers such areas as the establishment of seed and cattle production centres; control of animal diseases, regional water supply programme, regional floating weeds control, and environmental protection. However, the objectives of the agricultural development strategy remain largely unrealised. The impressive prescriptions on paper on how to attain food security in West Africa have not been accompanied by practical regional agricultural achievements. Some regional programmes however have many advantages and opportunities for Sierra Leone to potentially reap the benefits of economic regionalism. This section will evaluate some of these regional opportunities.

Regional Rural Water Supply Project

Regional rural water supply is part of the agricultural development strategy. It is geared towards harnessing water resources both to meet the requirements for irrigation purposes and as a means of boosting agricultural output and supplying safe drinking water to communities.

An important component of this ECOWAS co-ordinated project is the regional village water supply programme. Existing water supply projects are those undertaken by member states, IGOs or international agencies through bilateral agreements. Access to clean and safe drinking water has been a constant problem in ECOWAS countries and the social and health repercussions have been costly. The Community approach is an attempt to address this problem. The Community programme for the development of village and pastoral water resources involves the creation of 3,200 water points throughout the region: 200 water points per member state.[58] The first phase of the programme (1992-1996) targeted the needs of member states most seriously affected or threatened by drought and desertification. About 90 per cent of the programme has been implemented. The second phase comprises countries not seriously threatened, but which have serious problems with access to water in the rural areas. Sierra Leone falls within this category. The total costs of constructing 3,200 water points at the rate of 200 water points per country has been estimated at US $54,360.000 million.[59] ECOWAS has mobilised external funding for the construction of these water points. The focus on regional co-ordination is to harmonise on-going programmes with IGOs, provide information on water development policies and accelerate the pace of well construction especially for areas that do not have access to safe drinking water.

Sierra Leone is in the second phase of implementation of the regional rural water supply programme. Though the country does not suffer from the devastation of drought and desertification, access to clean and safe drinking water in rural and some urban areas has been a perennial problem. The governments' effort has been complemented by NGOs such as Water Aid, CARE International and the German sponsored Bo-Pujehun project. The ECOWAS rural water supply project is potentially a major benefit for the country. The second phase of the project, which commenced in 1998, involves the construction of 400 water points for coastal countries like Sierra Leone. The implementation of the Sierra Leone phase of the regional water wells project has been adversely affected by the civil war. However, through economic regionalism and co-operation, the country has the advantage of benefiting from the construction of 400 rural water points. This opportunity provides rural communities with access to clean and safe drinking water, thereby reducing health hazards like cholera which is common in the country.

Regional Marine Development and Protection

Developing and exploiting the marine resources of West African coastal states is gradually gaining recognition as a lucrative area of regional economic endeavour. The importance of the artisanal fisheries sector in food security, employment and revenue generation has led to a renewed approach to developing the marine sector. Fisheries in West Africa, if properly harnessed, have the potential to be a continuing source of food, income at local level and foreign exchange from exports. Industrial fisheries have been mostly undertaken by the national governments through public-private investments.

The ruthless exploitation of the marine resources of West African coastal states by foreign vessels has been aided by the lack of effective national or regional monitoring, control and surveillance mechanisms.[60] The United Nations Convention on the Law of the Sea (UNCLOS) recognises the coastal nation's rights to an exclusive economic zone (EEZ) up to 200 nautical miles wide, and its responsibility to take measures to assure the proper conservation and management of the EEZ. Policing and protecting the marine resources of West Africa is not a problem peculiar to the region. The South Pacific Forum which relies heavily on marine resources as the main foreign exchange earner, cannot police its sea zones because of lack of resources and the predominance of foreign fishery operators.

The exploitation of Sierra Leone's marine resources, the richest breeding zone in West Africa, has been systematically carried out by foreigners with the tacit support of individuals such as the Afro-Lebanese fishery and diamond tycoon, Jamil Sahid Mohamed. Fish production in 1988 was about 44,500 tons in the marine artisanal sector, 2,500 tons from industrial marine fisheries and 1,600 tons from inland waters. Industrial fishing statistics for 1990 - 91 show that of 89 vessels (demersal trawlers, tuna vessels, shrimpers, purse seiners) licensed to fish only 28 vessels were registered under the Sierra Leone flag. The other vessels were from Korea, Russia, Ukraine, Italy and Japan. Government documents indicate a projected revenue of US $8-10 million a year in 1989-1992, generated from licences fees, royalties, and transhipment fees. The exploitation of the country's marine resources has not been in the best interest of the nation. A Ministry of Agriculture memorandum observed that:

> the benefits accruing to Sierra Leone out of this arrangement [i.e. USSR-Sierra Leone fishing agreement] are not commensurate with the degree of exploitation of our marine resources over the years if one reckons the thousands of tonnes of fish and shrimps caught and sold to third countries in hard currency.[61]

According to World Bank statistics, Sierra Leone loses US $30 million annually as a result of poaching by foreign vessels in Sierra Leone's territorial waters.

In the absence of an effective Monitoring, Control and Surveillance (MCS) mechanism in the country, the government established a joint venture with a foreign private company. The Marine Protection Services - Sierra Leone (MPSSL) started operation in 1991, with a 51 per cent government ownership. The MPSSL venture was however a complete failure as it ended up costing more than the entire revenue for the fisheries industry.[62] Another aerial surveillance scheme sponsored by Luxembourg ended up in failure due to inadequate funding. The inability of Sierra Leone, like other ECOWAS coastal countries, to monitor its marine resources, especially foreign fishing fleets, means that the country is not receiving the full economic returns from its fisheries.

A regional fishing committee initiated an aerial watch scheme at the end of August 1996. Sierra Leone joined the regional effort using aerial monitoring to protect West African fisheries from poaching. The first flight over Sierra Leone territorial waters took place in August 1996. The monitoring was organised by a regional commission on fisheries and funded by Luxembourg. The countries participating in the aerial monitoring of fishing zones were Cape Verde, The Gambia, Guinea, Guinea-Bissau, Mauritania, Senegal and Sierra Leone. According to the Deputy Director of Fisheries at the Ministry of Marine Resources, 'The use of planes for surveillance of the country's territorial waters will greatly reduce poaching which has almost crippled the country's fishing industry'.[63] As a result of ECOWAS MCS co-operation, Sierra Leone now has the potential to halt the serious problem of poaching and thus protect its marine resources. The regional surveillance mechanism provides the opportunity for the country to exploit its marine resources better, and generate millions of dollars which have previously been lost through poaching. However, this rather optimistic conclusion is not borne out by realities as poaching of Sierra Leone's fishery resources continues unabated. The collapse of the state's governing institutions as a result of patronage politics and the civil war has further strengthened the dominance of foreign economic operators in the fishery industry.

Regional Environmental Protection

In the mid-1980s, West Africa became a constant source of international media attention dealing with the importation and depositing of toxic waste within the region. These mounting reports warranted a resolution in 1988 by the ECOWAS Heads of State and Government banning the importation of toxic waste into West Africa and called for adoption of appropriate national legislation. Member states undertook to enact and enforce appropriate legislation prohibiting the importation, movement or dumping of any such wastes in their territories. An ECOWAS Dump-Watch was established in 1990 to co-ordinate at regional level this environmental problem, in collaboration with national environmental protection agencies.

This is of particular relevance to Sierra Leone where the problem of toxic waste dumping was becoming a controversial national issue in the 1980s. The problem had earlier surfaced during the presidency of Siaka Stevens when a US based company proposed a secret deal with State House to bury toxic waste materials in Sierra Leone for a payment of US $25 million.[64] Abdul Karim Koroma explains that the arrangements collapsed due to the intervention of Sierra Leonean nationals in the US who, acting on covert information, responded with outrage against the issue. This problem surfaced again in July 1988 when the government was informed that arrangements had been made by a construction company together with two Sierra Leoneans to have toxic waste materials dumped at the KingTom garbage site in Freetown. According to Koroma's account, investigations proved their culpability and the government therefore decided that the three agents were to pay for the technical services necessary for the removal of the waste. In Brussels, a report was carried in a local newspaper of a 'two hundred and twenty million dollars scheme to ship household waste to Sierra Leone where it would be used to produce methane gas and electricity'.[65] The Sport and Import company of Mechelen responsible for the waste claimed that the project would be environmentally friendly, though it was condemned by the environmental Green Movement as a potential health hazard. Koroma further explained that, according to ecologist Francios Rodants, Belgian MEP and vice-president of the EEC Environmental Commission, the project was 'simply a waste-dumping scheme dressed up as a high technology venture'.[66]

The regional environment initiative and monitoring mechanism had advantages for the country because Sierra Leone was placed on the list of priority countries for constant and vigilant supervision. The Community rationale is that the serious health hazard resulting from dumping toxic waste in any member state will have a spillover effect in other Community countries. Through the Dump-Watch mechanism and reporting system, Sierra Leone was able to halt this environmental hazard because Community members were always ready to alert the Sierra Leonean public and civil society organisations about the movement of toxic waste bound for the country. Since the coming into operation of the ECOWAS resolution banning the importation and dumping of toxic waste, the threat of dumping of toxic waste in the country has been eliminated. Information is shared among Community countries on the activities of unscrupulous Sierra Leoneans and their Western cohorts with regards to toxic waste dumping. Regional environmental protection is therefore another potential benefit generated by ECOWAS regionalism and co-operation.

Sierra Leone and ECOWAS Infrastructural Development Strategy

The ECOWAS Infrastructural Development Strategy is an attempt to enhance the production and physical integration of the economic community. It is an acknowledged fact that the lack of adequate physical links between ECOWAS member states constitutes greater obstacles to trade than traditional tariff and non-tariff barriers. A large regional market can only function well if the national markets are effectively linked through infrastructural facilities such as roads and telecommmunitcations. The lack of these creates a situation wherein transaction costs are relatively high. This is what is referred to as the costs of non-integration. The regionalisation of production is an important means of generating tangible benefits for the people of the region. Without an adequate regional transportation and communications network, economic regionalism would have very little meaning in a region spread over 6,142,000 square kilometres. Economic regionalism of any group of countries by implication means easy access to each others' markets. This is what ECOWAS aims to achieve through its regional development strategy.

Against this background, the Community is implementing a regional network of roads and telecommunications development programmes to enhance the physical integration of the region. The ECOWAS Fund provides guarantees in respect of foreign investments, provides finances for and facilitates the financing of specific projects of member states geared towards the integration of production within the Community.

Regional Road Transport Sector

Road transport constitutes the dominant mode of transport accounting for over 85 per cent of the movement of the production factors. A Community Transport Programme was adopted in 1980 to promote effective linkage of member states of the Community. It was seen as a means to facilitate intra-Community economic and social activities and to ensure that the transport system helped achieve the objectives of economic regionalism and co-operation. In furtherance of the objective of regional physical integration, a road network, which constitutes the basic foundation of a well meshed sub-regional network, was adopted. It includes: i. the Trans-West African Coastal Highway which runs through Nigeria, Benin, Togo, Ghana, Côte d'Ivoire, Liberia, Sierra Leone, Guinea, Guinea-Bissau, The Gambia, Senegal and Mauritania; ii. the Trans-Sahelian Highway (Dakar-Niamey).[67]

The Mano River bridge linking Liberia and Sierra Leone in the south-east, and the Kambia bridge connecting Sierra Leone and Guinea in the north, form integral components of the Lagos-Nouakchott axis of the ECOWAS coastal road network. The pace of implementation of the regional road network project has been affected by the weak macro-economic environment and civil unrest within the Community.

Through the ECOWAS-donor multilateral agreements, the maintenance and rehabilitation of the existing transport infrastructure is being implemented. For example, the World Bank Sub-Saharan African Transport Programme (SSATP), and the ACP-EEC West African regional projects under the Lomé IV Convention. As a result of this Community approach to physical integration, Sierra Leone and other ECOWAS countries are at an advanced stage of implementing the World Bank transport sector adjustment programme. The regional approach in seeking multilateral funding for the maintenance and rehabilitation of the road network in the member states is a major infrastructural benefit derived from ECOWAS regionalism.

The current status of implementation of the trans-coastal highway indicates 84 per cent completion, and 79.2 per cent completion of the trans-Sahelian route. For the trans-coastal route, Sierra Leone is among the five countries with missing links, with a section of unpaved distance of 178.5 kilometres. The ECOWAS regional road network constitutes the main arterial link in the member states' national road network.

Through the Second United Nations Transport and Communication Decade for Africa (UNTACDA II), Sierra Leone roads projects were among the projects for roads and road transport approved in 1991. The Monrovia-Freetown highway (i.e., Bandajuma-Zimmi-MRU bridge section (95.5 km), being part of the trans-coastal highway, is one of the ECOWAS regional road network projects submitted for approval. The total cost of the approved project is US $52.50 million. In addition, approval for funding under UNTACDA II has been granted for the rehabilitation and upgrading of Rogbere Junction (northern Sierra Leone) and Pamelap road (Guinea-Sierra Leone border). This brings the total costs of these projects to US $104 million. The Bandajuma-Zimmi-MRU bridge section is part of the Freetown-Monrovia highway project. The objective is to link Sierra Leone and Liberia by means of an all-weather road in line with the physical integration desired by ECOWAS and MRU. This will complete the

ECOWAS trans-coastal road network link, boost economic activities and open up important agricultural zones. The project entails the tarring of the 95.5 km long Bandajuma-Zimmi-MRU bridge section. It also includes construction of bridges over the rivers Moa, Sewa and Bandajuma (see Map of Sierra Leone). The project will be constructed according to ECOWAS road safety standards. The climate of insecurity in the country as a result of the civil war has stalled the implementation of the project.

The donor funding for this road project includes: ECOWAS Fund - US $2.5 million; OPEC Fund - US $5 million; BADEA - US $8 million; ADB/Nigeria Trust Fund - US $7.6 million. The total amount pledged is US $23.1 million, leaving a gap of US $42.7 million.[68] However, the following donors have pledged to provide the shortfall: ECOWAS Fund, ADB, IDN, and the German government.

The benefits derived from the regional roads project is not limited to enhancing physical integration. The tarring of roads and construction of bridges in the country will help reduce the significant financial burden on the government. It will enable the government to re-allocate scarce resources to other needy areas such as health, agriculture and education. It is highly probable that against the background of Sierra Leone's deteriorating economic situation, it would be difficult for the government to undertake full scale construction of these bridges and roads. Consequently, the road network in the country will remain in a poor state, thereby hindering smooth economic activity, holding up the physical integration of the country and the sub-region. These bridges will remain in their 'traditional' state of neglect and its often disastrous effect with the loss of lives through accidents on these death-traps. For Sierra Leone to single-handedly finance the construction of roads and bridges to the tune of US $104 million is a Herculean task when one takes into account the increasing financial difficulties faced by the country. Through Sierra Leone's ECOWAS regionalism, the donors have further become partners in the country's development process.

The other aspect of this physical integration is the environmental destruction that goes with the project. The environmental impact would entail the destruction of forest reserves along the road construction route. It will also lead to the dislocation of small rural communities who have for decades lived in the area where the roads are being constructed. The disruption of the traditional life of the people also has a significant impact on their economic well-being. The negative aspects of the infrastructural gains could be regarded as the costs of regionalism.

Road transport measures taken to facilitate the international movement of goods between member states include: i. the establishment of an ECOWAS Brown Card relating to Motor Vehicle Third Party insurance liability which covers all member states; ii. a protocol relating to Inter-State Road Transportation between ECOWAS countries (TRIE). The protocol on inter-state road transit of goods has provided an economic opportunity for private investment in the transhipment of goods. Inter-state road transit allows for the transportation of goods by road from one customs border to another, free of duties, taxes and restrictions while in transit. A thriving transhipment of goods to neighbouring countries by Sierra Leonean entrepreneurs using cargo trucks is fast developing. The transhipment operators have close links with the West African Union of Road Transporters (UTRAO).

Conclusion

An economic balance sheet of Sierra Leone's ECOWAS regionalisms reveals both positive and negative effects. Sierra Leone's participation in the economic community illustrates the fact that economic regionalism requires participating governments to relinquish their freedom of action over progressively wider areas of economic and social policies. It also requires increasing diminution of sovereignty over some economic, fiscal and commercial policy areas. The elimination of customs duties and adoption of a common external tariff has serious financial implications for Sierra Leone in view of its dependence on international trade revenue. Furthermore, the free movement of the factors of production not only has debilitating economic and social consequences, but is sometimes politically unacceptable. However, these negative effects are not commensurate with the numerous economic benefits accruing to the nation as a result of ECOWAS regionalism and co-operation. Even in situations where immediate and tangible gains are not yet realised, the potential economic opportunities are there to be exploited by the country. The opportunity cost of Sierra Leone's contribution, financial or otherwise, far outweighs the economic gains it has brought to the state. The pooling of sovereignty, with its accompanying limitations, is the price that the country has to pay to achieve the benefits of economic regionalism and co-operation. Against the background of Sierra Leone's underdeveloped economy, with inadequate infrastructural facilities, pooling of sovereignty has been an advantage to the country. An inquiry into the opportunity costs of Sierra Leone's ECOWAS regionalism is an excellent way to determine the value of ECOWAS to the development of the country.

The traditional economic benefits derived from the freeing of trade have provided access to a larger West African market for the country. The underdeveloped nature of the country's economy and industrial base has made it difficult to fully exploit the potential of the economies of scale. It has, in the process, exposed domestic industries to stiff regional competition. However, the large regional market has provided access to cheaper goods and a broader choice of commodities for the ordinary people in the country. Investment opportunities through the ECOWAS-ACP-EU Industrial Forum is a major advantage for the governments' effort to liberalise its economy. Trade liberalisation has brought some positive effects to the traditional handicraft industry, though it has repercussions for the country's wild life and protection of endangered species. Limited intra-Community trade has made the country a net importer from the Community. Thus, Community partners take advantage of the protective tariff cover to flood the domestic market with cheap goods. Free movement has brought a variety of positive and negative effects, but its negative effects are mainly felt in the diamond industry, informal economy and the civil war. The ASYCUDA project has the potential to revolutionise the outdated Customs regime in the country, and will create the potential for enhanced revenue generation. The private sector in the country has been brought into the regionalisation process through their participation in the ECOWAS Trade Fairs. Taking into consideration the positive impact of some aspects of the regional agricultural and infrastructural development strategies, Sierra Leone, in economic terms, is a net beneficiary in ECOWAS regionalism. However, the underdeveloped economy and the nature of domestic politics based on clientelism and patrimonialism have all made it difficult for the country to fully exploit the potential and opportunities of ECOWAS regionalism and co-operation.

Notes and References

[1] See Commonwealth Report, *Trade Liberalisation in the Economic Community of West African States: An Assessment*, London: Commonwealth Secreatriat, May 1997; P. G. Elkan, 'Measuring the Impact of Economic Integration among Developing Countries', *Journal of Common Market Studies*, Vol. 14, 1975; S. K. B. Asante, *The Political Economy of Regionalism in Africa*, New York: Praeger, 1986.

[2] Commonwealth Report, *Trade Liberalisation in the Economic Community of West African States: An Assessment*, op. cit., 1997.
[3] Peter Elkan, 'Measuring the Impact of Economic Integration among Developing Countries', op. cit., 1975; Uka Ezenwa, *ECOWAS and the Integration of West Africa*, London: C. Hurst and Co., 1983.
[4] Caroline Thomas, *Global Governance, Development and Human Security: The Challenge of Poverty and Inequality*, London, Pluto, 2000, pp. 69-90.
[5] Asante, 1986, p. 112.
[6] Michael B. Brown, *Africa's Choices: After Thirty Years of the World Bank*, Middlesex: Penguin Books, 1997.
[7] Ibid.
[8] Asante, p. 31.
[9] Commonwealth Report, op. cit., 1995.
[10] Ibid.
[11] This researcher, during field trips in West Africa was not able to pay hotel bills in Naira (Nigerian currency). An explanation that Togo has removed all non-tariff barriers of a monetary nature was scorned by the hotel management. What came out clearly in the discussion was the apparent lack of information on ECOWAS trade liberalisation programme among economic operators.
[12] *Decision of the Heads of State and Government of ECOWAS relating to Trade Liberalisation in respect of traditional handicraft*, A/DEC:1/5/81.
[13] Commonwealth Report, op. cit.
[14] Ibid.
[15] Ibid.
[16] M. I. Mansaray, 'ASYCUDA: A Framework for an Integrated Socio-Economic Development of ECOWAS Countries' in S. C. Bhatnagar and M. Odedna (eds.), *Social Implications of Computers in Developing Countries*, New Delhi: Tata McGraw - Hill Publishing Ltd., 1992; See also, Monne Wolters and Peter Coffrey (eds.), *The Netherlands and EC Membership Evaluated*, London: Pinter, 1990.
[17] Ibid.
[18] P. Keating, *Ireland and EC Membership Evaluated*, London: Pinter, 1991, see also, Walters and Coffery, op. cit., 1990.
[19] M. I. Marsaray, op. cit., 1992.
[20] M. Wolters and P. Coffery (eds.), *The Netherlands and EC Membership Evaluated*, London, Pinter, 1990.
[21] Ibid. See also; Report by Commonwealth Secretariat, 1997; R. L. Allen, 'Integration in Less Developed Areas', Vol. XIV, 3, 1961.
[22] *Trade Liberalisation in the Economic Community of West African States* op. cit. 1997, p. 3.
[23] Ibid.
[24] *ECOWAS Handbook of International Trade*, Lagos, ECOWAS Secretariat, 1995, pp. 8-9.
[25] *The Economic Intelligence Unit Report* EIU-Country Report, 1st Quarter 1997, p. 22.
[26] Commonwealth Report, op. cit., 1997.
[27] Various issues, World Bank- *World Tables 1994*; IMF- *Trade Data 1995*; UNCTAD- *Commodity Yearbook*.
[28] UNCTAD, 1973, pp. 13-14.

[29] ECOWAS, *Protocol Relating to the Free Movement of Persons and Right of Residence,* 1979.
[30] *Commonwealth Report.*
[31] A. Deardorff & W. Stolper, 'Effects of Smuggling under African Conditions: A Factual, Institutional and Analytical Discussion' *Weltwirtschaft. Archive* Band 1126, Heft 1, 1990, p. 116-41.
[32] UNCTAD, *ASYCUDA-Trade Facilitation Programme,* 1996.
[33] M. l. Mansaray- 'ASYCUDA: A Framework for an Integrated Socio-Economic Development of ECOWAS Countries' in *Social Implications of Computers in Developing Countries* S. C. Bhatnagar & M. Odedra (eds.), 1992, pp. 244-60.
[34] Ibid.
[35] Ibid.
[36] Ibid.
[37] UNCTAD- *ASYCUDA-Trade Facilitation Programme,* 1996.
[38] Mansaray, op. cit.
[39] Ibid.
[40] UNCTAD-FALPRO- *ASYCUDA-Trade Facilitation Programme,* 1991.
[41] Mansaray, op. cit.
[42] Ibid.
[43] Ibid.
[44] *Trade, Customs, Immigration, Money and Payments Department Report,* Lomé, October 1997.
[45] *Report on the Seminar on Understanding the West African Clearing House Mechanism,* Lagos, Central Bank of Nigeria, January 1990.
[46] Ibid.
[47] Ibid.
[48] *WACH Annual Report,* Freetown, 1990, p. 89.
[49] Central Bank of Nigeria, op. cit.
[50] Ibid.
[51] *Harmonisation of Macro-Economic Policies of ECOWAS Member States: Surveillance Mechanism,* ECOWAS Secretariat, Lagos, July 1997.
[52] *Report on Sierra Leone Participation in the First ECOWAS Trade Fair in Dakar, 25 May - 4 June 1995,* Freetown: SLEDIC, 1995.
[53] *Report on Sierra Leone Participation in the First ECOWAS Trade Fair-Dakar,* 25 May-4 June 1995, SLEDIC, Freetown, 1995.
[54] The advantages of the private sector participation in the ECOWAS Trade Fairs are largely drawn from the SLEDIC reports.
[55] Ibid, p. 11.
[56] Ibid.
[57] ECOWAS Revised Treaty 1993, op. cit.
[58] UNDP/ECA/UNEP, *Multi-Sectoral Programme of Assistance to ECOWAS: Master Plan for Co-ordination of Programmes for Combating Desertification/Natural Resources Management in West African Sub-region,* (RAF/88/047), March 1993 and 1997.
[59] Ibid.
[60] Ibid.
[61] Memorandum of Ministry of Agriculture, 16 January 1990.
[62] A. K. Koroma, op. cit., 1996.

[63] Sierra Leone Web, September 1996, available at http:www.Sierra-Leone.org/.
[64] A. K. Koroma, op. cit., 1996, extensively discusses this issue. This section draws from Koroma's analysis of the toxic water controversy during the Stevens and Momoh regimes.
[65] Ibid.
[66] Ibid., p. 86.
[67] *Donor Co-ordination Meeting of ECOWAS Regional Road Transport Programme. Technical Consultation Meeting of Member States*, Lomé: ECOWAS Fund, March 1995.
[68] Ibid.

Conclusion

The analysis of Sierra Leone in ECOWAS reveals the nature, dynamics and complexity of the politics of economic regionalism in West Africa. The developments within ECOWAS regionalism are part of the wider transformation in the international system and global economy. The ECOWAS response to the new regionalism is an attempt to strategically position itself to realise the benefits of globalisation, i.e. freeing of trade, creating the enabling economic and political environment for the import of foreign direct investment, and access to information technology. ECOWAS regionalism has therefore provided the collective political and economic bargaining bloc and diplomatic forum for dealing with the outside world. It has also institutionalised co-operation in West Africa across a range of issues, and further provided the framework for managing intra-state conflicts and inter-state disputes. It remains to be seen whether the strategic positioning of ECOWAS within the context of the re-structuring of the global market economy will in fact benefit the weak and fragile economies, or whether the so-called 'trickle down' effects would create better welfare and support human security for the peoples of the sub-region. However, it is evident that the integration of ECOWAS into the global economy also simultaneously marginalises the economies of the sub-region. It has become evident that the benefits of globalisation are only available to those who have access to the opportunities of globalisation. The fact that the majority of the weak and developing economies in West Africa do not have the capability to exploit the benefits and opportunities of globalisation points to the further marginalisation of the region in the global economic and political processes. Is ECOWAS therefore doomed to remain in its peripheral status as 'producer of what it cannot consume and eats what it cannot produce'? The recent anti-capitalist demonstrations in Seattle, Washington and Prague illustrate the opposition to the effects of globalisation and direction the world economy is taking that further marginalises the poor and developing regions. Is this the dawn of a new economic and political order that would be transparent and favours the poor and developing regions? It would be premature to be optimistic about these recent developments because the political, financial and economic structures of the World Bank, IMF and WTO are entrenched in such a way that their vested interests will always remain their priority, even to the detriment of the developing regions.

It becomes obvious that more than two decades of ECOWAS regionalism have not been able to reverse the progressive economic deterioration of the sub-region. A variety of domestic and external factors have coalesced to make the achievement of the economic integration objectives difficult. But out of this relative economic failure, the ECOWAS political and security regionalisms have emerged as the most important aspects, and in the process have revamped what was then a moribund economic community. The ECOWAS expansion into the security domain with the establishment of the West African peacekeeping and intervention force, ECOMOG, the declaration of political principles in 1991 which enjoined member states to respect democratic principles, human rights and fundamental freedoms, and the revision of the Treaty in 1993 which specifically provided for political and security co-operation, have fundamentally changed the nature, scope and level of economic regionalism in West Africa. A major development is the signing of the ECOWAS protocol relating to the Mechanism for Conflict Prevention, Management, Resolution, Peacekeeping and Security in 1999. This protocol is the acknowledgement of the inextricable link between conflicts, economic development, democratisation, regional peace and security. The protocol provides an institutional framework to prevent conflict, manage and resolve regional conflicts and peacekeeping. The protocol is important because it creates a Mediation and Security Council which authorises all forms of regional intervention. The mediation and security council has similarity with the UN Security Council. Conflict prevention and peacebuilding are other relevant provisions of the protocol. These provisions demonstrate the fact that ECOWAS has learnt valuable lessons from its peacekeeping and conflict management efforts in West Africa. The focus on conflict prevention is an attempt to move away from its usual 'fire brigade' response to conflicts in West Africa, whilst peacebuilding not only potentially strengthens post-conflict transition and prevents a relapse into further violence, but also as a strategy to prevent conflicts in the sub-region escalating into armed violence. The protocol is an attempt to strengthen regional peace and security in West Africa. The institutionalised political, security and foreign policy co-operation has made it possible for the ECOWAS Defence and Security Council to periodically review the conflicts and security threats within the sub-region.

ECOWAS security regionalism, in spite of its limitations, has become part of the post-Cold War debate on security regionalism in world politics and, in the process, this relatively unknown regional player is now setting a new agenda in terms of co-operative security and burden-sharing with the UN for the maintenance of international peace and security. In comparison, the model for *sui generis* economic regionalism, the EU, has still yet to come to terms with the establishment of a EU security organ in the shape of a European Rapid Reaction Force, which enable the community to intervene in regional crises such as the Balkans. Within the context of West Africa, the novel initiative for a peacekeeping, peace enforcement and conflict management force fashioned by the ECOWAS community has considerable impact on the sub-region. ECOMOG's conflict management and peace support operation activities in Liberia, Sierra Leone and Guinea Bissau have helped to prevent further killings in these war-torn societies, restore fragile peace and security, and facilitate the process of state re-construction. The ECOWAS and ECOMOG peacekeeping and conflict management activities in West Africa have a considerable impact on African international relations. The ECOMOG example influenced the establishment of the OAU Mechanism for Conflict Prevention, Management and Resolution in 1993, and even the creation of the SADC Organ for Politics, Defence and Security. The peacekeeping and intervention operations in West Africa have considerably eroded the salience of the traditional principle of sovereignty and non-intervention. ECOWAS has therefore abrogated to itself the right of collective intervention in domestic conflicts to prevent humanitarian catastrophes, gross violations of human rights, war crimes and state collapse. Therefore, ECOMOG could be a model for the establishment of an African peacekeeping and intervention force.

However, the experiment with security regionalism within the context of economic integration and co-operation is not without problems. It becomes evident that this purely military response to conflicts and insecurity in West Africa would be inadequate to address non-military security threats such as poverty, underdevelopment, diseases such as HIV/AIDS, environmental problems, and ethno-religious identities. In effect, ECOMOG cannot provide long-term security in West Africa, especially against the background of the increasing reluctance of the sub-regional hegemon, Nigeria, to provide the financial and economic resources needed for the maintenance of regional peace and security. The purely military response to insecurities and conflicts in West Africa is a very expensive enterprise and it has become increasingly difficult for ECOWAS governments to justify the diversion of millions of dollars from national development to regional peace and security. The fact that ECOMOG operates without a defined doctrine for peacekeeping and peace support operations means that the security organ has not conducted its peace enforcement operations according to the norms of international law relating to the conduct of warfare. The excesses of ECOMOG's peacekeeping and peace enforcement in Sierra Leone which were graphically portrayed by Samura's *Out of Africa* documentary shows the lack of neutrality of the West African peacekeepers. But this is a difficult issue because the manner in which ECOMOG was deployed in the civil war with no peace to keep made it inevitable that the regional intervention force would become embroiled in the conflict. Despite these limitations, ECOWAS has demonstrated its 'regionness', i.e., it has been transformed from a mere object to the subject of international politics with the capacity to articulate the interests of West Africa.

Sierra Leone's ECOWAS regionalism has brought to the fore the political, diplomatic and security relevance of economic regionalism. Sierra Leone's regionalisation process since 1975 demonstrates that economic regionalism is an aspect of development that is essentially political. It is arguable whether Sierra Leone is a net 'beneficiary' or 'loser' in ECOWAS regionalism. Economically, the country has not been able to exploit the advantages and opportunities of ECOWAS regionalism because of the nature of domestic politics, the underdeveloped nature of the economy, poor infrastructural facilities, and the manner in which the state had been incorporated into the international economic system through colonial rule. The external dependent nature of the economy deflects attention from ECOWAS regionalism and intra-regional trade. However, the ECOWAS free movement, in spite of its pressures on the economy, has created a new community spirit and provided socio-economic opportunities for the informal sector and ordinary Sierra Leoneans. The ECOWAS declaration against dumping of toxic waste, its regional water supply programme, the ASYCUDA project to revolutionise the customs regime, and infrastructural development strategy are potential benefits of ECOWAS regionalism on Sierra Leone. But the responsibility rests with the government of Sierra Leone to formulate and implement realistic policies that would strengthen the country's participation in ECOWAS and further exploit practical avenues on how to maximise the economic benefits of ECOWAS regionalism.

Arguably, the most significant benefit of Sierra Leone's ECOWAS regionalism is in the realm of politics. The political implications of Sierra Leone's ECOWAS regionalism have repercussions far beyond the region itself. ECOWAS, as an instrument of foreign policy for a small and relatively insignificant state such as Sierra Leone has provided opportunities for the country to expand its political and diplomatic influence through the collective solidarity of the economic community. The institutionalised political, foreign and security co-operation in West Africa has provided an 'alibi' for the country on controversial international issues. It is this foreign and security co-operation that made it possible for ECOWAS to facilitate peace making, peacekeeping, peace enforcement and conflict management in Sierra Leone. The defence of democracy and constitutional rule in Sierra Leone has been regarded as the most important benefit derived from ECOWAS regionalism. But in the process it has brought into question the propriety of intervention by ECOMOG to restore constitutional order in West Africa. Though some political analysts perceive this as a monumental development in the political history of ECOWAS in terms of collective intervention to overthrow a military regime, others criticised the *realpolitik* interests of the then Nigerian military junta under late General Abacha, and asked why similar actions have not taken in the case of Niger, Guinea Bissau and Côte d'Ivoire. The ECOWAS defence of democracy in Sierra Leone also highlights another criticism in that the regional organisation is often anti-change and always intervenes on behalf of beleaguered regimes such as Doe in Liberia, Kabbah in Sierra Leone and Viera in Guinea Bissau. The pre-occupation of ECOWAS to preserve the status quo, no matter how corrupt and oppressive the system may be, is a solid reminder that ECOWAS is really about regime protection and survival. The peacekeeping and intervention operations of ECOMOG in Sierra Leone, as in Liberia, have serious implications for the civil war peace settlement and the consolidation of peace and security in post-war Sierra Leone. The involvement of ECOMOG in the criminal exploitation of the war economy, especially the diamond resources, has inadvertently contributed to fuelling and prolonging the war in Sierra Leone. The exploitation of the criminalised war economy by those entrusted with the responsibility to keep and enforce the peace, more than anything else, advances the case for regulation, accountability and transparency of ECOMOG operations.

ECOWAS conflict management in West Africa has led to the evolution of a new kind of partnership with the UN. The ECOWAS-UN co-operative security for peacekeeping and conflict management in West Africa has further strengthened UN task-sharing with regional organisations. ECOWAS, in the case of Liberia and Sierra Leone, has rescued the UN in the maintenance of international peace and security. The ECOWAS-UN partnership helped to focus international attention on the brutal conflict in Sierra Leone. Sierra Leone therefore became a useful entry point to focus international attention on African problems at the dawn of the new millennium. ECOWAS-UN co-operative security in Sierra Leone has, amongst other things, led to the fundamental strategic rethinking of traditional UN peacekeeping as a result of the humiliation of UN peacekeepers after the withdrawal of the ECOMOG contingent.

Against the background of the significant role played by ECOWAS regionalism in the civil war peace settlement and conflict management in Sierra Leone, the post-war foreign policy approach of the country should adopt a tripartite policy based on constructive engagement with: i. ECOWAS regionalism; ii. African international relations; and, iii. proactive continuity with the West. This new political economy of post-war foreign policy is based on a pragmatic blend of African and Western-centred engagements for peace, security and development in Sierra Leone. The African-centred approach would provide the forum to address issues such as conflict diamonds and the role of regional states in fuelling wars in other African countries such as the covert involvement of Charles Taylor and Blaise Campaoré in Sierra Leone. On the other hand, the Western-centred approach would make it possible to focus international attention and international diplomatic support at the UN and amongst key western governments to support the African initiatives for peace, security and conflict management. Despite the erosion of national sovereignty within the context of ECOWAS economic and security regionalism, Sierra Leone has, on the whole been a net beneficiary from the politics of economic regionalism. What is needed is sustained political and diplomatic support and commitment for ECOWAS regionalism in order for the country to strategically position itself to better maximise the benefits of regionalism, but at the same time put into place mechanisms that would limit the costs of Sierra Leone's ECOWAS regionalism. However, the civil war, the destruction of infrastructure and the collapse of governing institutions have greatly hindered the capability of the country to reap the benefits of economic regionalism. The economic and development dislocation caused by the war are major obstacles for Sierra Leone's ECOWAS regionalism.

Bibliography

Abdullah, I. (1998), 'Bush Path to Destruction: The Origin and Character of the Revolutionary United Front/Sierra Leone.', *Journal of Modern African Studies*, vol. 36, no. 2, pp. 207-213.

Abraham, A. (1997), 'War and Transition to Peace: A Study of State Conspiracy in Perpetrating Armed Conflict', *African Development*, vol. 22, no. 3-4.

Adibe, C. (1994), 'ECOWAS in Comparative Perspective', in Shaw, T. and Okolo, J. (eds), *The Political Economy of Foreign Policy in ECOWAS*, St. Martin's Press, New York.

Adler, E. and Barnet M. (eds) (1998), *Security Communities*, Cambridge University Press, Cambridge.

African Leadership Forum (1992), *The Kampala Document: Towards a Conference on Security, Stability, Development and Co-operation*, African Leadership Forum, New York.

Ajami, F. (1992), 'Somalia: the Work of Order and Mercy', *US News and World Report*, 21 December.

Alagappa, M. (1995), 'Regionalism and Conflict Management: A Framework for Analysis', *Review of International Studies*, vol. 21, no. 4, pp. 359-387.

Alagappa, M. and Inoguchi, T. (eds) (1999), *International Security Management and the United Nations*, UN University Press, Tokyo.

Alao, A., Mackinlay, J. and Olonisakin, F. (1999) *Peacekeepers, Politicians and Warlords: The Liberian Peace Process*, United Nations University, Tokyo.

Aluko, O. (ed.) (1977), *The Foreign Policies of African States*, Hodder and Stoughton, London.

Amin, S. (1976), *Unequal Development*, Monthly Press Review, New York.

Asante, S.K.B. (1986), *The Political Economy of Regionalism in Africa: A Decade of Economic Community of West African States*, Praeger, New York.

Bach, D.C. (1983) 'The Politics of West African Economic Co-operation: CEAO and ECOWAS', *Journal of Modern African Studies*, vol. 24, no. 4, pp. 605-613.

Bach, D.C. (ed.) (1999), *Regionalisation in Africa: Integration and Disintegration*, James Curey, Oxford.

Baldwin, D. (1997), 'The Concept of Security', *Review of International Studies*, vol. 23, no. 1, pp. 5-26.

Baylis, J. and Smith, S. (eds) (1997), *Globalization of World Politics: An Introduction to International Relations*, Oxford University Press, Oxford.

Berdal, M. and Malone, D. (eds) (2000), *Greed and Grievance: Economic Agendas in Civil War,* Lynne Rienner, London.
Boutros-Ghali, B. (1992), *Agenda for Peace,* UN Publications, New York.
Bradshaw, S. (1996) 'The Coming Chaos?' *Moving Pictures Bulletin,* Issue 25, February, pp. 18-19.
Brehun, L. (1991), *Liberia: The War of Horror,* Adwinsa Publications, Accra.
Brown, C. (1997), *Understanding International Relations,* Macmillan, London.
Bundu, A. (1999), 'Beyond Peace-keeping', *West Africa,* 6 December - 12 December.
Butler, F. (1997), 'Regionalism and Integration', in J. Baylis and S. Smith (eds), *Globalization of World Politics,* Oxford University Press, Oxford.
Buzan, B. (1991), 'New Patterns of Global Security in the Twenty First Century', *International Affairs,* vol. 67, no. 3, pp. 431-451.
Callaghy, T.M. (1990), 'Lost between State and Markets' in J. Nelson (ed.), *Economic Crisis and Policy Choice: The Politics of Adjustment in the Third World,* Princeton University Press, New York.
Chazan, N., Lewis, P., Mortimer, R., Rothchild, D. and Stedman, S. (1999), *Politics and Society in Contemporary Africa,* 3rd edition, Lynne Rienner, Boulder.
Cheru, F. (1989) *The Silent Revolution in Africa: Debt, Development and Democracy,* Zed Books, London.
Clapham, C. (1982), *Private Patronage and Public Power: Political Clientelism and the Modern State,* Frances Pinter, London.
Claude, I. (1965), *Swords into Ploughshares: The Problems and Progress of International Organisation,* London University Press, London.
Coleman, J.S. and Rosberg, C.G. (1966) *Political Parties and National Integration in Tropical Africa* University of California Press, Berkeley.
Collier, P. (2000), 'Doing Well out of War: An Economic Perspective', in M. Berdal and D. Malone (eds), *Greed and Grievance: Economic Agendas in Civil War,* Lynne Rienner, London.
Commonwealth Report (1997), *Trade Liberalisation in the Economic Community of West African States: An Assessment,* Commonwealth Secretariat, London.
Creveld, M. van (1992), *On Future of War,* Brasseys, London.
Damrosch, L.F. (ed.) (1993), *Enforcing Restraint: Collective Intervention in Internal Conflicts,* Council of Foreign Relations, Inc., New York.
Davies, A. (1983), 'Cost-benefit Analysis within ECOWAS', *The World Today,* May.
Deng, F., Kimaro, S., Lyons, T., Rothchild, D. and Zartman, I.W. (1996), *Sovereignty as Responsibility: Conflict Management in Africa,* The Brookings Institutions, Washington D.C.

Deutsch, K., Burrell, S. and Kann, R., (1958), *Political Community and the North Atlantic Area: International Organization in the Light of Historical Experience*, Princeton University Press, New Jersey.

Dickson, A.K. (1997), *Development and International Relations: A Critical Introduction*, Polity, Cambridge.

Drucker, P.F. (1993), *Post-Capitalist Society*, Butterworth-Heinemann, London.

Dunn, J. (ed.) (1978), *West African States: Failure and Promise: A Study in Comparative Politics*, Cambridge University Press, Cambridge.

ECA (1983), *ECA and African Development 1983-2008*, ECA Secretariat, Addis Ababa.

ECA (1985), *Proposals for Strengthening Economic Integration in West Africa*, ECA Secretariat, Addis Ababa.

ECA (1989), *African Alternative Framework to Structural Adjustment Programmes for Socio-Economic Recovery and Transformation*, ECA Secretariat, Addis Ababa.

Economic Intelligence Unit Country Report 1st Quarter 1997, EIU Ltd.

ECOWAS : Achievements, Challenges and Future Prospects, ECOWAS Publications, Lagos, n.d.

ECOWAS (1975), *Treaty of the Economic Community of West African States (ECOWAS) 1975*, ECOWAS Secretariat, Lagos.

ECOWAS (1979), *Protocol Relating to the Free Movement of Persons, Residence and Establishment*, ECOWAS Secretariat, Lagos.

ECOWAS (1981), *Decision of the Authority of the Heads of State and Government of the Economic Community of West African States Relating to Trade Liberalisation in Respect of Traditional Handicrafts*, Decision A/DEC. 1 May 1981.

ECOWAS (1993), *Revised Treaty of the Economic Community of West African States (ECOWAS) 1993*, ECOWAS Secretariat, Abuja.

ECOWAS (1995), *ECOWAS Handbook of International Trade*, ECOWAS Publication, Lagos.

ECOWAS (1995), *National Accounts of ECOWAS 1998*, ECOWAS Publications, Lagos.

ECOWAS (1995), *Report and Audited Accounts 1995*, ECOWAS Fund Secretariat, Lomé.

ECOWAS (1997), *Final Communiqué - Meeting of Minister of Foreign Affairs of ECOWAS 26 June 1997*, Conakry, Guinea.

ECOWAS (1997), *Memorandum on the Status of Ratification of the Revised Treaty, Protocols and Conventions as at 15 March 1997*, ECWW/AFC/XX/ August 1997, Executive Secretariat, Lagos.

ECOWAS (1999), *Protocol Relating to the Mechanism for Conflict Prevention, Management, Resolution Peace-keeping and Security*, ECOWAS Secretariat, Abuja.

El-Ayoutu, Y. (ed.) (1994), *The Organization of African Unity Thirty Years On,* Praeger, Westport.

Ero, C. (2000) *Sierra Leone's Security Complex,* The Conflict, Security & Development Group, Centre for Defence Studies, London.

Evans, G. (1994), 'Co-operative Security and Intra-state Conflict', *Foreign Policy,* No. 96.

Ezenwa, U. (1983), *ECOWAS and the Economic Integration of West Africa,* C. Hurst & Co., London.

Falk, R. (1999), *Predatory Globalization: A Critique,* Polity Press, Cambridge.

Fawcett, L. and Hurrell, A. (eds.) (1995), *Regionalism in World Politics: Regional Organization and International Order,* Oxford University Press, Oxford.

First Progress Report of the United Nations Military Observer Mission in Sierra Leone (UNAMSIL), 12 August 1998, (available at http:/www.sierra-leone.orglslnews.html).

Footpaths to Democracy towards a New Sierra Leone (1995), The Revolutionary United Front of Sierra Leone.

Fowler, M. and Bunck, J. (1996), 'What Constitutes the Sovereign State?' *Review of International Studies,* vol. 22, pp. 381-404.

Francis, D.J. (1998), *Sierra Leone in ECOWAS: Political and Economic Implications,* (unpublished PhD. Thesis), University of Southampton.

Francis, D.J. (1999), 'Mercenary Intervention in Sierra Leone: Providing National Security or International Exploitation?' *Third World Quarterly,* vol. 20, no. 2, pp. 319-338.

Francis, D.J. (1999), 'The Economic Community of West African States, the Defence of Democracy in Sierra Leone and Future Prospects', *Democratization,* vol. 6, no. 4, pp. 139-165.

Francis, D.J. (2000), 'ECOMOG: A New Security Agenda in World Politics' in B.T.Bakut and S. Dutt (eds), *African at the Millennium: A Mature Approach to Development* Palgrave, London, pp. 177-202.

Francis, D.J. (2000), 'Torturous Path to Peace: The Lomé Peace Agreement and Post-war Peacebuilding in Sierra Leone', *Security Dialogue,* vol. 30, no. 3, pp. 357-373.

Francis, D.J. (2001), 'The Fire Next Door: Regional Diplomacy and Conflict Management in West Africa', *African Review of Foreign Policy,* vol. 2, no. 2.

Francis, D.J. (2001), 'Nigeria and West Africa', in Darryl Howlett and John Glenn (eds.) *Realism versus Culture,* Aldershot, Ashgate.

Frank, A.G. (1969), *Capitalism and Underdevelopment in Latin America,* Monthly Press Review, New York.

Friedberg, A.L. (1993-4) 'Ripe for Rivalry. Prospects for Peace in a Multipolar Asia', *International Society,* vol. 18, no. 3.

Fyle, C.M. (1995), *Conflict and Population Dispersal: The Refugee Crisis in the Mano River Tri-State Area,* CODESRIA, Dakar.

Gaddafi, M. (1994), *The Green Book*, Benghazi, n.d.

Galtung, J. (1968), 'Structural Theory of Integration', *Journal of Peace Research*, vol. 4.

Gambari, I. (1991), *Political and Economic Dimension of Regional Integration: The Case of ECOWAS*, Humanities Press International, New Jersey.

General Jetley, V. (2000), *Report on the Crisis in Sierra Leone*, May 2000, Freetown.

Gerth, H. and Wright, C. (eds) (1958), *From Max Weber: Essays in Sociology*, Oxford University Press, Oxford.

Gibbens, A. (1990), *The Consequences of Modernity*, Polity Press, Cambridge.

Global Witness (2000), *Conflict Diamonds: Possibilities for the Identification, Certification and Control of Diamonds*, Global Witness, Ltd., London.

Government of Sierra Leone (1997) *Restoration of Democratic Civilian Rule in Sierra Leone: A 90 Day Programme* Ministry of Presidential Affairs and Public Service, Government of Sierra Leone, Guinea.

Government of Sierra Leone (1997), *The Conakry Peace Plan - Report of the Meeting of the Ministers of Foreign Affairs of the Committee of Five on Sierra Leone, 23 October 1997*, Conakry.

Government of Sierra Leone (1999), *The Lomé Agreement: Peace Agreement Between the Government of Sierra Leone and the Revolutionary United Front of Sierra Leone, 7 July 1999*, Lomé.

Gray, H.P. (1993), 'Globalisation versus Nationhood: Is Economic Integration a Useful Compromise?' *Development and International Co-operation*, vol. IX, no. 16, pp. 35-49.

Groom, A.J.R. and Heraclides, A. (eds) (1978), *International Relations Theory*, Pinter, London.

Haas, E. (1968), *The Uniting Europe*, Stanford University Press, Stanford.

Haas, E. (1975), 'The Study of Regional Integration: Reflections on the Joy and Anguish of Pretheorising', in L. Lindberg and S. A. Scheingold (eds), *Regional Integration: Theory and Research*, Harvard University Press, Cambridge, MA.

Haas, E. (1975), 'Turbulent Fields and the Theory of Regional Integration' *International Orgainization* vol. 3, no. 2.

Harding, J. (1997), 'The Mercenary Business: 'Executive Outcomes', *Review of African Political Economy*, vol. 24, 71, pp. 87-99.

Harvey, D. (1989), *The Condition of Post-Modernity*, Blackwell, Oxford.

Hazelwood, A. (ed.) (1967), *African Integration and Disintegration*, Oxford University Press, Oxford.

Hettne, B., Inotai, A. and Osvaldo, S. (1998 and 1999) *Studies in the New Regionalism*, vol. I-V, Macmillan, London.

Hettne, B, Inotai, A. and Sunkel, O. (eds) (1999), *The New Regionalism: Implications for Global Development and International Security*, UNU/WIDER, Helsinki.

Hettne, B. and Söderbaum, F. (1998), 'The New Regionalism Approach', *Politeia*, vol. 17, no. 3, pp. 6-21.

Hirst, P. and Thompson, G. (1996), *Globalisation in Question*, Polity Press, London.

Hoogvelt, A. (1997), *Globalisation and the Postcolonial World: The New Political Economy of Development*, Macmillan, London.

Huntington, S. (1993), 'The Clash of Civilisations?' *Foreign Affairs*, vol. 72, pp. 22-49.

Inegbedion, E.J. (1994), 'ECOMOG in Comparative Perspective' in T. Shaw and J. Okolo (eds), *The Political Economy of Foreign Policy in ECOWAS*, St. Martin's Press, New York.

Kamara, J. (2000), 'Annan Talks up Peacekeeping', *West Africa*, 4-10 September, p. 15.

Kandeh, J.A. (1992), 'Politicization of Ethnic identities in Sierra Leone' *African Studies Review*, vol. 35, no. 1. pp. 81-99.

Kandeh, J.A. (1992), 'Sierra Leone: Contradictory Class Functionality of the 'Soft' State', *Review of African Political Economy*, no. 55, pp. 30-31.

Kandeh, J.D. (1999), 'Ransoming the State: Elite Origins of Subaltern Terror in Sierra Leone', *Review of African Political Economy*, no. 81, pp. 349-366.

Kaplan, R. (1994), 'The Coming Anarchy', *Atlantic Monthly*, February, pp. 44-76.

Keen, D. (1998), 'The Economic Functions of Violence in Civil Wars', *Adelphi Paper 320*, Oxford University Press for the IISS, pp. 1-88.

Kegley, C. and Wittkopf, E. (1995), *World Politics: Trends and Transformation*, 5th edition, St. Martins Press, New York.

Keller, E. and Rothchild, D. (eds) (1996), *Africa in the New International Order: Rethinking State Sovereignty and Regional Security*, Lyne Rienner, London.

Keohane, R. and Hoffmann, S. (eds) (1991), *The New European Community: Decisionmaking and Institutional Change*, Westview, Boulder.

Keohane, R. and Nye, J. (1989) *Power and Interdependence*, Harper Collins, New York.

Kieh Jr., G.K. (1994), 'The Obstacles to the Peaceful Resolution of the Liberian Civil Conflict', *Studies in Conflict and Terrorism*, vol. 17, pp. 97-108.

Koroma, A.A. (1996), *Sierra Leone: The Agony of a Nation*, Andromedra Publications, London.

Laan van der, H.L. (1965), *The Sierra Leone Diamonds: An Economic Study Covering the Years 1952-61*, Oxford University Press, Oxford.

Lancaster, C. (1991), ' The Lagos Three: Economic Regionalism in Sub-Saharan Africa', in J. Harbeson and D. Rothchild (eds), *Africa in World Politics*, Westview Press, Boulder.

Lavergne, R. (ed.) (1997), *Regional Integration and Co-operation in West Africa: A Multidimensional Perspective*, International Development Research Centre, Ottawa.

Lémarchand, R. (1988), 'The State, the Parallel Economy, and the Changing Structure of Patronage System', in D. Rothchild and N. Chazan (eds), *The Precarious Balance: State-Society in Africa,* Westview Press, London.

Lewis, M. (1993), *Making History in Somalia: Humanitarian Intervention in a Stateless Society,* Discussion Paper 7, Centre for the Study of Global Governance, London School of Economics, London.

Luttwak, E.N., (1995), 'Great-powerless Days', *Times Literary Supplement,* 16 June, p. 9.

Machiavelli, N. (1995), *The Prince,* (translated by S.J. Miller), Phoenix Paperback, London.

Mahdavy, H. (1970), 'The Pattern and Problems of Economic Development in Rentier States: The Case of Iran', in M.A. Cook (ed.) *Economic History of the Middle East,* Oxford University Press, Oxford.

Mansfield, E. and Milner, H. (eds) (1998), *The Political Economy of Regionalism,* Columbia University Press, New York.

Marchand, M., Bøas, M. and Shaw, T. (1999), 'The Political Economy of New Regionalisms', *Third World Quarterly,* vol. 20, no. 5, pp. 897-910.

Mayall, J. (ed.) (1996), *The New Interventionism 1991-1994: United Nations Experience in Cambodia, former Yugoslavia and Somalia,* Cambridge University Press, Cambridge.

Mclean, I. (1996), *The Oxford Dictionary of Politics,* Oxford University Press, Oxford.

Mitrany, D. (1966), *A Working Peace System,* Quad, Chicago.

Mittelman, J. (ed.) (1996), *Globalization: A Critical Reflection,* Lynne Rienner, Boulder.

Moravcsik, A. (1993), 'Preferences and Power in the European Community: A Liberal Intergovernmentalist Approach', *Journal of Common Market Studies,* vol. 31, no. 4, pp. 474-480.

Morrison Taw, J. and Grant-Thomas, A. (1999), 'US Support for Regional Complex Contingency Operations: Lessons from ECOMOG', *Studies in Conflict and Terrorism,* vol. 22, no. 1, pp. 53-77.

Musah, A.-F. and 'Kayode Fayemi, J. (eds) (2000), *Mercenaries: An African Security Dilemma,* Pluto Press, London.

Neild, R. (2000), 'Expose the Unsavoury Business Behind Cruel Wars', *International Herald Tribune,* 17 February.

Nwachukwu, I., Oboizor, G. et al. (1991), *Nigeria and the ECOWAS since 1985: Towards a Dynamic Regional Integration,* Fourth Dimension Publishing Co., Nigeria.

Nyang'oro, J. E. and Shaw, T. (eds) (1992), *Beyond Structural Adjustment in Africa: The Political Economy of Sustainable and Democratic Development,* Praeger, London.

Nye Jr., J.S. (ed.) (1968), *International 'Regionalism Readings'*, Little, Brown & Co., Boston.
Nye Jr., J.S. (1970), 'Comparing Common Markets: A Revised Neo-Functionalist Model', *International Organization*, vol. 24, no. 4, pp. 796-835.
OAU (1980), *Lagos Plan of Action for Economic Development of Africa, 1980-2000*, OAU Publication, Addis Ababa.
OAU (1991), *Treaty of the African Economic Community, 1991*, OAU Publications, Addis Ababa.
Ojo, O. (1980), 'Nigeria and the Formation of ECOWAS', *International Organization*, vol. 34, no. 4, pp. 571-604.
Okolo, J. and Wright, S. (eds) (1990), *West African Regional Co-operation and Development*, Westview Press, Boulder.
Olonisakin, F. (1997) 'African "Homemade" Peacekeeping Initiatives', *Armed Forces & Society*, vol. 23, no. 3, pp. 349-372.
Olonisakin. F. (1998) 'Sierra Leone and Beyond: Nigeria and Regional Security' *Jane's Intelligence Review*, June.
Onwuka, R.I. and Sesay, A. (eds) (1985), *Future of Regionalism in Africa*, Macmillan, Basingstoke.
Payne, A. and Gamble, A. (eds) (1996), *Regionalism and World Order*, St. Martin's Press, New York.
Penaherrera, G.S. (1980-1981), 'Viable Integration and Economic Co-operation Problems in the Developing World', *Journal of Common Market Studies*, vol. XIX, no. 1&2.
Pratt, D. (1999) *Sierra Leone: The Forgotten Crisis*, Report to the Canadian Minister of Foreign Affairs from the Special Envoy to Sierra Leone, 23 April, Ottawa.
Prebish, R. (1950), *The Economic Development of Latin America and its Principal Problems*, United Nations, New York.
Ramsbotham, O. (1997), 'Humanitarian Intervention: A Need to Re-conceptualise?', *Review of International Studies*, vol. 23, no. 4, pp. 445-468.
Reno, W. (1995), *Corruption and State Politics in Sierra Leone*, Cambridge University Press, Cambridge.
Reno, W. (1998), *Warlord Politics and African States*, Lynne Rienner, Boulder, Colorado.
Richards, P. (1996), *Fighting for the Rain Forest: War, Youth and Resources in Sierra Leone*, James Curry, Oxford.
Riley, S.P. (1996), *Liberia and Sierra Leone: Anarchy or Peace in West Africa?* Conflict Studies 287, Research Institute for the Study of Conflict and Terrorism, London.
Robertson, R. (1992), *Globalisation*, Sage, London.
Rodney, W. (1972), *How Europe Underdeveloped Africa*, Bogle L'Overture, London.

Rosecrance, R. (1991) 'Regionalism and the Post-Cold War Era' *International Journal, vol. 46.*

Rostow, W.W. (1960), *The Stages of Economic Growth*, Cambridge University Press, Cambridge.

Roy-Maculey, C. (2000), 'Sierra Leone Diamond Trade Targeted', *Associated Press*, 16 January.

Rupert, J. and Farah, D. (2000), 'The Man in the Middle: Liberia President Taylor May Hold the Key to Peace in Sierra Leone', *The Washington Post,* 30 May.

Russet, B. (1967), *International Regions and the International System: A Study in Political Ecology*, Rand Mcnally, Chicago.

Sesay, A. (1994), 'Peacekeeping by Regional Organisations: The OAU and ECOWAS Peacekeeping Forces in Comparative Perspective' in D. Charters (ed.), *Peacekeeping and the Challenge of Civil Conflict Resolution,* Centre for Conflict Studies, University of New Brunswick, New Brunswick.

Sesay, M. (1993), *Interdependence and Dependency in the Political Economy of Sierra Leone* (Unpublished Ph.D. Thesis), Southampton University.

Sesay, M. (1995), 'Collective Intervention or Collective Disaster? Peace-keeping in West Africa', *Security Dialogue,* vol. 26, no.2, pp. 205-222.

Sesay, M. (1997), 'Sierra Leone's Intractable War', *Africa World Review,* November 1997-March 1998, pp. 6-9.

Shaw, T. (1985) 'Towards a Political Economy of Regionalism in Africa', in R.I. Onwuka and A. Sesay (eds), *Future of Regionalism in Africa,* Macmillan, Basingstoke.

Shaw, T. (1994), 'The South in the "New World (Dis) Order": Towards a Political Economy of Third World Foreign Policy in the 1990s', *Third World Quarterly*, vol. 15, no. 1.

Shaw, T. and Aluko, O. (eds) (1984), *The Political Economy of African Foreign Policy,* St Martin's Press, New York.

Shaw, T. and Okolo, J (eds) (1994), *The Political Economy of the Foreign Policy in ECOWAS,* St. Martin's Press, New York.

Shearer, D. (1997), 'Exploring the Limits of Consent: Conflict Resolution in Sierra Leone', *Journal of International Studies,* vol, 26, no. 3, pp. 845-860.

Shearer, D. (1998), *Private Armies and Military Interventions,* Adelphi Paper 316 IISS, Oxford University Press, Oxford.

Smillie, I., Gberie, L. and Hazelton, R. (2000), *The Heart of the Matter: Sierra Leone, Diamonds and Human Security* Ottawa: Partnership Africa Canada.

Söderbaum, F. (1998), 'The New Regionalism in Southern Africa', *Politeia,* vol. 17, no. 3, pp. 75-94.

Soetendorp, B. (1999), *Foreign Policy in the European Union,* Longman, London.

Sorensen, G. (1993), *Democracy and Democratization: Processes and Prospect in a Changing World,* Westview Press, Oxford.

Strong, M. (1995), The 'New South', *The World Today,* November, pp. 215-219.

Thomas, C. (1987), *In Search of Security: The Third World in International Relations*, Harvester Wheatsheaf, Hemel Hempstead.

Thomas, C. (1998), 'International Institutions and Social Economics and Cultural Rights: An Exploration', in T. Evans (ed.), *Human Rights Fifty Years On*, Manchester University Press, Manchester.

Thomas, C. (1999), 'Where is the Third World Now?' *Review of International Studies*, vol. 25, December, pp. 225-243.

Thomas, C. (2000), *Global Governance and Human Security: The Challenge of Poverty and Inequality*, Pluto, London.

Toffler, A. and Toffler, H. (1994), *War and Anti-war: Survival at the Dawn of the 21st Century*, Little Brown & Co., London.

UNCTAD (1973), *Current Problems of Economic Integration : The Distribution of Benefits and Costs in Integration among Developing Countries*, United Nations, New York.

UNDP, (1999), *Human Development Report 1999*, Oxford University Press, New York.

UNRISD (1997), *States in Disarray: The Social Effects of Globalisation*, United Nations, Geneva.

Vogt, M.A. (ed.) (1992), *The Liberian Crisis and ECOMOG*, Gabumo Publishing Company, Lagos.

Weeks, J. (1992), *Development Strategy and the Economy of Sierra Leone*, St. Martin's Press, New York.

Weiss, T. (ed.) (1998), *Beyond UN Sub-contracting. Task Sharing with Regional Security Arrangements and Service-Providing NGOs*, Macmillan, London.

Werner, S. (1997), 'In Search of Security: Relative Gains and Losses in Dyadic Relation', *Journal of Peace Research*, vol. 34, no. 3.

Wheeler, N. (1997), 'Humanitarian Intervention and World Politics', in J. Baylis and S. Smith (eds), *Globalization of World Politics*, Oxford University Press, Oxford.

Wilkin, P. (1996), 'New Myths for the South: Globalisation and the Conflict between Private Power and Freedom', *Third World Quarterly*, vol. 17, no 2, pp. 227-238.

Wilson, K.B. (1992), 'Cult of Violence and Counter-Violence in Mozambique', *Journal of Southern African Studies*, vol. 18, no. 3, pp. 527-582.

World Bank (1989), *Sub-Saharan Africa: From Crisis to Sustainable Growth*, World Bank Publication, Washington DC.

Wright, S. (ed.) (1999), *African Foreign Policies*, Westview Press, Boulder.

Wyse, A.J.G. (1989), *The Krios of Sierra Leone: An Interpretative History*, Okrafor-Smart, Freetown.

Yates, D.A. (1996), *The Rentier State in Africa: Oil Rent Dependency and Neo-colonialism in the Republic of Gabon*, Trenton, New York.

Zack-Williams, A.B. (1990), 'Diamond Mining and Underdevelopment in Sierra Leone', *Africa Development,* vol. XV, no. 2.

Zack-Williams, A.B. (1995), *Tributors, Supporters and Merchant Capital: Mining and Underdevelopment in Sierra Leone*, Avebury Press, Aldershot.

Zack-Williams, A.B. (1999), 'Sierra Leone: The Political Economy of Civil War 1991-98', *Third World Quarterly,* vol. 20, no. 1, pp. 143-169.

Zartmann, I. (ed.) (1995), *Collapsed States: The Disintegration and Restoration of Legitimate Authority,* Lynne Rienner, London.

Index

AAF 33
Abdullah, I. 122n
Acharya, A. 55, 61n
ACP-EEC 14, 89, 194
ACRI 46
Adedeji, A. 21
adhocery 49
Adibe, C. 55, 61n, 177
Adler, E. 54, 60n
ADMS 124
AEC 8
AFRC 51, 78, 110
African High Command 53
African Leadership Forum 48
Agenda for Peace 45
Ajami, F. 62n
Alagappa, M. 47, 53, 60n
Alie, J. 104n
Aluko, O. 106n
American Government 180
Americo-Liberian 40-41
Amin, S. 37n, 82
Anglophone 18, 20, 31
ANSWE 216
Antwerp 123, 125-126, 132-133, 141
AOF 17
APC 51, 78, 84-87, 108, 109
Arab-Israeli war 16
Asante, S. 31, 37n, 194, 196, 188n, 238
Asanti Stool 219
ASEAN 65
ASYCUDA 209-212, 227, 234
authority 93

Babangida, I. 41
Baldwin, D. 60n
Bangura, Y. 116, 121n
Barhimi, L. 187n
BBC 107, 111
Bedie, K. 166
Beirut 126
Benghazi 108
Berg report 32
Berri, N. 126
Biafra civil war 18, 21
Biddle, K. 175
bi-polar international system 2
Big, M. 110
Binkolo Mafia 84
Blair, T. 175, 187n
Böas, M. 5n, 74n, 244n
Bo-Pujehun project 219
Boutros Ghali 44, 59n
Bradshaw, S. 120, 122n
Brehun, L. 40, 59n, 122n
Britain 175
British Crown Colony 78
Bunck, J. 176, 188n, 241n,
Bundu, A. 61n, 99
Burrell, S. 240n
Butler, 64, 74n
Buzan, B. 35n

Callaghy, T. 239n
capitalist world system 9, 30, 70
    capitalist economies 11
    economic marginalisation 12
    enclave economy 29
    global economy 4, 65
    globalisation 65-70, 73

liberal international economic order 15
CARE International 219
Caribbean Common Market 2
Casamance 51
CAST 124
CCC 209
CCMS 126
Cecchini Report 3
Charters, D. 59n, 246n
Chazan, N. 18, 36n, 239n
Cheru, F. 37n, 239n
civil defence forces 110, 118, 161
    Donors 121n
    Kamajors 110, 121n
    Kapras 121n
    Tamaboros 121n
civil society 111
civil war 38, 107-111
Clapham, C. 82, 105n, 239n
Clarkson, T. 77
Claude, I, 68, 239n
Clinton, B. 41, 45
CMS 125-126
Cold War 2, 13, 52, 62
    ideological divide 41
Coleman, J. 84, 105n, 239n
collective security 52-53
collective self-reliance 15, 32, 90
Collier, P. 116-117, 239n
COMESA 6
commodity power 15
common agricultural policy 218
common foreign policy 43
common market 1, 25
Commonwealth 158, 166
community citizens 28, 204-5
Compaore, B. 108, 109
complex emergency operation 48, 56
conflict 105-111, 114-120
conflict diamonds 123, 129-143
Contractgate 83

Cook, M. 105n, 244n
Co-operative Security 52, 58, 166
CPLP 51
CSO 125, 132
customs 212-219
customs union 191, 195
customs union theory 13

Da Cintra, P. 77
Damrosch, L. 61n, 239n
Davies, A. 239n
DDR 174
De Beers 124-125, 130-133, 144n
Deardorff, A. 208, 229n
Demby, A. 160
Democratisation 3, 69
Deng F. 60n, 239n
Dependency 29, 81
    African dependency Frankien model 30
Deutsch, K. 53-55, 60n, 240n
developmental regionalism 29, 31, 90
diamond(s) 79, 84-85, 123-143
    diplomacy 88
    political economy of 4
DiamondWorks 164
Dickson, A. 11, 35n, 240n
Doe, S. 39, 108-109, 208
domino effect 42
Drucker, P. 2, 5n, 240n
Dump-Watch 221
Dunn, J. 35n, 240n

EAC 33
ECA 6, 20, 21, 32-33, 240n
ECCAS 7
ECLA 6, 29
ECOMOG 38, 48-51, 57-58, 67-70, 101, 111-113, 164,

170-1, 177-8, 182, 191, 232-6
conflict management 45, 48-49
contingent 42
creation of 39, 41
democratic intervention 4
Field Commander 113
humanitarian intervention 49, 56-57
Liberian civil war 39-40, 47
mandate 42
peacekeeping and enforcement 42, 48-52, 56-57
ECOWAS 1, 7, 159-160, 162-166, 171, 177-184, 210, 240n
  aims and objectives 22-23
  authority 23, 183
  Executive Secretary 22-23, 99
  formation 12, 20
  formation, reasons for 12, 13, 15-17, 19
  free movement 27, 182-3, 204-7
  Fund 22-23, 27, 98
  Guinea Bissau 51
  industrialisation 9
  institutional framework 23
  integration 25, 35
  Liberia 41, 49
  main features of 25
  member states 7
  National Units 93, 95
  peace plan for 4
  regionalism 2, 4, 25, 48, 53, 70-72, 87-88, 91-94, 99-100, 102, 189-226
  sectoral development 23
  Sierra Leone 50
  specialised commissions 24
  Trade Fair 102, 215-7, 227
  Travellers Cheque 26
  Treaty 22
  trilingual cultural heritage 8
  UN Co-operative security 4

EEZ 219
Eire 8
EIU 240n
Ekutay 84, 105n
El-Ayoutu, Y. 59n, 241n
Ero, C. 241n
European Colonialism 8, 16
  Berlin Congress 8
  colonial race 8
  Portuguese imperialism 9
European Integration 6
  Commission Eurocrats 24
  ECSC 6
  EEC 6, 19, 62, 200
  EU 217, 233
European Union 2
Evans, G. 187n, 241n
Ezenwe, U. 17, 36n

Falamakata 118-119
Falk, R. 60n, 241n
FAO 79
Farah, D. 246n
Fawcett, L. 2, 3, 5n, 68, 241n
Fayemi, J. 59n
FDI 193
foreign policy 13, 88-92
Fourah Bay College 82
Fowler, M. 176, 188n, 241n
France 14, 16, 18, 19, 26
Francis, D. 59n, 105n, 121n, 168, 185n, 186n, 187n, 241n
Francophone 19, 21, 30, 162
Frank, G. 29, 36n, 81, 241n
Freetown 77
Friedberg, A. 2, 5n, 241n
Führerism 83
functional co-operation projects 6
functionalism 30
Fyle, M. 127, 144n, 242n

Gaddafi, M. 108, 119, 122n, 242n
Galtung, J. 242n
Gambari, I. 13, 35n, 242n
Gamble, A. 74n
GDP 10, 78, 201, 214-5
General Gowon, Y. 20, 21, 22
General Jetley, V. 170-1, 187n, 242n
General Opande, D. 171
Gereffi, G. 67
Gerth, H. 242n
Giddens, A. 65, 74n, 242n
global market economy 33
Global Witness 242n
Globalisation 65-67
GNP 10, 27, 80, 217
Grant-Thomas, A. 61n, 244n
Gray, H. 242n
Gray, P. 182, 188n
Green Book, 108, 119
Green, G. 126
Groom, A. 5n, 242n
Guaz, M. 125
Gulf war 41

Haas, E. 5n, 14, 30, 242n
Hain, P. 168
handicraft industry 197-8
Harding, J. 242n
Harford, C. 14
Harvey, D. 66, 74n, 242n
Hawkins, J. 77
Hazelwood, A. 17, 36n, 242n
Heininger, J. 186n
Heraclides, A. 5n, 242n
Hettne, B. 3, 5n, 64-65, 74n, 243n
Hirst, P. 67, 74n, 243n
Hodges, M. 5n
Hoffman, S. 243n
Holbrooke, R. 187n
Hoogvelt, A. 75n, 243n
Hoon, G. 175, 187n
Horton, A. 14

Houphouet-Boigny, F. 10
Huntington, S. 121n, 243n
Hurrell, A. 2, 3, 5n, 67, 241n

IGOs 91, 218
Indian 80
Inegbedion, E. 60n, 243n
Inoguchi, T. 59n
Inotai, A. 74n, 242n
INPFL 39
interdependence 4
International Criminal Court 173
International Financial
  Institutions (IFIs) 10, 90-91
    IMF 10, 89, 110, 175, 209,
      213-4, 232
    World Bank 6, 32, 35n, 89,
      110, 175, 209, 220, 224,
      232, 248
IPE 65
ISI 29

Jawara, D. 179
Johnson, P. 39
Jonah, J. 122n, 143

Kabbah, T. 51, 78, 110
Kalamanowitch, S. 125
Kamara, J. 172, 187n, 243n
Kandeh, J. 83, 85, 105n, 121n,
  243n
Kann, R. 240n
Kaplan, R. 1, 5n, 11, 114-115,
  121n, 243n
Karim Koroma, A. 89, 104n,
  112, 121n, 222, 230n,
  243n
'Kayode Fayemi, J. 244n
Keen, D. 243n
Kegley, C. 243n
Keller, E. 60n, 243n
Keohane, R. 59n, 243n

KFOR 49
Kieh, G. 40, 58n, 243n
Kimaro, S. 239n
King Jimmy Market 77
Kodjoe, O. 30
Koindu 207-8
Koroma, J. 110
Kouyate, L. 34
Kwame Nkrumah 11, 15, 53

Laan van der, H. 243n
LAFTA 2
Lagos Plan of Action 7, 32
Lancaster, C. 243n
landlocked states 7
Lansana, D. 78
Lavergne, R. 243n
LDCs 11
Lebanese 81, 125-6, 194
Lémarchand, R. 104n, 244n
Lewis, M. 186n, 244n
Liberia 126
Lindberg, L. 5n, 243n
London 123
Lord Chief Justice Mansfield 77
LPC 49
lumpen proletariat 109
Luttwak, E. 120, 122n, 244n
Lyons, T. 239n

Machiavelli, N. 112, 244n
Madingos 126
Maghreb Union 7
Mahdavy, H. 104n, 244n
Malu, V. 50
Mane, A. 51
Mane invasion 77
Mansfield, E. 64, 74n, 244n
Marchand, M. 64, 71, 73n, 244n
Margai, M. 78
Mayall, J. 186n, 244n
McInnes, C. 187n

Mclean, I. 36, 244n
MCS 220
mercenaries 107
    Liberian 118
migration 9
Milner, H. 64, 74n, 244n
Mitrany, D. 30, 36n, 244n
Mittelman, J. 65, 67, 73n, 244n
MNCs 9, 91, 123, 193,
MOD 175
modernisation 29, 192
Momoh, J. 77, 108-109, 112,
    113, 127-128
Monetary Union 17, 26
    CFA Franc Zone 16, 26, 197,
    207
    single currency 26
monkey trade 206-8
Moravcsik, A. 73n, 244n
Morrison-Taw, J. 60n, 244n
MPSSL 220
MRU 21, 200, 206-8, 224
Musah, A. 59n, 244n

NAFTA 2, 65
NAM 87
NATO 178
nature of domestic politics 8
    ethnic corporation 84
    Neo-patrimonialism 82-83
    patrimonial politics 81-86
    patron-clientelism 81-83
    political ethnicity 8
    prebendal politics 84
    rentierism 83-84
NDMC 124
Neild, R. 244n
Neo-functionalism 30
Neo-liberal economic philosophy
    32, 63, 193
Neo-marxist 120
new barbarism 115

NFPL 39, 42, 112-113
NGOs 174, 219
NIEO 12, 15
Nigeria 17, 53, 58
   Chamber of Commerce, Industry and Agriculture 19
   leadership role 18
   Naira diplomacy 21
   oil diplomacy 18, 21
   pax-Nigeriana 42
   West Africa and 18
North-South Relations 15
NPRC 50, 96, 127-128, 138, 153
NRA 64
Nwachukwu, I. 245n
Nyang'oro, J. 37n, 244n
Nye, J. 5n, 59n, 243n
Nyerere, J. 46

OAU 32, 47, 57, 86, 245n
   try Africa first 44, 58, 59n
Obasanjo, O. 35, 58, 180
ODA 210
oil crisis 9
Ojo, O. 20-21, 37, 245n
Okello, F. 167
Okolo, J. 20, 36n, 59n, 60n, 245n, 246n
Olatunde, O. 19, 36n
Olonisakin, F. 245n
Onwuka, R. 37n, 245n
OPEC 15
open regionalism 34, 63
Operation Liberty 42

PADRIGU 65
Pan-African force 45
Pan-Africanism 14, 55, 89, 120
   Africa Political Unity 14
   Micro-nationalists 14
   National Congress of British West Africa 14

Pan-West African Solidarity 14
Radical Nationalists 14
Paramount Chief 125
Paris Club 80
Payne, A. 73n, 245n
peace settlement 110
   Abidjan accord 110, 166
   Blanket Amnesty 110
   Conakry accord 110
   Lomé accord 110, 158, 160, 167
   power sharing 110
peace support operation 48, 56
peacekeeping 169-172
Penaherrera, G. 14, 36n, 245n
Pickering, T. 176
PMMC 124
political alliances 14
political economy 11, 75, 81
political independence 8
political systems 10
   democratic pluralism 10
   military dictatorship 10
   multi-party politics 10
   one-partison 11
   popularist 10
   Socialist and Marxist-Leninist 10
Pompidou, G. 19
popular participation 76, 99-103
post-Cold War 2, 41, 52, 56, 91
   Africa 4
   international neglect 40-44
   West Africa 10, 11, 47
post-colonial Africa 8, 15
   West Africa 8
pragmatic incrementalism 52-53
Pratt, D. 245n
pre-colonial West Africa 16
Prebisch, P. 29, 36n, 245n
President Clinton, B. 176-7

President Eyadema, G. 21
President Tobman, W. 20
private military companies 45
    EO 45, 110
    MPRI 45
    Sandline International 45, 110
private sector 215-7
pro-integrationists 19, 20
protective evacuation 40
Protocol on mutual assistance in defence 43-44
Protocol on non-aggression 43
PTA 7

Ramsbotham, O. 62n, 245n
Ravenhill, J. 37n
Regional co-operation 4
    identity 3
    integration 3, 4, 62, 92
regionalisation 3, 47, 52, 101-103
    trans-border 4
regionalism 1-5, 63-70
    economic 1, 4, 6, 43, 52, 69
    new 4, 63-64, 193
    old 2, 3, 63-64
    politics of 1, 2
    resurgence of 2, 5n
Regionness 3
RENAMO 118
Reno, W. 86, 105n 121n, 126, 128, 134, 144n, 245n
rentier state 84
Richards, P. 86, 105n 114-116, 119, 121n, 245n
Riley, S. 245n
Robertson, R. 65, 73n, 245n
Rodants, F. 222
Rodney, W. 36n, 245n
Rosberg, C. 84, 104n
Rosecrance, R. 246n
Rostow, R. 29, 36n, 246n
Rothchild, D. 60n

Roy-Maculey, 246n
RUF 50, 80, 107, 118, 168-171
Rupert, J. 246n
Russet, B. 53, 60n, 246n

SACU 201
SADC 2, 6, 34, 57, 201, 233
SADCC 34
Sahid Mohamed, J. 84, 124, 220
Samora, S. 114, 178
Sankoh, F. 50, 107-108, 167-8
Sapes 76
SAPs 10, 32, 80
SCD 212
Scheingold, S. 5n, 243n
SDR 213
Sectoral Industrial Forum 70
security 46
    community 54-56
    complex 69
    human 3, 68, 79
    privatisation of 110
    regionalism 1, 4, 38-39, 43, 51-52, 56, 185
Seers, D. 3
Senghor, L. 21
Sesay, A. 59n, 246n
Sesay, M. 60n, 104n, 186n, 246n
shadow state 86
Sharpe, G. 77
Shaw, T. 5n, 27, 60n, 74n, 106n, 244n, 246n
Shearer, D. 59n, 246n
Sierra Leone post-colonial 87
SLA 107, 118
slavery 76
SLEDIC 93, 215-7, 229n
SLPP 77, 110
SLST 124-125, 137
Smillie, I. 115, 124-125, 132, 138, 144n, 246n
smuggling 206-9

sobel 127-128, 157
Söderbaum, F. 3, 5n, 31, 64, 70-71, 74n, 243n, 246n
Soetendrop, B. 246n
SOFA 113
Somalia syndrome 45, 170
Soo Gil, P. 187n
Sorensen, G. 104n, 246n
South 66-68, 72
South-South Co-operation 15, 90-91, 194
South Pacific Forum 220
Squandergate 84
SSATP 224
SSD 87
Standing Mediation Committee 41-42
State House 82
Stevens, S. 10 78, 83, 88, 100, 124-126, 139, 182
Stohl, R. 176, 187n
Stolper, W. 208, 229n
Strasser, V. 77, 109-110
Strong, M. 68, 74n, 246n
Suez crisis 48
Sultanism 84
Sunkel, O. 73n, 243n
supranationality 24, 94

Tarawalli, M. 121n
task-sharing 58
Taylor, C. 39-40, 42, 50, 108, 111-112
Taylor, T. 5n
Tel Aviv 123
teleological nature 4
The Economist 1, 5n
Third Wave 10
Third World 12, 29
    ideology 15, 16
    solidarity 15

Thomas, C. 36n, 60n, 67, 70, 74n, 75n, 193, 228n, 247n
Thomas, S. 109
Thompson, G. 66, 74n, 243n
TNCs 67, 72
Toffler, A. 120, 247n
Toffler, H. 247n
Tolbert, W. 39, 109
toxic waste 221-2, 234
trade creation 190
trade diversion 190
trade liberalisation 25, 27, 194, 196-200
    intra-regional trade 25-26, 32, 201, 204, 213-5
traditional ends of politics 18
trans-border regionalisation 64, 208-9
trans-Saharan trade 16
trans-West African highway 27
transatlantic slave trade 77
Triad 66

ULIMO 49
UMEOA 200
UNAMSIL 110, 169-174
UNCLOS 219
UNCTAD 209, 228n, 247n
UNDP 209, 217, 247n
underdevelopment 9
UNEF 48
United Nations 4, 44, 57
    Human Development Index 32
    Human Development Report 10
    Special Initiative for Africa 32
    task-sharing 44
units of account 98
UNOMIL 49
UNOMSON 49

UNPAAERD 32
UNPROFOR 49
UNRISD 247n

Vaitsos, C.
Van Greveld, M. 115, 121n, 239n
Via 8
Viera, N. 51
Vogt, M. 247n
Vouchergate 84

WACH 26, 213
WAMA 26, 99, 213
war
    economy 116-117
    conduct of 114
    contagion effects 38, 48, 50
    fire next door 38
    inter-state 42
    intra-state 38, 46
warlords 91
Weber, M. 84, 105n
Weeks, J. 247n
Weiss, T. 186n, 247n
Werner, S. 248n
West Africa 1, 8-12
West African Chamber of Commerce, Industry, Mines and Agriculture 20
West African Currency Board 16
West African economies 9
    external dependent 9, 26

West African Integration and Co-operation 5, 20
    economic unions 17
    Free Trade Area 20
    functional co-operative 16
    geographical expression 7
West African Produce Board 17
West Side Boys 175
Westminster model 78
Wheeler, N. 61n, 247n
White, R. 111-112
WIDER/U 65
Wilberforce, W. 77
Wilkin, P. 69, 75n, 247n
Williams, S. 182
Wilson, K. 122n, 247n
Wittkopf. E. 243n
Wright, C. 242n
Wright, S. 36n, 59n, 92, 106n, 186n, 245n, 247n
WTO 89
Wyse, A. 77, 104n, 247n

Yates, D. 104n, 247n
Yoruba 8

Zack-Williams, A. 89, 105n, 125, 186n, 248n
Zartman, I. 61n, 186n, 239n, 248n

West African Integration and
  Co-operation 5, 17
Scarcity scheme 17
Free Trade Area 20
Intergovernmental co-operation
  strategies of movement in
West African Production Board
West State Boys, 148
re: Cabinet model, 12
Wheat, W. S., 85n, 242n
Wentz, B., 117-118
Wolpe, H. n.
Wilberforce, W., 7, 27n.
Wickert, F. R., 74n, 242n
Williams, S., 182
Wright, R. R138, 247n
Wilmot, E., 24
Bentsen, 1 A3n
Willink, E. 26b, 70n, 41, 160n
  Report, 18n, 217n
WPP 193
Wyse, A. 77, 104n-175n

Yates, D., 165n, 217n
Yu, G. T., 5

Zaki-Williams, Said, S., 126, 169, 179
  136n, 216n
Zartman, I. W., 18n, 219n